RICHARD HOLMES's first book was *Shelley: The Pursuit* which won the Somerset Maugham Prize in 1974. *Footsteps: Adventures of a Romantic Biographer* was first published in 1985 and was described by Michael Holroyd as 'a modern masterpiece'. *Coleridge: Early Visions* won the 1989 Whitbread Book of the Year Prize; his next book *Dr Johnson & Mr Savage* won the James Tait Black Prize and in 1996 he published *Coleridge: Selected Poems*, an anthology of 101 poems which gives a fresh and enlarged sense of Coleridge's creative powers. In 1998, he published *Coleridge: Darker Reflections*, which won the Duff Cooper Prize. Richard Holmes is also the author of *Sidetracks: Explorations of a Romantic Biographer* (2000). He is a Fellow of the British Academy and in 1992 was awarded an OBE. He lives in Norwich and London with the novelist Rose Tremain.

From the reviews of *Footsteps*:

'This exhilarating book, part biography, part autobiography, shows the biographer as sleuth and huntsman, tracking his subjects through space and time.' HILARY SPURLING, *Observer*

'Nothing is simple in this intricate, complicated and fascinating book, which is like a set of Russian dolls, biography containing travel-writing containing autobiography containing and so on. Holmes is indeed a biographer and a romantic in every sense.' RICHARD BOSTON, *Guardian*

'His purpose is to locate "the personal life that is hidden in, and below, the printed page" and then to understand that life by an act of identification. There is nothing more eloquent in this book than Holmes' account of the biographer's obsession with the past – that feeling of being "haunted".' PETER ACKROYD, *Sunday Times*

FOOTSTEPS

ADVENTURES OF A
ROMANTIC BIOGRAPHER

RICHARD HOLMES

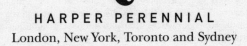

HARPER PERENNIAL

London, New York, Toronto and Sydney

Harper Perennial
An imprint of HarperCollins*Publishers*
77–85 Fulham Palace Road
Hammersmith
London W6 8JB

www.harperperennial.co.uk

This edition published by Harper Perennial 2005

4

First published by Hodder & Stoughton 1985

A catalogue record for this book is available from the British Library

ISBN 0 00 720453 1

Set in Baskerville

Printed and bound in Great Britain by Clays Ltd, St Ives plc

For Vicki and those children

Contents

Illustrations

Robert Louis Stevenson in 1879
(photo courtesy of Albert E. Norman collection, California Historical Society,
San Francisco)

Fanny Osbourne in 1876
(photo courtesy of Stevenson collection at Beinecke Library,
Yale University)

William Wordsworth in 1798
(reproduced by kind permission of The National Portrait Gallery)

Mary Wollstonecraft *circa* 1797
(reproduced by kind permission of The National Portrait Gallery)

Looting during The French Revolution
(reproduced by kind permission of the Mary Evans Picture Library)

Paris, 1968
(photo: Popperfoto)

Percy Bysshe Shelley in Rome, 1819
(reproduced by kind permission of The National Portrait Gallery)

Claire Clairmont in Rome, 1819
(reproduced by courtesy of Nottingham Museums, Newstead Abbey)

The Garden at Casa Bertini
(from the author's own collection)

Casa Magni *circa* 1875

Gérard de Nerval in Paris, 1855
(photo: Bibliothèque Nationale, Paris)

Théophile Gautier *circa* 1854
(photo: Bibliothèque Nationale, Paris)

ONE

1964 : Travels

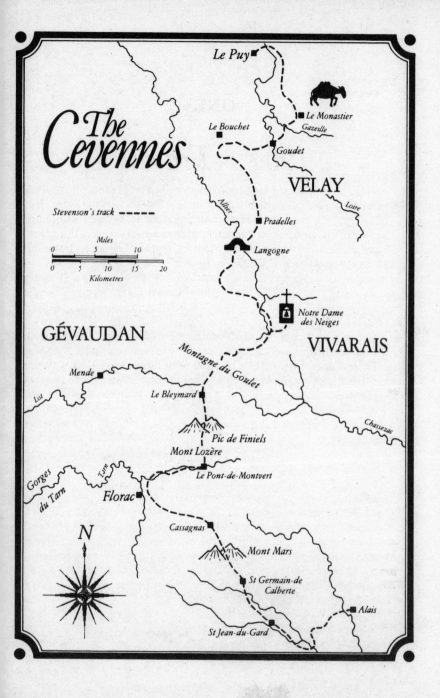

1

All that night I heard footsteps: down by the river through the dark trees, or up on the moonlit road from Le Puy to Le Monastier. But I saw nothing except the stars, hanging over me where I wanted to be, with my head on a rucksack, and my rucksack on the grass, lying alone somewhere in the Massif Central of France, dreaming of the dead coming back to life again. I was eighteen.

I had started a travel-diary, teaching myself to write, and trying to find out what was happening to me, what I was feeling. I kept it simple:

> Found a wide soft dry ditch under thorn hedge between the track and the little Loire. Here lit candle once more, studied ground for red ants, then set out bed-roll with all spare clothes between me and my waterproof cloak-sheet. Soon I was gazing up at stars, thinking of all the beats and tramps and travellers *à la belle étoile* from RLS to JK. Story of snakes that are drawn to body-heat and slide into your sleeping-bag. Cicadas and strange sounds river makes at night flowing over rocks. Slept fitfully but without disturbance from man or beast, except a spider in my ear. Saw a green glow-worm like a spark.

I woke at 5 a.m. in a glowing mist, my green sleeping-bag blackened with the dew, for the whole plateau of the Velay is above two thousand feet. I made a fire with twigs gathered the night before, and set water to boil for coffee, in a *petit pois* tin with wire twisted round it as a handle. Then I went down to the Loire, here little more than a stream, and sat naked in a pool cleaning my teeth. Behind me the sun came out and the woodfire smoke turned blue. I felt rapturous and slightly mad.

I reached Le Monastier two hours later, in the local grocer's van, one of those square Citroëns like a corrugated garden privy, which smelt of camembert and apples. Monsieur Crèspy, chauffeur and patron, examined my pack and soaking bag as we jounced along through rolling uplands. Our conversation took place in a sort of no-man's-land of irregular French. M. Crèspy's patois and Midi twang battled for meaning against my stonewall classroom phrases. After initial skirmishing, he adopted a firm line of attack.

"You are walking on foot?" he said, leaning back into the depths of the van with one arm and presenting me with a huge yellow pear.

"Yes, yes. I am searching for *un Ecossais*, a Scotsman, a writer, who walked on foot through all this beautiful country."

"He is a friend of yours? You have lost him?" enquired M. Crèspy with a little frown.

"No, no. Well . . . Yes. You see, I want to find him." My chin streamed hopelessly with pear juice.

M. Crèspy nodded encouragingly: "The pear is good, *n'est-ce pas?*"

"Yes, it is very good."

The Citroën lurched round a bend and plunged down towards a rocky valley, broken with trees and scattered stone farmhouses, with pink tiled roofs and goats tethered in small bright pastures where the sun struck and steamed. The spire of a church, perched on the far hillside, pointed the horizon.

"There is Le Monastier. Look! Perhaps your friend is waiting for you," said M. Crèspy with great confidence.

"No, no, I don't think so," I said. But it was exactly what I hoped.

I rummaged in my rucksack. "You see, here is his book. It tells the story of his walk on foot."

M. Crèspy peered at the little brown volume, and the Citroën swung back and forth across the road, the sound of rolling fruit growing thunderous behind us. I hastily propped the book up on the dashboard, being careful not to cover the St Christophe medal or the picture of Our Lady mounted above a cone of paper flowers. I ran my finger down the sketch map on the title page: Le Monastier, Pradelles, Langogne, Notre Dame des Neiges, Montagne du Goulet, Pic de Finiels, Le Pont-de-Montvert, Florac, Gorges du Tarn, St Jean-du-Gard—to me already magic names, a litany of hills and rivers, with a lone figure striding along them, laughing, beckoning, even mocking: follow! follow!

M. Crèspy considered the map, and then my face, then the map again, and changed gear with a reflective air. "It is far, it is far."

"Yes," I said, "it is two hundred and twenty kilometres."

M. Crèspy raised a finger from the steering wheel. "And you, you are Scottish then?"

"No, no. I am English. My friend—that is to say, Mr Stevenson

—was Scottish. He walked on foot with a donkey. He slept *à la belle étoile*. He . . ."

"Ah, *that!*" broke in M. Crèspy with a shout, taking both hands from the steering wheel, and striking his forehead. "I understand, I understand! You are on the traces of Monsieur Robert Louis Steamson. Bravo, bravo!"

"Yes, yes, I am following his paces!"

We both laughed and the Citroën proceeded by divine guidance.

"I understand, I understand," repeated M. Crèspy. And I believe he was the first person who ever did.

Robert Louis Stevenson came to Le Monastier in September 1878. He was twenty-seven, spoke good French, and had already spent several summers abroad; near Fontainebleau, and on the canals of Holland, paddling a canoe with a friend. The experience had produced his first book, *An Inland Voyage*, which despite its whimsical style captured an attitude to travel that enthralled me, a child of the Sixties.

I take it, in short, that I was about as near Nirvana as would be convenient in practical life; and if this be so, I make the Buddhists my sincere compliments . . . It may be best figured by supposing yourself to get dead drunk, and yet keep sober to enjoy it . . . A pity to go to the expense of laudanum, when here is a better paradise for nothing! This frame of mind was the great exploit of our voyage, take it all in all. It was the farthest piece of travel accomplished.

That was the kind of travel which interested me too: as far out in Nirvana as possible. After ten years of English boarding schools, brought up by Roman Catholic monks, I was desperate to slip the leash. Free thought, free travel, free love was what I wanted. I suppose a foreign *affaire de coeur* would have been the best thing of all; and that, in a way, was what I got.

It did not immediately occur to me to wonder what Stevenson himself was doing in that remote little town "in the French highlands". I knew he wanted to be a writer, had published essays in the London reviews, but was still struggling to establish his independence from his family in Edinburgh. They had brought him up a strict Calvinist, an outlook which he had rejected; and they had wanted him to be an engineer. Instead he had adopted the life of a literary bohemian, was a friend of Edmund Gosse and Sidney Colvin, affected wide-brimmed hats and velvet jackets, and fled to France whenever he could.

Staying at the little hotel at Le Monastier that autumn, he made friends with the local doctor and "Conductor of Roads and Bridges" and completed a little sketch of the place, *A Mountain Town in France*. His account had immediately captivated me.

Le Monastier is the chief place of a hilly canton in Haute-Loire, the ancient Velay. As the name betokens, the town is of monastic origin; and it still contains a towered bulk of monastery and church . . . It stands on the side of a hill above the river Gazeille, about fifteen miles from Le Puy, up a steep road where the wolves sometimes pursue the diligence in winter . . .

Stevenson had decided to pursue the road south himself, but on foot, in the company of a donkey to carry his baggage. This second voyage resulted in his second book—the little brown volume I now carried as my bible—his *Travels with a Donkey in the Cévennes*.

At Le Monastier that morning, the question of Stevenson's donkey bulked large. Unloaded from the van, I was taken into the backroom of the *épicerie* and given breakfast by Madame Crèspy.

"When Monsieur Steamson was here, they used to make lace," she said, also using the local pronunciation. "But you will want your donkey, like him. You must go and see Le Docteur Ollier."

Mlle Crèspy, who looked at me with dark dancing eyes, was deputed to take me to the doctor. "It's no fun without the donkey," she observed, prettily rolling the colloquial word, *rigolo*, and seizing me by the hand. Mlle Crèspy was about nine.

Le Docteur, a tall patient man, ushered me into his surgery and poured me a yellow medicine, which turned out to be a liqueur. "Of course, there is the question of the donkey. You will have to consult the Mayor. Everyone takes a donkey."

"Everyone?"

"Mlle Singer took a donkey. She was lost in a storm, on the Lozère. It is high up there. The fire brigade from Bleymard went out to find her with lanterns."

I accepted another yellow medicine. "This was recently, Miss Singer?"

"Oh yes, this was in 1949. You must pay attention to the vipers," concluded Dr Ollier.

"So you desire to hire a donkey," said the Mayor, as we paced in the cobbled courtyard of the old Bishop's palace.

I looked abashed. "I am following Stevenson. But I have my sack."

The Mayor reflected. "You see, Monsieur Steamson, he had a

donkey. It is in his book. It is *charming* for a writer to have a donkey. It is his companion of the route."

The sun beat down, the liqueur rose in my head, I had a vague sense that things were getting out of hand even before I had started. The reality of Stevenson's presence in Le Monastier was uncanny. I asserted myself rather desperately. "No, no, I do not desire a donkey. My companion of the route—is Monsieur Stevenson himself!"

The Mayor stopped short, took off his small gold spectacles and tapped me on the chest. "Of course, of course," he said, beaming suddenly. "You are young, indeed you are young, and I wish you a good journey with all my heart." He replaced his spectacles and shook my hand many times, and I shook his quite as often. "You know," added the Mayor as we parted, "Monsieur Steamson purchased his donkey for sixty-five francs. I could not easily find you such a bargain. But still, after all, if you should desire . . ."

Stevenson purchased his donkey for sixty-five francs "and a glass of brandy". He christened her "Modestine", and described her as the size of a large Newfoundland dog and the colour of "an ideal mouse". She was to play a large part in his story. With her, he intended to cross over some of the highest and wildest country in France, moving across the remote borderlands of four *départements*—the Haute-Loire, the Lozère, the Ardèche, and Gard—and over the top of two notable peaks or highland ridges, the Goulet and the Pic de Finiels, between four and five and a half thousand feet. (For comparison, Snowdon is 3,650 feet and Ben Nevis 4,405 feet.) He intended to be solitary and self-sufficient, and loaded up his donkey with a huge sleeping-sack of his own design, six foot square of green waterproof cart-cloth, lined inside with blue sheep's fur: "there was luxurious turning-room for one; and at a pinch the thing might serve for two." The last phrase seemed rather at odds with the rest of his plans. The sack had open sheep's-fur flaps at both ends, to act as pillow and foot-warmer by night, and as the double mouth of an enormous saddle-bag by day.

I considered his equipment with professional interest, from the point of view of minimum necessities. It included the following items: two complete changes of warm clothing; several books, among them Father Peyrat's *Histoire des Pasteurs du Désert*; a Scottish railway plaid; a spirit-lamp and cooking pan; a lantern and candles; a twenty-franc jack-knife with assorted blades, openers, and instruments for removing stones from donkey's hooves; a leather water-flask; an eighty-page blue-lined schoolboy's exercise book, which he used for the first draft of the *Travels*, composed en route usually in the mornings or at inns where he lunched; many blocks of black chocolate and tins of Bologna sausage (as hard rations); and, on his first morning, a basket containing a leg of cold mutton and a bottle of Beaujolais. He also packed an egg-whisk, to make the egg-and-brandy nog he loved to take at breakfast with his café au lait.

In the pocket of his country-velveteens he secreted a revolver, a brandy-flask and a large tin of tobacco and papers for rolling cigarettes. Most intriguing item of all, he wore on his wedding finger—though not married—a large silver gypsy ring. At first I assumed that he simply wanted to be taken for a gypsy or a pedlar himself, in the true "bohemian" spirit. Needless to say, I had started wearing one myself; to be exact, a large tin ring—being the best I could afford—previously bought from a gypsy stall at Les Saintes-Maries, two hundred miles south in the Camargue.

Stevenson's journey lasted a mere twelve days. But its shortness was made up for by its intensity: it was a complete pilgrimage in miniature. He started from Le Monastier at dawn on Sunday, 22 September 1878—though Modestine's reluctance to become his beast of burden meant that everyone had gone to midday church by the time he made any visible progress on the further hill; and eventually arrived at St Jean-du-Gard on the afternoon of 3 October. On his way, he spent three nights sleeping in the open—*à la belle étoile*; seven nights in country inns; and one at the Trappist monastery of Notre Dame des Neiges. He wrote some twenty-three thousand words of journal entries (slightly more than half the length of the final *Travels*); made a dozen or so pencil sketches; and expended—according to his frugal notes—eighty-five francs ten sous.

I set out to follow him as accurately as I could, without modern maps (until Florac) but going by the old tracks and roads between every village and hamlet that he mentioned. I also took twelve days, spending one night in a country hotel at Langogne; seven nights in fields and woods; two nights in barns; and one night—my last—under a venerable spreading chestnut tree in the valley of St Germain-de-Calberte. I spent ninety-eight francs fifty centimes —but I had only one hotel bill, and people gave me refreshments almost all the way. Most of my money went on the evening meal. I always saved a bit of bread, some sugar and sometimes a piece of pâté for my dawn *petit-déjeuner* in the fields. Lunch was usually a bottle of Pelforth beer and a handful of black olives. At farms, when I asked for water for my bottle, I was almost invariably given cold *citron* or red wine as well; or black coffee made as in Greece, very strong, with sugar poured into it, from a saucepan often kept on an open-fire stove. I smoked a pipe, which was often a useful point of conversation with people I met on the road: shepherds, woodsmen, old grandfathers out for a stroll near the village cemetery, farmers working the corner of a remote upland field. I exchanged tobacco as many times as words, and English flake could be sweet under the loneliness of the stars.

I also wore a hat, a brown battered felt object, somewhat like an old fedora, with a wide brim, and a curious leather band round the crown which gave it a backwoods character. I have had many hats since, but except for a certain cap from Dublin none of them ever quite achieved such talismanic properties and powers. This hat, Le Brun, besides performing the normal hat-like functions of keeping sunstroke at bay, and mildly redirecting heavy rain on to my left or right shoulder (at choice), had several magical virtues. One was deflecting lightning. Another was helping me see in the dark. A third was giving me the most vivid dreams about Stevenson whenever I slept with it tipped over my nose.

But most important of all, perhaps, was Le Brun's power to make other people laugh. It is a vital point. A stranger with a bag, when he appears at your door, perhaps at dusk; or knocks at your café window before the bread and milk have been delivered; or comes clambering over your gate, or surging out of your wood, or lumbering down your path making the dogs bark—such a stranger is not always a welcome figure. When he does not speak your language properly he is even more dubious and unwanted; and when he clumsily enquires about his friend "who came here a hundred years ago, with a donkey" you can be forgiven for thinking that you may have *un fou ou un méchant* on your hands. But not with Le Brun. It is quite impossible to be menaced by someone wearing Le Brun. You can only smile at such an apparition—*un type au chapeau incroyable!*

The girl in the *pâtisserie* at Florac, the prettiest blonde in the whole of the Cévennes, was so overcome with laughter at the way Le Brun doffed himself with a sudden farcical stream of rainwater flowing on to the polished tiles of her shop that she offered him a plate of éclairs *gratuit* if only Monsieur would go out and do it again in five minutes, "*quand mon amie Sylvie est descendue.*"

But these are lighter considerations. The beginning of the journey was hard for us both. For the whole of the first day, from Le Monastier to Le Bouchet, a distance of twenty-five kilometres over steep country roads, baked in hot golden dust, Stevenson had endless and humiliating trouble with Modestine. She refused to climb hills, she shed her saddle-bag at the least provocation, and in villages she swerved into the cool of the beaded shop-doors. He was forced to beat her relentlessly, first with his own walking-cane and then with a thorn-switch cut from a hedge by a peasant on the long hill up to Goudet. At Costaros, the villagers even tried to intervene, taking the side of French donkey against foreign tyrant: " 'Ah,' they cried, 'how tired she is, the poor beast!' " Stevenson lost his temper: "Mind your own affairs—unless you would like to help me carry my basket?" He departed amid laughter from the Sunday loiterers, who had just come out of church and were feeling charitable.

Yet as he flogged her over the rocky gorse-covered hillsides under a blazing afternoon sun Stevenson's own heart revolted against the apparent brutality of donkey-driving. He later wrote in his route journal: "The sound of my own blows sickened me. Once when I looked at Modestine, she had a faint resemblance to a lady of my acquaintance who once loaded me with kindness; and this increased my horror of my own cruelty."

As I laboured up the same noviciate slopes, sweating under my own pack, I found myself puzzling over these words. Were they just the famous Stevensonian whimsy? Or was he thinking of some particular woman? It was intriguing; I would have liked to have asked him about it. But it is true that when travelling alone your mind fills up strangely with the people you are fond of, the people you have left behind.

Stevenson was soon made further aware of Modestine's personality:

> We encountered another donkey, ranging at will upon the roadside; and this other donkey chanced to be a gentleman. He and Modestine met nickering for joy, and I had to separate the pair and stamp out the nascent romance with a renewed and feverish bastinado. If the other donkey had had the heart of a male under his hide, he would have fallen upon me tooth and nail; and this is a kind of consolation, he was plainly unworthy of Modestine's affections. But the incident saddened me, as did everything that reminded me of my donkey's sex.

He eventually discovered that Modestine was on heat for almost their entire journey. This disturbed him; for as I gradually came to suspect, problems of friendship, romance and sexuality were much on his mind throughout this lonely autumn tour.

Sitting up to my chin in the cool brown waters of the Loire tributary, on a sandy bank below the little bridge at Goudet, I mused on these questions and whistled to myself. I was wearing Le Brun, but nothing much else, and was dissolving in the glittering flowing water which seemed, for a moment, like time itself, a fluid gentle medium through which you might move at will, upstream and down, wherever you chose, with a lazy kick of your feet. A sharp giggle overhead recalled me: two children hung over the parapet pointing: "*Mais qu'est-ce-que c'est que ça! c'est un nomade—non, c'est un fou!*" I retreated to my clothes under the shadow of a tree, hot with embarrassment. Not so easy to slip out of time, or clothes, or conventions, even here. Le Brun hung on a branch and mocked me gently. I turned again to the dusty road.

Despite his donkey troubles, Stevenson got into the inn at Le Bouchet shortly after nightfall, well ahead of me on this first day's run. I began to appreciate how physically tough he must have been. Coming down to Costaros, in a hot low red sun, I began to shiver with exhaustion and at one point tumbled headlong into a ditch. My shoulders were bruised from the pack, my right foot was spectacularly blistered, my morale low. I fell asleep on the bench of a little dark-panelled café, knocked over my green glass of *sirop*, and was turned out into the twilit street by an angry *madame la patronne*. I felt I was not managing things very well.

"*Désolé, madame,*" I murmured; and that's exactly how I felt: desolate. I was soon to grow familiar with this feeling. It is how every traveller feels at the approach of night, and the lighting up of windows in houses where he does not belong, and cannot enter in.

An old man stopped me, and talked, and took me by the arm. "*Mais oui, la route de Monsieur Steamson—c'est par ici, prenez courage . . .*" He led me to the outskirts of the town and showed me the *vieux chemin*, a glimmer of cart-track heading into the darkening, pine-fringed hills for Le Bouchet. Then, inexplicably, he took me back again, and I was suddenly sitting in a little shoemaker's cottage, under a yellow print of Millet's *Angelus*, eating omelette and drinking red wine from a pitcher and laughing. I remember the old man's dungaree blues, his black beret, his arthritic hands, still nimble and expressive, on the red check tablecloth. He was one of those who knew the story, as if it were part of village history. He spoke of Stevenson as if he had done his *Travels* in living memory, in some undefined time "*avant la guerre*" when he himself was a young lad, full of adventures.

"You see," said the old man, "there is a time to kick up your heels and see the world a bit. I was like that too. And now I make shoes. That's how things are, you will see."

I slept out that night under an outcrop of pines, facing east on a slight incline, with the lights of Costaros far away to my left. The turf was springy, and the pine needles seemed to discourage insects. As I lay in my bag, a number of late rooks came winging in out of

21

the gloaming, and settled in the pine branches, chuckling to each other. They gave me a sense of companionship, even security: nothing could move up through the trees below me without disturbing them. Once or twice I croaked up at them (it was the wine), and they croaked back: "*Tais-toi, tais-toi.*" This night I fell asleep quickly. Only once, waking, I drank two ice-cold mouthfuls of water from my can and, leaning back, saw the Milky Way astonishingly bright through the pine tops, and felt something indescribable—like falling upwards into someone's arms.

At Le Bouchet, Stevenson slept in the same inn room as a married couple from Alais. They were travelling to seek work at St Etienne. Sharing rooms was normal practice in country *auberges* till the very end of the nineteenth century, but the woman was young and Stevenson was shy, for all his bohemian manners. "*Honi soit qui mal y pense*; but I was sufficiently sophisticated to feel abashed. I kept my eyes to myself as much as I could, and I know nothing of the woman except that she had beautiful arms, full white and shapely; whether she slept naked or in her slip, I declare I know not; only her arms were bare."

In the morning the innkeeper made a goad for Modestine, while his wife briskly advised Stevenson about what should go into his travel-book. "'Whether people harvest or not in such and such a place; if there were forests; studies of manners, what for example I or the master of the house say to you; the beauties of nature; and all that.'" Stevenson wrote her words down in his most winning manner, adding that the wife—unlike the husband—could read, had a share of brains, but was not half so pleasant. "'My man knows nothing,'" he recorded her as saying with an angry toss of her chin. "'He is like the beasts.' And the old gentleman signified acquiescence with his head as if it were rather like a compliment."

Their youngest daughter, who looked after the cattle, was rude and mischievous, until her father—without a flicker of expression—abruptly announced that he had sold her to the foreign *monsieur* to be his servant-girl. He appealed to Stevenson for confirmation.

Stevenson solemnly took up the game. "'Yes,' said I, 'I paid ten half-pence; it was a little dear, but . . .'

'But,' the father cut in, 'Monsieur was willing to make a sacrifice.'"

A little while after, the girl hurried out of the stone-flagged kitchen, and the sound of sobs came through from the stable next door, along with the munching and stamping of the cows and horses. Instantly Stevenson hurried after her, and put all right, closing the game in wild laughter. He had a quick rapport with children, and would play instinctively on their sense of mystery and adventure, half-entrancing and half-terrifying them. To be sold to a long-haired foreign traveller with a huge blue woollen sack was not much better than to be pursued by Blind Pew tap-tapping with his stick at the door of the Admiral Benbow inn.

Stevenson's route now swung almost due south, up over the last high farmlands of the Velay to Pradelles, then down to the little market town of Langogne on the River Allier. Here he came to wild country, and a new phase in his pilgrimage of the heart.

He described the bleak prospect with the relish of an Edinburgh lowlander set free:

> On the opposite bank of the Allier, the land kept mounting for miles to the horizon; a tanned or sallow autumn landscape, with black dots of firwood, and white roads wandering far into the Gévaudan. Over all this, the clouds shed a uniform and purplish shadow, sad and somewhat menacing . . . It was a cheerless prospect, but one stimulating for a traveller. For I was now upon the limit of the Velay, and all that I beheld lay in another country – wild Gévaudan, mountainous, uncultivated, and but recently disforested from *the terror of wolves.*

All that morning, as I tried to catch Stevenson up, I thought of wolves. Clambering over the flint farm-tracks, I watched the dark hills of Gévaudan before me, and saw no one but the figures of distant labourers working in the shimmering fields.

A curious gnawing pain began at my heel. Before Pradelles, the ball of my right foot split open, leaving something like a slice of best back bacon, which I held mournfully under the village pump. The doctor at Landos, with half-moon gold spectacles, hung out of his window and announced that he was having lunch. Then, seeing Le Brun very crestfallen, he added, "*Mais montez, montez quand même.*"

Scissors snapped, patent ointments oozed, and my proffered francs were waved aside. I limped out of Landos in a cloud of Pernod fumes, menthol and cocaine-gel.

Beyond Pradelles I bathed in another stream, this time discreetly shrouded by bulrushes. The heat was still stunning, and I lay back in the cool water, holding my bandaged foot solemnly in the air like a demented heron. I dozed, and the grumbling of distant thunder mixed in my dreams with the growling of those wolves of long ago.

But Stevenson was still three or four hours ahead of me. He crossed the stone bridge into Langogne in the early afternoon of Monday, 23 September 1878, "just as the promised rain was beginning to fall". Here, however, he decided to settle for the rest of the day at the inn, and this I knew would give me my chance to catch up with him. Modestine was fed and stabled, and Stevenson sent his knapsack out for repair, then sank into a corner-seat to read up about the legendary "Beast of Gévaudan".

This Napoleon Bonaparte of Wolves had terrorised the whole region in the mid-eighteenth century. Its exploits held a peculiar fascination for Stevenson. Roving in the remote hills between Langogne and Luc, it had viciously attacked small children guarding sheep, or lone women returning from markets at dusk. These attacks lasted throughout the 1760s. When the victims were found their bodies were always drained of blood, though not wholly devoured, and there were wild rumours of vampirism, or worse. The Bishop of Mende ordered public prayers to be said in the country churches on Sundays, and the Intendant of Languedoc organised armed wolf-hunts with parties of dragoons. The King himself eventually offered a reward of six thousand *livres* to whoever should slay the Beast.

It proved strangely elusive for several seasons, and the myths about the animal grew: its appearance on nights of the full moon, its liking for thunderstorms, its power to leap from one hilltop to the next or to appear in two places at once. Finally, in September 1765, a local shepherd called Antoine shot a huge wolf weighing nearly ten stone. Its body was stuffed and sent to the court at Versailles amidst great rejoicings. The local people felt a curse had been lifted from them.

How great was their horror when, less than two years later, in the spring of 1767, the attacks began again with even more frenzied violence. On the hills of the Lozère two teenage boys were virtually torn to pieces. The entire population of the Gévaudan lapsed into a state of superstitious panic; farming went neglected and almost no one would cross their doorsteps after dark.

The end when it came was curiously muted. One late June evening in 1767, Jean Chastel, a local woodsman, out hunting for the Beast, was attacked in a forest clearing by a large wolf which he shot at point-blank range with a single musket-ball. The kill really did bring the reign of terror to an end, and Chastel became a folk hero. Yet this second wolf was a common enough animal, with a tatty pelt, and weighing two stone less than its predecessor. The mystery of the Beast of Gévaudan always remained, and continued to haunt the region even in Stevenson's time. He read a novel on the subject by Elie Berthet at Langogne.

"If all wolves had been as this wolf," Stevenson remarked thoughtfully, "they would have changed the history of man."

Modern studies of the subject, rich in explanations, were each more fantastic than the last. One school followed a vampire theory; another proposed a sadistic Gévaudan landowner who terrorised his tenants with a trained pack of hunting wolves; and a third, deeply psychological, produced Jean Chastel himself as a pathological killer dressed up in wolf-hides. But my favourite had a sinister simplicity. It proposed, as a strict zoological possibility, a rogue family of *three* wolves (like The Three Bears) who, ostracised from the main pack, had tasted the delights of human flesh, and thereafter attacked in combination. Hence the inexplicable ferocity of the Beast; and also its ability to be in two places at once. This theory had the great attraction of leaving *one wolf still unaccounted for*. I liked this very much.

It was sheer coincidence that on the final leg of my walk over the hills to Langogne, I had my first brush with a Cévennes storm. These storms are peculiar to this highland region, local and intense, fast-moving from one hilltop to the next, and teethed with forked lightning that terrified me. It overtook me rapidly from the west, and seemed to chase me over the bare pastures, until to my immense relief I came upon a hamlet in the fold of the hill, with a tiny *café-épicerie* where I took shelter for an hour, while the storm passed, banging and snarling and flashing overhead.

The café-owner, a small man in an extravagantly dirty apron, polished glasses philosophically in the doorway. The rain beat on the green awning while we talked disjointedly of Stevenson and storms.

"It is not always wise to go over the hills," he observed, while cigarette ash from his yellow *papier-maïs* fell on his apron in the hot damp wind. There was something lugubrious about his down-turned mouth. He craned his head outside, looked sharply up at the lowering clouds and shrugged. "There, he is clearing away now." He returned to the little zinc-topped bar, flapped at the thunder flies, coughed, shook his head (more ash) and wished me well in his own fashion. "So, you are going into Gévaudan. You will see him again, *alors*."

I departed, draped in my waterproof sheet, my hat at a combative angle. The sun came out, and I made the last descent to Langogne, through drenched fields of grass full of gleaming buttercups. I felt oddly elated.

At a little after eight in the evening I at last crossed the bridge over the Allier into Langogne, the shadows lengthening along the streets. The shopkeepers were closing up their stalls, and the air was full of the smell of crushed fruit and frying garlic. It was the biggest place I'd been in for days, with a fine eleventh-century church and a medieval covered market. It was cheerful and bustling, with family groups sitting out on the pavements, couples strolling arm in arm along the river and children fishing for minnows with pink and yellow nets.

But here something strange happened. The feeling that Stevenson was actually waiting for me, in person, grew overwhelmingly strong. It was almost like a hallucination. I began to look for him in the crowds, in the faces at the café doors, at hotel windows. I went back to the bridge, took off my hat, rather formally as if to meet a friend, and paced up and down, waiting for some sort of sign. People glanced at me: I felt an oddity, not knowing quite what I was doing, or looking for. The twilight thickened; bats began to dart over the river. I watched their flickering flight over the gleaming surface, from one bank to the other.

And then I saw it, quite clearly against the western sky, the old bridge of Langogne. It was about fifty yards downstream, and it was broken, crumbling, and covered with ivy. So Stevenson had crossed *there*, not on this modern bridge. There was no way of following him, no way of meeting him. His bridge was down. It was beyond my reach over time, and this was the true sad sign.

The discovery put me in the blackest gloom. It was stupid, but I was almost tearful. I could not bear to stay in Langogne, and after a distracted supper I climbed the steep hill of rustling plane trees towards St Flour and Fouzilhac. It was pitch-black (my eyes had lost their "country" vision by dining under bright lights) but I was anxious to plunge into the Gévaudan. Below, to my left, I could hear a small river running through what I took to be a gentle-sloping water-meadow, and I fancied I would camp there. Turning off through the plane trees I jumped over a low stone wall and seemed to drop into a bottomless pit.

In fact, it was a fifteen-foot, stone-banked wall ending in a mass of thorn briars; below them, the ground shelved away directly into the river and, skidding and cursing through the blackness, I went with it. An hour later, wet to the waist, I was signing myself into the only hotel in Langogne that would take a doubtful traveller after midnight. Le Brun did his best, but the joke was thin. In my pocket I found my pipe broken off at the stem.

As I dropped off to sleep in my luxurious broom-cupboard I thought I would give the whole damn thing up.

I had mad dreams about children dancing round me in a mocking circle. They were waving nets and singing:

> *Sur le pont d'Avignon*
> *On y danse, on y danse . . .*

I thought a good deal about this dream. It seemed, in part, to be a projection of Stevenson's own experiences, when, the following night, he was lost on the paths between Fouzilhac and Fouzilhic. He could find nowhere to stay as the darkness came on, and no one to give him directions. Instead he too met strange and dreamlike children.

> As I came out on the skirts of the woods, I saw near upon a dozen cows and perhaps as many more black figures, which I conjectured to be children, although the mist had almost unrecognisably exaggerated their forms. These were all silently following each other round in a circle, now taking hands, now breaking up with chains and reverences . . . at nightfall on the marshes, the thing was eerie and fantastic to behold.

Partly also I came to think that my dream was a warning: a warning not to be so childish and literal-minded in my pursuit of Stevenson. The children were dancing and singing of the old bridge of Avignon: the bridge that is broken, just like the old bridge of Langogne. You could not cross such bridges any more, just as one could not cross literally into the past.

Even in imagination the gap was there. It had to be recognised; it was no good pretending. You could not play-act into the past, you could not turn it into a game of make-believe. There had to be another way. Somehow you had to produce the living effect, while remaining true to the dead fact. The adult distance—the critical distance, the historical distance—had to be maintained. You stood at the end of the broken bridge and looked across carefully, objectively, into the unattainable past on the other side. You brought it alive, brought it back, by other sorts of skills and crafts and sensible magic.

Have I explained myself at all? It is the simplicity of the idea, the realisation, that I am after. It was important for me, because it was probably the first time that I caught an inkling of what a process (indeed an entire vocation) called "biography" really means. I had never thought about it before. "Biography" meant a book about someone's life. Only, for me, it was to become a kind of pursuit, a tracking of the physical trail of someone's path through the past, a following of footsteps. You would never catch them; no, you would never quite catch them. But maybe, if you were lucky, you might write about the pursuit of that fleeting figure in such a way as to bring it alive in the present.

I awoke next morning in a different mood, and climbed the same hill in bright sunlight, in the company of a shepherd with his small black-and-white collie dog. The shepherd had been on the road eight days, he said, going to his cousins' farm across the Tarn. He mended my pipe with a piece of waxed twine, cunningly tied.

Stevenson had a rough day on those hills. The weather was bad. He fell into bogs, lost his way in woods and finally found himself benighted in a storm at the inhospitable village of Fouzilhac. No one would cross their doorsteps to put him on the path for Cheylard. *"C'est que, voyez-vous, il fait noir,"* they told him. Stevenson implies that it was memories of the Beast of Gévaudan that made the men so reluctant. But he himself could not have looked an inviting figure by then: gaunt, long bedraggled hair, trousers caked in mud, and a strong whiff of the brandy-flask. No wonder everyone refused his requests to be shown the way with a lantern. The hour grew later, the rain heavier. He blundered on, alone.

Stevenson, for all his reputation as a dilettante, was determined and resourceful. The Scottish grit came out in just such a minor crisis as this. Abandoning all thoughts of civilisation, he pitched camp alone in the howling wind, under the lee of a dry-stone wall, tethering Modestine to a nearby pine branch and carefully feeding her chunks of black bread. He spread his sleeping-sack by the light of his spirit-lamp tucked into a crack of the wall. After removing his soaking boots and gaiters, he drew on a pair of long, dry woollen stockings, stuck his knapsack under the canvas top flap of the bag for a pillow, slid down into the woolly interior of the bag (still containing his books, pistol and spare clothes) and strapped himself in with his belt "like a bambino". Here he proceeded to dine on a tin of Bologna sausage and a cake of chocolate, washed down with plenty of brandy from his flask, rolled and smoked "one of the best cigarettes in the world", and dropped off to sleep like a child, contentedly lulled by the stormy sounds of wild Gévaudan. It struck me as an admirable feat in the circumstances.

The next morning, Wednesday, 25 September, he woke warm and refreshed, beneath the clear grey light of dawn and a brisk dry wind. Closing his eyes, he reflected for a moment how well he had survived, without once losing his temper or feeling despair. Opening them again, he saw Modestine gazing across at him with an expression of studied patience and disapproval. Hastily pulling on his boots, he fed her the remaining black bread, and wandered about the little beech wood where he now found himself, cheerfully consuming more chocolate and brandy. He was filled by one of those sensations of early-morning rapture which seem to affect people who have slept rough in the open. He later wrote:

Ulysses, left on Ithaca, and with a mind unsettled by the goddess, was not more pleasantly astray. I have been after an adventure all my life, a pure dispassionate adventure, such as befell early and heroic voyagers; and thus to be found by morning in a random woodside nook in Gévaudan—not knowing north from south, as strange to my surroundings as the first man upon the earth, an inland castaway—was to find a fraction of my daydream realised.

I loved this idea of the "inland castaway". It seemed to me such a subtle, almost poetic idea, as if real travel were concerned with disorientation rather than merely distance. It was losing yourself, then finding yourself again: casting yourself, at least for one moment, into the lap of the gods, and seeing what happened. Of course I could understand that his literary talk of Homer, and later Bunyan, was partly self-mockery. But then it seemed to me it was partly serious as well, and that the "daydream" was a real thing for Stevenson, and that his travels were also a pilgrimage.

What puzzled me again was that "goddess". Did he have some particular Circe in mind? Some woman who had cast a spell over him, perhaps? Were his own thoughts secretly "unsettled" by her, and was this pilgrimage an attempt to escape her—or appease her? As I padded along the silent woodland trails, deeper and deeper into Gévaudan, it slowly dawned on me that I might be pursuing a woman as well. Beyond Fouzilhac, which I never found at all, even in daylight, I stopped for an adder slowly uncurling itself off a large flat rock in my path. It was small and handsomely zigged, glossy black on soft beige, and moved aside with perfect dignity. At Cheylard, which is little more than a clearing with a few farms and a shrine, I stood for a long time beneath the wooden statue of Our Lady of All Graces.

We were now heading for the Trappist monastery of Notre Dame des Neiges. Stevenson, I supposed, had a conscience to examine. Our path went eastwards, over high moorland beyond the shelter of the Forêt de Mercoire, to Luc; then turned south again down a remote valley of the Allier towards La Bastide, where the Trappists lived on a thickly wooded hillside, in their ancient vows of poverty, chastity, obedience—and silence. Lay people from the outside would occasionally be granted permission to stay there "on retreat", sharing the monks' harsh routine, meditating and praying, and taking stock of their lives. For a lapsed Calvinist like Stevenson it was a not entirely foreign idea; for a lapsed Catholic like me it was only too familiar. A brief visit seemed unavoidable.

This leg of the journey took two days, broken by a night at Luc.

Stevenson slept at the comfortable *auberge*, after his Fouzilhac adventure; while I crossed the river and camped in a fragrant barn full of new-mown hay. I had again been caught by a storm crossing the moors between Cheylard and Luc, and I was glad of a roof-beam and the friendly, reassuring sound of munching cattle.

I had another dream. My path was an endless track of grey stone chippings that mounted through mauve heather to a bare sky. It seemed deserted but was full of unknown presences and pine stumps, as far as the eye could see. All were lightning-struck, a dead and ghastly white. A storm approached me from behind, trailing fingers of rain. Thunder booms set me running and gasping as my pack grew heavier and heavier. Someone was coming, chasing me, and prongs of lightning snapped down on the hill—to my right, to my left, then directly overhead. My heart beat with fear, and I ran and ran over the lonely moor, and my hair turned snow-white. I sat up and it was the whiteness of dawn. The cattle were chomping and the hay smelt sweet.

In the morning a farmer gave me a large bowl of coffee and *tartines*, and I was sick. I went down to the Allier, and bathed from a rock, and scrubbed some clothes. A fisherman, carrying a long cane rod, walked by with a sideways glance, curious. Long after he was gone I could see the gleaming tip of the rod moving on down the valley in the direction of La Bastide, like the antenna of some predatory insect. I felt like another species myself, a sort of animal cut off from the human world. I lay on the rock all morning in the hot sun, listening to the call of peewits and the sounds of the river.

I found that Stevenson wrote that day in his journal:

Why anyone should desire to go to Cheylard or to Luc is more than my much inventing spirit can embrace. For my part, I travel not to go anywhere, but to go; I travel for travel's sake. And to write about it afterwards, if only the public will be so condescending as to read. But the great affair is to move; to feel the needs and hitches of life a little more nearly; to get down off this feather bed of civilisation, and to find the globe granite underfoot and strewn with cutting flints.

It is one of his most memorable formulations, and I learnt it by heart. At night I would mumble it to myself, almost like a prayer, in the solitariness of my sleeping-bag. Again, I took it quite literally, on trust. Or rather, I was compelled to take it—this, I felt, is what I had to do; though if anyone had asked me why I could not have explained. The fact that Stevenson was also making something of a profession of his bohemian wanderings, and deliberately searching for picturesque copy, did not occur to me at first. (He did not use that sentence about his reading public in the published version of his *Travels*; it revealed his hand too clearly.) But I now think that my critical innocence allowed me to learn other things, far more important, about the personal life that is hidden in, and below, the printed page. To learn by heart has more than one meaning.

On Thursday, 26 September Stevenson turned east again away from the Allier, climbed along the high forested ridge above La Bastide, and with much misgivings came down with Modestine to the gateway of Our Lady of the Snows. He stayed there for one night and most of two days. I came to think of this as one of his most complicated human encounters. It threw into relief for me much of his Scottish inheritance and upbringing, and eventually revealed some of the deepest preoccupations of his journey.

The faintly jocular tone in his journal was, I was sure from the start, a disguise. I felt the same real twinges myself.

Here I struck left, and pursued my way, driving my secular donkey before me and creaking in my secular boots and gaiters, towards the asylum of silence. I had not gone very far 'ere the wind brought to me the clanging of a bell; and somehow, I can scarce tell why, my heart sank within me at the sound. I have rarely approached anything with more hearty terror than the convent of Our Lady of the Snows; this is what it is to have had a Protestant education.

His first sight of the monk Father Apollinaris planting out a long avenue of birch trees, in his flapping robed habit, immediately touched off childhood memories. It reminded him of the old prints of the medieval friars in the Edinburgh antique shops. The white gown, the black pointed hood, the half-revealed yellow pate, all stirred forgotten terrors. Moreover, what was the etiquette for dealing with the Trappist vow of silence? "I doffed my fur cap to him, with a faraway, superstitious reverence."

He was surprised to find, however, that a foreign traveller was most kindly and indeed volubly greeted. Once it was established that he was not a pedlar "but a literary man" he was regaled with a liqueur, assigned a whitewashed cell in the guest wing, and bidden to attend the community services and meals at will. Father Apollinaris asked Stevenson if he were a Christian, "and when he found that I was not, or not after his way, he glossed over it with great goodwill". Later, an Irish brother, when he heard that the guest was a Protestant, "only patted me on the shoulder and said, 'You must be a Catholic and come to heaven'".

Stevenson read the notice pinned over the table in his cell, for those attending official retreats, with a mixture of amusement and gravity. "What services they were to hear, when they were to tell their beads, or meditate, when they were to rise or go to rest. At the foot was a notable N.B.: '*Le temps libre est employé à l'examen de conscience, à la confession, à faire de bonnes résolutions, etc.*'" But he was decidedly impressed by the severe régime of the Trappists themselves: rising at two in the morning to sing the office of prime in the choir, then regulating the entire day between work duties and prayer accordingly as the bell rang, maintaining a sparse vegetarian diet and never speaking—except by special dispensation to strangers like himself.

At the same time La Trappe had its measure of worldly good sense. Every monk was encouraged, indeed required, to work at a hobby of his own choice. Stevenson found monks binding books, baking bread, developing photographs, keeping rabbits or peacefully cultivating potato patches. The monastery library was open to all, with a collection that included not only the sacred texts and holy fathers of the Church but Chateaubriand, Molière and the *Odes et Ballades* of Victor Hugo. "Let me whisper in addition what I only heard by way of a report, a great collection in another room, under orthodox lock and key, where Voltaire and Walter Scott, in God knows how many volumes, led the dance."

That night, in the conduct of the kind old Irish brother, he attended the service of Compline in the candle-lit choir, greatly moved by the stern simplicity of the plain, white-painted chapel, and the "manly singing" of the cowled figures, alternately standing and bowed deep in prayer. "These things have a flavour and significance that cannot be rendered in words. Only to the faithful can this be made clear; or to one like myself who is faithful all the world over and finds no form of worship silly or distasteful."

As he retired to his cell for the night Stevenson began to think about the force of prayer—a somewhat uneasy subject to his tolerant but sceptical mind. Partly he was thinking back to the old childish certainties of his Presbyterian boyhood, the attendance at the kirk, the teachings of his beloved nanny, Cummie, and the nostalgic confidences of the counterpane which he was to capture so brilliantly in the land of Leerie the Lamplighter, of *A Child's Garden of Verses* (1885). But partly also he was realising that, even as a man, he had continued to pray; only in a different sense. Not in the form of superstitious supplications or "gasping complaints", which he could no longer regard as real prayers at all, but in the form of deliberate meditations, a particular turning and concentrating of the mind when alone. Sometimes, he recollected, he had even found himself taking pleasure in giving these prayers literary form, "as one would make a sonnet".

He realised that his voyage through the Gévaudan had been peculiarly fruitful in this respect: that through the physical hardships and the plodding loneliness a particular kind of consciousness had been released in him. And this consciousness made him more, not less aware of his place in the scheme of things outside; of his friendships, his loves, his duties; of his common fate. He wrote: "As I walked beside my donkey on this voyage, I made a prayer to myself, which I here offer to the reader, as I offer him any other thought that sprung up in me by the way. A voyage is a piece of autobiography at best."

He then entered not one, but three short prayers in his journal, of which the last is a Prayer for Friends.

God, who hast given us the love of women and the friendship of men, keep alive in our hearts the sense of old fellowship and tenderness; make offences to be forgotten and services to be remembered; protect those whom we love in all things and follow them with kindness, so that they may lead simple and unsuffering lives, and in the end die easily with quiet minds.

I sensed in all this that Stevenson was telling himself, quite simply, that he was not made to be alone, either in the human or the divine scheme of things. Paradoxically, the Trappists were teaching him that he belonged outside: he belonged to other people, and especially to the people who loved him.

It is here that I later discovered one of the most suggestive differences between the original journal and the published *Travels*. For, on reflection, Stevenson removed all these passages from the published version. They were, I think, just too personal and became part of an emotional "autobiography" he was not prepared, at that date at least, to deliver up to his readers. Instead he struck a more romantic, raffish pose, remarking only of his feelings after the Compline service: "I am not surprised that I made my escape into the court with somewhat whirling fancies, and stood like a man bewildered in the windy starry night." Cutting out all mention of the prayers, he reverted to his bohemian persona, and added instead a snatch of bawdy French folk-song:

Que t'as de belles filles,
Giroflé Girofla!

It served to remind him, he said, that the Trappists were after all "the dead in life—there was a chill reflection". He could only bless God that he was "free to wander, free to hope, and free to love". An interesting contradiction.

But then La Trappe is full of contradictions. They knew all about Stevenson when I passed through: a hundred years, they told me, is not so long in the eyes of eternity. Father Apollinaris's line of birch trees still stood. There were the white blocks of the monastic buildings perched bleakly on the forested hillside, rows of square unrelieved windows, part-military and part-industrial in appearance, and a bell chiming a flat commanding note—what memories it stirred!—from the rugged church tower. Yes, they said, it was all rather like a power-station: so think of it as a spiritual generator, pumping out prayers.

The original buildings which Stevenson saw had been burnt down in 1912. His small guest wing for travellers and retreat-makers had been replaced by a brightly painted café-reception house astride the main drive, constructed like a Swiss chalet, with a self-service food bar and souvenir counter. Under the trees a score of cars were parked, transistors played, and families picnicked at fixed wooden tables. I walked through like a ghost, dazed with disappointment, and headed for the church, remembering now what my farmer at Luc had said: "Ah, La Trappe, they make an *affaire* of the holy life up there"; though he had added with a Gallic shrug, "But good luck to them. We must all live in our own way, and le Bon Dieu has always liked a little money, as proof of good intentions."

In the church a young monk, with a Cicero haircut and penetrating grey eyes, suddenly rose out of the sacred bookstall and gently tugged at my rucksack. English? On the trail of Stevenson? Sleeping rough? Ah yes, he had wanted to be a writer himself. That too was a vocation! Well, it was a happy chance that had brought me to La Trappe. A happy Providence. So now I must lay down my burden (he said this with a smile, the grey eyes suddenly teasing) and he would take me to visit the monastery. But first things first! And here he peered at me with what I took to be a frown, and I thought I was to be put through my catechism. Le Brun, who had doffed himself politely enough at the church porch, now shifted uneasily from hand to hand, ready for a sharp retort and a swift retreat. Protestant, lapsed Catholic, atheist, poetic agnostic . . .

"You are hungry, my friend," Father Ambrose cut into my thought, "so come with me." And he gave me another of those Trappist smiles.

I was whisked away without ceremony to the kitchens, and sat down at a huge wooden table. Behind me, a large electric dishwasher turned like a Buddhist prayer-wheel. All round, tiles gleamed and scoured pots bubbled on brand-new gas ranges. The kitchen monk in a pressed white apron considered me thoughtfully. "One must feed the corpse as well as the spirit," he observed in a heavy Provençal accent, and grinned seraphically. He was as thin as a fence-pole, with the marks of asceticism like the marks of an axe over his long face and frame. He disappeared into an echoing pantry and came out with plate after plate balanced on his arm. I could not believe such a feast, and later listed it all in my diary: dish of olives, black and green; earthenware bowl of country pâté with wooden scoop; whole pink ham on the bone, with carving knife; plate of melon slices; bowl of hot garlic sausage and mash; bowl of salad and radishes; board of goats' cheeses; basket of different breads; canister of home-made butter; two jugs of wine, one white, one red. *Spécialité de la maison*, thin slices of fresh *baguette* spread very thickly with a heavy honey-coloured paste which turned out to be pounded chestnuts, *marrons*, and tasted out of this world. I was told simply: "*Mangez, mais mangez, tout ce que vous voudrez!*" And he was right; I had the hunger of the devil.

Much later I smoked my pipe and fell asleep in the monastery gardens, under a mulberry tree, wondering at the wisdom of monks. Father Ambrose woke me as his sandals came tapping along the terrace. "Better now?" was his only comment. I was taken on a tour of the buildings: long bare corridors of polished pinewood, a chapter-house full of afternoon sunlight and smelling of beeswax, a library like an academic college with a special history section including the complete works of Winston Churchill. Then a large bleak dormitory, with iron bedsteads in rows of cubicles, which brought back bad memories; and a shadowy choir-stall with, for me, the eternally ambiguous smell of incense.

The monks' timetable had shifted little since Stevenson's day. Prime began a little later, at three thirty in the morning; but the vegetarian fast was maintained from January till Eastertide. Prayer and hard physical work remained the staple of their lives. The cemetery stood behind a wall of the vegetable garden, a cluster of plain white crosses on a neat lawn, like a war grave in Passchendaele.

"And here at La Trappe," said Father Ambrose as we stood again upon the terrace, "the summer visitors soon depart. We are alone again with Our Lady. Her snows fall from November until April. Sometimes we are cut off for days. Cut off from everything . . .

except from God. And sometimes it is so ... But you must pray for us. Pray for us on your road. You will do that, my friend, I think? And come back again, we will be here. Your rucksack is a light one."

Father Ambrose smiled and turned rapidly away, slipping his hands into the long white sleeves of his habit and stepping off into silence. The sound of his sandals retreated along the stone-flagged terrace. I was left strangely confounded, perplexed; this was not what I had expected. In a sense I felt they had found me out.

2

Stevenson's reactions to the Trappists were greatly complicated by the presence of two other visitors in the guest wing, a local Catholic priest and a retired soldier. The priest had walked over from his country parish at Mende for four days' solitude and prayer; the *ancien militaire de guerre*, a short, grizzled and somewhat peppery personage in his fifties, had come to La Trappe as a visitor—like Stevenson—and remained to study as a novice. Neither had the simplicity or the wisdom of the monks; they were "bitter and narrow and upright" in their beliefs, "like the worst of Scotsmen", reflected Stevenson. But it was only in the morning that they discovered that a Protestant heretic was in their midst: "My kindly and admiring expressions as to the monastic life around us, and a certain Jesuitical slipperiness of speech," observed Stevenson slily, "which I had permitted myself in my strange quarters, had probably deceived them, and it was only by a point-blank question that the truth came out." There was an immediate explosion. "*Et vous prétendez mourir dans cette espèce de croyance?*" burst out the priest.

Clergyman and army officer now attempted to convert Stevenson with righteous fervour. They took it for granted that he was secretly ashamed of his faith as a Protestant; disdained all theological discussion, brushed aside Stevenson's appeal to family loyalties, and crudely urged the horrors of hell-fire. He must go to the Prior of La Trappe and declare his intention to convert; there was not a moment to lose; he must instantly become a Catholic. The atmosphere became quite embarrassing. "For me who was in a frame of mind bordering on the effusively fraternal, the situation thus created was painful and a little humiliating." He escaped on a long walk round the monastery grounds, but on returning for lunch was again attacked by the proselytising pair. This time they began to mock him for his stubbornness and ignorance, and unwisely referred to his beliefs as those of a "sect"—for they thought "it would be doing it too much honour to call it a religion". His attempts at explanation were received with "a kind of ecclesiastical titter". Finally Stevenson's temper—which could be formidable: he had once broken a bottle of wine against a wall in a Paris café during an argument with the management—began to get the better of him. Trembling with emotion and going rather white, he leant across the table to the parish priest: "I shall continue to answer your questions with all politeness; but I must ask you not to laugh. Your laughter seems to me misplaced; and you forget that I am describing the faith of my mother." An awkward silence fell, and the priest, remarked Stevenson, "was sadly discountenanced".

However, dignity was restored, the *ancien militaire de guerre*—no doubt recognising another kind of fighter—made soothing noises, and the curé hastily assured him that he had no other feeling but interest in Stevenson's soul. The incident was closed, and they parted on friendly terms. But Stevenson was probably taught something after all: for here he was hotly defending a religion, the Presbyterianism of his childhood, in which he had supposed he had no formal belief whatsoever. It led him to reflect, towards the end of his journey, on the mysterious nature of belief itself, on its profound roots in the heart and the sense of identity; and the degree to which formal creeds were inadequate to contain and express one's deepest moral convictions.

In the *Travels* he added a friendly, if somewhat patronising, *envoi* to the priest as a fellow-traveller on the rough road of life:

> Honest man! he was no dangerous deceiver; but a country parson, full of zeal and faith. Long may he tread Gévaudan with his kilted skirts—a man strong to walk and strong to comfort his parishioners in death! I daresay he would beat bravely through a snowstorm where his duty called him; and it is not always the most faithful believer who makes the cunningest apostle.

The experience of the monastic life, even—and perhaps especially—in a passing glimpse, was both vivid and unsettling for Stevenson. In some ways it was weird, even repellant: Father Apollinaris's "ghastly eccentricity" as he suddenly raised his arms and flapped his fingers above his tonsured head, to indicate that the vow of silence had come back into force at the monastery gate, became a comic symbol of this. Yet in other ways it was obviously attractive to Stevenson. And what it attracted, I think, was paradoxically not the religious man, but the artist in him. He was drawn and fascinated by the idea of the celibate life within a community. The ascetic standards—the silence, the physical discipline, the solitary spiritual endeavour—appealed to him as a writer. The clarity of purpose, the absence of distraction, the lifelong sense of self-commitment were exactly the kind of ideals he felt he should be nourishing in himself as a professional author. The monks represented a sort of Flaubertian perfection. In their own way they had given up the world for an art form. Should he not do the same?

To begin with I had conceived of Stevenson's journey—and experienced it for myself—as a physical trial, a piece of deliberate "adventuring", a bet undertaken against himself, that he could survive on his own. His ill-health, his struggle against consumption, together with the real wildness of the Cévennes a hundred years ago made this trial a genuine enough affair.

But here was a new element, a metaphysical one. Stevenson was making a pilgrimage into the recesses of his own heart. He was asking himself what sort of man he should be, what life-pattern he should follow. Many hints had already suggested strongly to me that he was in love with someone. The incident with the young married couple in the inn at Le Bouchet was one obvious pointer; and the whole slightly mannered drama with Modestine seemed to me to contain some element of a private joke, a comic (but none the less serious) little allegory about his relations with the opposite sex.

The question he seemed to be formulating at La Trappe came down to this. As a writer, as an artist, should he be living and working on his own, celibate (or at least unmarried) and dedicated purely to the ideals of a literary community? Or should he commit himself emotionally to something, and someone else: to domesticated love, to marriage, to a professional life undertaken in partnership? For a young and ambitious Victorian writer this was no light or hypothetical question. He could survive comfortably as a single man on an allowance from relatively wealthy and well-meaning parents; and artistically he could flourish in the London literary world of clubs, pubs, reviews and masculine "bohemia". It required the most fundamental decisions about his future. Most of all, from a man of Stevenson's unusual temperament, to whom the enclosed Scottish world of his boyhood was so imaginatively important, it meant a choice about how far he could afford to grow up, to come fully into man's estate.

Reflecting on the life of the Trappists, Stevenson added a revealing passage to the *Travels*. Once again its lightness of tone was curiously deceptive. He wrote:

. . . Apart from any view of mortification, I can see a certain policy, not only in the exclusion of women, but in this vow of silence. I have had some experience of lay phalansteries of an artistic not to say bacchanalian, character; and seen more than one association easily formed and yet more easily dispersed. With a Cistercian rule, perhaps they might have lasted longer. In the neighbourhood of women it is but a touch and go association that can be formed among defenceless men; the stronger electricity is sure to triumph; the dreams of boyhood, the schemes of youth, are abandoned after an interview of ten minutes, and the arts and sciences, and professional male jollity, deserted at once for two sweet eyes and a caressing accent.

What was this lay *"phalanstère"* or commune to which Stevenson was referring? (The odd term was invented by the French utopian socialist Charles Fourier, and always appealed to the dreamer in Stevenson.) More important, to whom did the "two sweet eyes" belong? From my reading of his letters I could now guess a little at this.

The "artistic not to say bacchanalian" place was the village of Grez, some sixty miles south-west of Paris on the River Loing. Grez lies on the edge of the Fontainebleau forest, on the opposite side from the more fashionable Barbizon, already beginning to be associated with the Impressionists and "plein-air" school of painters. Stevenson had spent a part of the three previous summers at Grez, taking rooms at the Hotel Chevillon, idyllically placed by the low stone bridge, with its shadowy arches, over the placid river. He and his dashing elder cousin, Bob Stevenson, and a small group of Francophile painters, mostly Irish or American, including William Low and Frank O'Meara, all ate and worked in common in the grounds of the hotel. The place was soon to become famous for its resident artists—Delius was later to do much of his composing at Grez, and Sisley to commemorate it in his sunlit pictures. It was in the early days of this *phalanstère* that Stevenson met the Osbourne family from San Francisco, with their two young children. And it was the eyes of Mrs Osbourne which had entranced him—for life, as it turned out. As he later wrote in his *Songs of Travel*:

> Trusty, dusky, vivid, true,
> With eyes of gold and bramble-dew,
> Steel-true and blade-straight,
> The great Artificer made my mate . . .

3

I knew little of Fanny Vandergrift Osbourne at the time I followed Stevenson through the Gévaudan. The story of their tempestuous but largely successful marriage—which took them through California, back to Edinburgh, down to Hyères, and finally out again to America, the South Seas, Tahiti and Samoa, with Stevenson all the time writing, his professional path found, *Treasure Island* (1883), *Dr Jekyll and Mr Hyde* (1886), *The Master of Ballantrae* (1889) and the posthumous *Weir of Hermiston* (1889)—belongs to the mature part of his biography. But what I subsequently learned of Fanny's early life, and her personality, confirmed a great deal of what I was already seeing in Stevenson's own nature at this time—his needs, his strengths, his weaknesses. The difficulties of their early love affair also showed me more clearly the hidden significance of his pilgrimage through the Cévennes: a preparation for his journey of emigration the following year to San Francisco—also undertaken alone—to claim his bride.

Fanny Vandergrift broke the rules, almost all of them, and that was her first and enduring charm. She was a spirit quite as original and adventurous as Stevenson. Born in Indianapolis, Indiana, in March 1840, she was thirty-six when she first met him at Grez in 1876. Her ancestors were Dutch and Swedish; her parents were pioneer farmers who let her run wild on a series of small ranches. They had her baptised in the Presbyterian faith—an interesting emotional link with Stevenson—in one of the total immersion ceremonies in the White River when she was two. By her teens she had grown up into a strong, dark-haired, gypsy-looking girl, who could ride, use a rifle, grow vegetables, make wine, and hand-roll cigarettes. Her passion was painting, and because she was not thought a belle her style was that of the tomboy artist, dashing and devil-may-care. She had big, dark eyes, a determined jaw, and a powerful, stocky body with great sexual presence that remained with her late into middle-age. "God made me ugly," she used to say with sultry good humour, and the result was that everyone

40

thought her a handsome gal of spirit. She was popular, and her sister Nellie recalled that "there was scarcely a tree in the place that did not bear somewhere the name or initials of Fanny Vandergrift".

She was married at seventeen—probably already pregnant—to a young lieutenant on the Governor's staff, Sam Osbourne. He was blond, six-foot, quixotic, amiable and incurably unfaithful, and she loved him passionately. They went West to seek their fortunes, living in mining towns in Nevada, and when the gold-boom was over settling in San Francisco, in 1866. Sam was frequently away, fighting Indians with the army, prospecting in Montana with friends, or having affairs with saloon ladies. But he was always back when the children were born: Isabel ("Belle") in 1858; Lloyd in 1868; and Hervey in 1871. Jealous rows and passionate reconciliations became the pattern of the household, but gradually Fanny emerged as the stronger, more capable and more stable figure: her children were devoted to her, and remained emotionally dependent on her for the rest of their lives. Moreover Fanny, far from becoming embittered and frumpish, seemed almost to grow younger and more carefree as her family grew up. She lost none of her dash, good humour or energy; she always seemed game for anything. During the 1870s strangers often mistook her and Belle for sisters. When Belle was sent to finish her education at the San Francisco School of Design, Fanny enrolled too as a mature student, and a whole new circle of friendships opened out for her among the artistic "European" set in the city. In particular Fanny became friendly with a young Irish-American lawyer, Timothy Rearden, who was Head of the Mercantile Library, and knew writers like Bret Harte. Rearden became her mentor, possibly for a time her lover. He encouraged her to paint and write, read French and German, think about a new life—a second chance.

Fanny seized the opportunity in a way that would have been almost impossible for her contemporaries in Victorian England or Second Empire France. In 1875, when Belle was seventeen, Lloyd seven and Hervey four, she set off with her three children to study art in Antwerp. Sam Osbourne stayed behind in San Francisco, promising to pay a small allowance. Fanny was at last *une femme indépendante*, a triumph of spirit over circumstance. A photograph of her at this time shows a distinctly romantic heroine: a dark, determined woman apparently in her late twenties (she was actually thirty-five) with a mass of wild hair brushed impatiently back behind her ears. She wears a velvet-edged jacket over a tight-fitting black dress that carelessly shows off her figure. Knotted round her throat is a large white neckerchief, tied like a man's tie, loose and full, faintly provocative. The eyes are large and frank, the mouth strong and beautifully formed. She combined force of character with a certain indefinable vulnerability. Her daughter Belle recalled that on the steamer from New York "when in any difficulty, she only had to look helpless and bewildered, and gallant strangers leaped to her assistance".

Life was not easy in Antwerp. Money was scarce, the lodgings poor, and worst of all the Antwerp Academy would not accept women students. The American Consul tried to help her and Belle find private tuition, but then little Hervey fell ill with fever, and they were advised to take the child to a specialist in Paris. By December they were living in rooms in Montmartre, but in the spring of 1876 Hervey was still ailing, and Lloyd had vivid memories of hanging about hungrily outside *pâtisserie* windows because all their money was spent on doctors' bills. Fanny sent a telegram to Sam Osbourne in San Francisco, telling him their son was dangerously ill. He arrived in Paris to be at Hervey's death-bed. Bemused with grief, Fanny went back to her life-classes at the *atelier*, but had fainting fits and hallucinations, and trembled on the edge of a nervous breakdown.

Their French doctor strongly advised them to take Lloyd out of Paris to spend the summer in the country. Fanny discussed this with her friends at the *atelier*, and a young American sculptor told them about the Hotel Chevillon at Grez-sur-Loing. Sam agreed to come with them, at least for a time; they put their belongings in store and climbed aboard a train.

It was too early in the summer for many others to be in residence, and the hotel was quiet and friendly. Lloyd began to eat and run about like a young colt; Fanny and Belle sat peacefully painting riverscapes and walking in the water-meadows; Sam drank and chatted with Will Low. Gradually other painters turned up at the *phalanstère*, and each accepted the Osbournes as a picturesque addition to the bohemian enclave. Frank O'Meara fell in love with Belle, and there was much talk of what would happen when the mad Stevensons, Bob and Louis, finally arrived to complete the party. Days were spent swimming, lunching out under the trees, painting in the fields under white umbrellas.

First to arrive at Grez was Bob Stevenson, a tall erratic figure with Mexican moustaches and a ceaseless, brilliant flow of mocking talk. He was generally regarded as the "genius" of the two cousins: painter, musician, linguist, drinker and unreformed rake. He dazzled but also rather frightened Fanny; she described him as "exactly like one of Ouida's heroes".

Then, one evening in early July 1876, cousin Louis made his appearance. Young Lloyd Osbourne, who was soon to hero-worship him, remembered the scene vividly. It was dinner-time, with some fifteen of the *phalanstère* sitting round the long wooden table in the main room of the Chevillon. Oil-lamps stood along the board, pitchers of wine circulated, laughter flew back and forth. The main windows of the dining-room stood open to let in the sweet night air. Occasionally moths flew in from the darkness and fluttered against the bright glass chimneys of the lamps. Fanny and Belle were the only women in the company, and all attention was on them. Then little Lloyd heard a faint noise outside the window, and saw a shadow moving and hesitating beyond the light. There was a clatter of boots, a thin brown forearm on the window-sill, a sharp exclamation, and a dusty figure wearing a slouch hat and carrying a knapsack vaulted lightly into the room. Bob rose gravely from his chair and, turning to the Osbournes, announced like a conjuror: "My cousin, Mr Louis Stevenson." It was a grand entrance, never to be forgotten, and often to be embroidered. Stevenson himself later said he had waited many minutes outside in the dark, gazing into the bright room, transfixed by Fanny's face, acknowledging his destiny. Perhaps he did. Certainly Sam Osbourne left Grez and returned to America in September; and when Fanny returned with Belle and Lloyd for the winter to her lodgings at 5 rue Douay in Montmartre, Stevenson soon moved to rooms nearby. As Lloyd put it with delight, "Luly is coming."

Yet the affair took two years, with much coming and going between Paris and London and Grez, before it became really serious for both of them. Stevenson had other elder Muse figures on hand, notably Mrs Fanny Sitwell, the confidante and future wife of his friend Sidney Colvin. While Fanny Osbourne, for her part, was equally attracted by Bob Stevenson to begin with. Indeed, there is some reason to think that initially Bob was the favourite. She described them both, in a suitably colourful style, in a letter of April 1877 to Timothy Rearden, in San Francisco. It told me a good deal about the Stevenson family penchant for romancing about themselves, and playing incorrigible, boyish bohemians. She wrote:

Bob Stevenson is the most beautiful creature I ever saw in my life, and yet somehow, reminds me of you. He spent a large fortune at the rate of eight thousand pounds a year . . . studied music and did wonderful things as a musician, took holy orders to please his mother, quit in disgust, studied painting and did some fine work, and is now dying from the effects of dissipation and is considered a little mad. [In fact Bob soon married, had a family, and comfortably outlived Louis.]

Louis, his cousin, the hysterical fellow, is a tall gaunt Scotchman with a face like Raphael, and between over-education and dissipation has ruined his health, and is dying of consumption. Louis reformed his habits a couple of years ago, and Bob, this winter. Louis is the heir to an immense fortune which he will never live to inherit. His father and mother, cousins, are both threatened with insanity, and I am quite sure the son is.

Madness, sickness, lost fortunes and wasted genius: it all sounded like a delicious game to Fanny. Yet pretending that she will never meet them again (both cousins had returned home to Britain until the next summer), she added a warmer and truer note:

. . . The two mad Stevensons with all their suffering are men of spirits, but so filled with joyfulness of mere living that their presence is exhilarating . . . I never heard one of them say a cynical thing, nor knew them to do an unkind thing. With all the wild stories I have heard of them fresh in my mind, I still consider them the truest gentlemen . . .

"Gentlemen" she uses in an American sense; not snobbishly, but virtuously—men of honour, manners, sincerity.

Fanny became serious about Louis Stevenson after the second summer at Grez. Bob went back to Edinburgh, but Louis returned with her again to Montmartre, and here he was really taken ill, not with consumption but with a form of conjunctivitis which threatened to leave him blind. Fanny, suddenly thrown into the role of nurse and mother, took one of her headstrong decisions which even in Paris might have been considered socially foolhardy. She moved Stevenson into her own apartment, put him to bed and throughout October 1877 looked after him like one of her own family. When he grew no better she sent another of her telegrams to Sidney Colvin in London, and in November took Stevenson over on the boat-train. It was thus that she suddenly found herself introduced into Stevenson's London literary circle—meeting Colvin himself, Henley, Gosse, and even his Muse Mrs Sitwell.

Fanny was now dealing with the realities, as well as the dreams, of Stevenson's existence. She was his nurse as much as his mistress; though Stevenson himself hardly seems to have been aware of this subtle shift of emotional balance. What he saw was a beloved companion who had proved herself true and practical, and utterly regardless of conventions. What his friends saw—and they all liked her instantly—was summed up by Sidney Colvin:

> Her personality was almost as vivid as his. She was small, dark-complexioned, eager, devoted; of squarish build—supple and elastic; her hands and feet were small and beautifully modelled, though busy; her head a crop of close-waving thick black hair. She had a build and character that somehow suggested Napoleon, with a firm setting of jaw and beautifully precise and delicate modelling of the nose and lips; her eyes were full of sex and mystery as they changed from fire or fun to gloom or tenderness.

In fact Fanny was rather formidable.

Stevenson recovered his health, if not his heart, and went back to Edinburgh for a parental Christmas, while Fanny returned to Paris. It was at this time that Stevenson finally spoke of the relationship to his father and mother, and it seems clear that he was now thinking of marriage. They were hardly pleased: an American woman ten years older than Louis, and moreover a married woman with two children to support. In January 1878 Stevenson went back to Paris, and in February his father Thomas Stevenson joined him there for a man-to-man talk. "Don't be astonished," Stevenson wrote to Sidney Colvin, "but admire my courage and Fanny's. We wish to be right with the world as far as we can." There is no evidence that his father actually met Fanny, but in the event the vital allowance of a hundred pounds a year was not cut off, as Stevenson had feared; and he seems to have reached a better understanding with his father about his free-thinking religious beliefs.

But what was going on in Stevenson's mind? By far the most revealing document to me consisted of a linked series of four essays which he wrote for the *Cornhill* magazine and Henley's *London* magazine between 1877 and 1879. He later collected them in 1881 under the general title of *Virginibus Puerisque* ("To Youths and Maidens"). The first two essays concern marriage and the marriage relationship; the third is headed "On Falling in Love", with the Shakespearian epigraph—"What fools these mortals be!"; and the fourth is called, severely, "Truth of Intercourse". But all four are evidently drawn from his passion for Fanny, and they represent an entirely new note in his work and outlook.

The tone Stevenson adopted was ironic, mildly facetious, even slightly misogynic. Considering the circumstances under which he was composing this surprised me very much. It runs right through all four essays, from the famous definition of marriage as "a sort of friendship recognised by the police" to the long peroration on the terrors of the righteous wife. "Times are changed with him who marries; there are no more by-path meadows, where you may innocently linger, but the road lies long and straight and dusty to the grave . . . To marry is to domesticate the Recording Angel. Once you are married, there is nothing left for you, not even suicide, but to be good." What is one to make of all this?

Part of the answer seems to be that Stevenson, having really fallen in love with Fanny, was genuinely frightened—even terrified —by the implications. She was not the first woman he had flirted with, played bohemians with or slept with. But she was undoubtedly the first woman to become so important to him that she made his life incomplete, and challenged his identity. All the rapid shuttlings between England and France vividly suggest this, and everywhere the essays bear it out.

There is the frank avowal: "The fact is, we are much more afraid of life than our ancestors, and cannot find it in our hearts to marry or not to marry. Marriage is terrifying, but so is a cold and forlorn old age." Or there is the mocking paradox: "Marriage is a step so grave and decisive that it attracts light-headed, variable men by its very awfulness." There is even the rather knowing and hopeful: "It is to be noticed that those who have loved once or twice already are so much better educated to a woman's hand; the bright boy of fiction is an odd and most uncomfortable mixture of shyness and coarseness, and needs a deal of civilising."

Above all, there is Stevenson's hymn to the eternally boyish in man, the Peter Panish element (though that is an anachronism), which he felt intuitively it was dangerous, even a crime, to deny. The true threat of marriage, as he saw it, came down finally to this: that it would kill the boy in him. This passage is one of the best in the *Virginibus Puerisque*, and evidently links with Stevenson's meditations on those threats to "the dreams of boyhood, the schemes of youth" during his night at La Trappe. He is considering the "unfading boyishness of hope", what he defines as the piratical quality, the refusal to be quite tamed or rational or responsible, Tom Sawyer's "Ah, if he could only die *temporarily*". Turning aside for a moment from the imminent threat of marriage, he suddenly stops to wonder if boyishness is not, after all, an irreducible quality even in the most sage and settled of his fellow-citizens. The thought develops in a now characteristic way, in which a journey through a harsh landscape is already foreseen, even predicted:

> Here we recognise the thought of our boyhood; and our boyhood ceased—well, when?—not, I think, at twenty; nor perhaps altogether at twenty-five; nor yet at thirty; and possibly, to be quite frank, we are still in the thick of that arcadian period. For as the race of man, after centuries of civilisation, still keeps some traits of their barbarian fathers, so man the individual is not altogether quit of youth, when he is already old and honoured, and Lord Chancellor of England. We advance in years somewhat in the manner of an invading army in a barren land; the age that we have reached, as the phrase goes, we but hold with an outpost, and still keep open our communications with the extreme rear and first beginnings of the march. There is our true base; that is not only the beginning, but the perennial spring of our faculties; and grandfather William can retire upon occasion into the green enchanted forest of his boyhood.

In a literary way, this idea is central not only to the kind of books Stevenson went on to write (with their mixture of boyish adventure and very adult nostalgia), but to a whole tradition of late Victorian and Edwardian fiction. J. M. Barrie, Kenneth Grahame and Rudyard Kipling are all foreseen. But I saw only the immediate and personal situation.

The spring of 1878 did not bring Stevenson anywhere nearer a practical decision about Fanny. Though he had published *An Inland Voyage* in May, and gone some way to establishing himself in his own eyes as a professional author, their shared future still seemed unassured. Stevenson returned to London to work as an assistant editor on Henley's *London* magazine, and suddenly in July Fanny announced that she was returning to California. If it was an ultimatum Stevenson did not respond; but it is likely that Fanny—still married to Sam—was in just as much turmoil as he. Lloyd recalled with feeling: "I had not the slightest perception of the quandary my mother and RLS were in, nor what agonies of mind their approaching separation was bringing."

The three Osbournes left on the boat-train from London in August, and Stevenson, pale and silent, came to see them off. He could not bear to wait till the train pulled out but, wrapping his long brown ulster coat round his thin shoulders, strode off down the platform without glancing back. In September he reached the Cévennes, and only then did he dare to look about him.

4

After La Trappe there seemed to be a new sense of determination about Stevenson's route. He was rested, and certain issues must now have been clearly in the forefront of his mind. He and Modestine now embarked on the great upland peaks of the central Cévennes: the Montagne du Goulet at 4,700 feet; and, a day's walk beyond it, the Pic de Finiels at 5,600 feet. It is a different landscape from the Gévaudan, bolder, wilder, more dramatically plotted. It is visionary highland country: steep woods of scented pine climb sharply upwards to windy expanse of bare moorland, heath, rolling grass or scree; then drop back down in precipitous alpine meadows, or rocky gorges, rushing streams and deep green-and-gold terraces of chestnut trees. You walk against the sky, with chain after chain of hills rolling southwards at your feet.

This is also the beginning of the "country of the Camisards", the Protestant rebels of the regional insurrection of 1702–3, whose history had fascinated Stevenson from adolescence, when he sketched out *The Pentland Rising* about a similar upheaval in the eighteenth-century Scottish highlands.

The last eight chapters of the *Travels* are largely concerned with this Camisard history, together with Stevenson's reflections on the nature of religious belief and bigotry. The effect of this in the published text is to give the last third of his journey a curiously impersonal feel, an essay in regional history, which is quite at odds with the almost confessional tone of the previous days. He retells the stories of the various Camisard commanders—"Spirit" Séguier, Roland and Joani—together with the atrocities performed by the Catholic generals like Maréchal Julien in suppressing the movement (despite promised English aid) on the orders of the French King. It is a saga not unlike that of twelfth-century Cathars, persecuted by the armed forces of the Inquisition, further south in the Basses-Pyrénées; and it shows the nascent historical novelist in Stevenson.

When he stands on the top of Mont Mars, after a long, lonely, exhausting climb, his reflections appear to be totally absorbed in the long-ago struggles of these French covenanters:

I was now on the separation of two vast watersheds; behind me all the streams were bound for the Garonne and the Western Ocean; before me, was the watershed of the Rhône. Hence, as from the Lozère, you may see in clear weather the shining of the Gulf of Lyons, and perhaps from here the soldiers of Salomon may have watched for the topsails of Sir Cloudesley Shovel, and the long-promised aid from England. You may take this ridge as lying in the heart of the country of the Camisards; four of the five legions camped all round it and almost within view—Salomon and Joani to the north, Roland and Castanet to the south—and when Julien had finished his famous work, the devastation of the High Cévennes, which lasted all through November and October, 1703, and during which four hundred and sixty villages were utterly subverted, a man standing on this eminence would have looked forth on a silent, smokeless, and dispeopled land.

It is a vivid picture; and standing on the same high, lost ridge myself, it was easy to imagine Stevenson's gaze traversing the wild horizon, and conjuring up the shades of the lost Camisards: Spirit Séguier leaping to his death from the window of a surrounded house in Le Pont de Montvert, Roland fighting to the end with his back against an olive tree.

Yet such an image of Stevenson, immersed in historical reflections on his last days, struck me as false. In his original journal there is only one single glancing mention of the Camisards, while he is talking to a poacher—"a dark military-looking wayfarer, who carried a game-bag on a baldrick"—on the general theme of the local Protestantism. For the rest, the colourful accounts and anecdotes of Camisard history are much later additions to the text, worked up from Peyrat's *Pasteurs*, the novels of Dinocourt and Fanny Reybaud, and half a dozen other sources, long after Stevenson's return to England.

The visions of the Camisards in fact serve to cover up Stevenson's completely different preoccupations at the time. The original journal becomes brief, disjointed, dreamlike and in places highly emotional. Though he travels with increasing speed and purpose he is sunk in his own thoughts, physically driving himself—and Modestine—towards the point of exhaustion.

As I followed him, I was aware of a man possessed, shut in on himself, more and more difficult to make contact with. The narrative of the trip became at the same time more intense, more beautiful, and on occasions almost surreal. His wayside meetings were fewer, but obviously more significant to him. The general descriptions take on a visionary quality: strangely awestruck meditations on the huge, shadowy chestnut trees overhanging his route; the dusty track glowing eerily white under the moon (it is noticeable how often now he seems to be travelling after dark); a solemn night spent high up amidst the pines on the side of Mont Lozère; another deeply troubled camp with drawn pistol on the precipitous terraces above the gorge of the Tarn; and a period of black depression walking through the deserted valley of the Mimente below Mont Mars:

> But black care was sitting on my knapsack; the thoughts would not flow evenly in my mind; sometimes the stream ceased and left me for a second like a dead man; and sometimes they would spring up upon me without preparation as if from behind a door . . . the ill humours got uppermost and kept me black and apprehensive. I felt sure I must be going to be ill; and at the same time, I was well aware that a night in the open air and the arrival of holy and healthy dawn would put me all right again with the world and myself.

The moody fluctuations of this entry are typical: the way the real river has become confused with the inward stream of his thoughts; the way the knapsack has become a more than physical weight; the way he longs for a "holy and a healthy" dawn. These were all, I knew, symptoms of the solitary walker travelling too long alone in high bare places. But for Stevenson they had a special source, a specific pain. Introspection had reached a critical point, and I was hardly surprised to discover one entry which refers to "this disgusting journal". I followed him now with a kind of trepidation.

Over the first of the "high ridges", the Montagne du Goulet, Stevenson abandoned the zigzag donkey track, and tried to push Modestine straight up through the trees, beating her—"the cursed brute"—with a savagery he later shamefully regretted. She was bleeding frequently now "from the poop", but it seems to have been some time still before he realised she was on heat. He crossed over the high bare crest, marked only by upright stones posted for the drovers, and came down to Le Bleymard, tucked in the valley, with "no company but a lark or two".

I crossed the same ridge shortly after dawn, having spent the night on a corner of the village green at L'Estampe, observed by a patient farm dog, who accompanied me almost all the way up, grinning at Le Brun and chasing rabbits. After he left, the sound of

cocks crowing and wood being chopped rose from far below, clear
and minute, like tiny bubbles of sound bursting up through liquid.
I felt alone in the world, half-floating, tethered by some fragile
thread, sweating and light-headed. My diary remarks tersely:
"Homesick. White stones on the track scattered like broken trail,
tramps' messages. Read RLS poems out loud to attentive clouds.
But when I come to 'Dark brown is the river, Golden is the sand'
I burst into tears. Go down the track crying. What a fool. At
Bleymard write letters."

I am still not sure quite what significance that little poem had.
But it is to do with travelling, or at least a childish dream of travel;
and perhaps even more the idea of landfall, of coming home. I
suppose it is intolerably sentimental, yet it does capture something
pristine about the Stevenson notion of "going away", and just
because it was written for children by a thirty-year-old man (it
comes from *A Child's Garden of Verses*) this does not make the core of
the feeling any less permanent a part of Stevenson's adult make-up.
It is called "Where Go the Boats?" and I give it here as a kind of
touchstone:

> Dark brown is the river,
> Golden is the sand.
> It flows along forever,
> With trees on either hand.
>
> Green leaves a-floating,
> Castles of the foam,
> Boats of mine a-boating—
> Where will all come home?
>
> On goes the river,
> And out past the mill,
> Away down the valley,
> Away down the hill.
>
> Away down the river,
> A hundred miles or more,
> Other little children
> Shall bring my boats ashore.

Stevenson was restless at Le Bleymard, and although it was already
late in the afternoon he set out to scale a portion of the Lozère.
Objects continued to strike him in an odd way: the ox carts coming

down from hills, packed with fir-wood for the winter stocks, stood out against the sky strangely: "dwarfed into nothing by the length and bushiness of what they carried; and to see one of them at a steep corner reliefed against the sky, was like seeing a dragon half-erected on his hind feet with forepaws in the air." This was in fact the first of all his nights in which Stevenson deliberately set out to lose himself in the remote landscape and camp out alone. (The night at Fouzilhac had been *faute de mieux*.) The experience dominates these latter days, and produced by far the longest consecutive entry in the original journal. It is of decisive importance in his pilgrimage.

Stevenson pushed on past the dragons, out of the woods, and struck east along a stony ridge through the gathering dusk. The ground here is very high, some four and a half thousand feet, on the last fold before the Pic de Finiels, the topmost point of the entire Cévennes. The highland nature of the country gives way to something much more sweeping and alpine, with curving rocky crests, distant cairns of stone and constant rushing winds. The whole place is alive with streams, that spring directly from the steep turf. The source of each spring is marked by a perfectly round, clear pool of water, not more than two foot across but perhaps twice as deep, and still as glass except for a tiny twirl of movement dancing across the bottom. This constant pulse of life is formed from a cone of fine, golden gravel. I have never drunk water so sweet and cold and refreshing—like pure peppermint—as from these springs of Finiels; they remain for me the archetype of the word "*la source*"—whether as literal water or as some metaphor of origins.

Stevenson followed the sound of one of these tiny streams a little way back down the ridge into "a dell of green turf", below the wind-line, and three-quarters surrounded by pines: "There was no outlook except north-eastward upon distant hilltops, or straight upward to the sky; and the encampment felt secure and private like a room." The streamlet made a little spout over some stones "to serve me as a water tap". Modestine was tethered, watered and fed black bread; the big blue wool sack spread. Stevenson buckled himself in with his supper of sausage, chocolate, brandy and water; and as soon as the flush of sunset disappeared from the upper air he pulled his cap over his eyes and went to sleep, exhausted.

He awoke some five hours later, at 2 a.m. It was the hour of the Monks, what is usually considered the dead of night. Yet in the open air, on Finiels, he described it as the moment of "resurrection", a secret time known only to shepherds and countrymen: "Cattle awake on the meadows; sheep break their fast on dewy hillsides, and change to a new lair among the ferns; and houseless men, who have lain down with the fowls, open their dim eyes and behold the beauty of the night." He was thirsty, and sitting up in his sack he drank half the tin of spring water lying in the grass at his side. He pulled out his pouch and began meditatively to roll a cigarette. At his feet he could see the dark shape of Modestine, tethered by the pack saddle, gently turning in a circle and munching the grass. Above him were the black fretted points of the pines, and the faint silvery vapour of the Milky Way; the stars were clear and coloured, "neither sharp nor frosty"; there was no moon. Apart from Modestine's soft cropping "there was not another sound, except the indescribable, quiet talk of the runnel over the stones."

He lay back, lit his cigarette and studied the sky. He was wearing his silver gypsy ring, "to be like a pedlar if possible", and the cigarette cupped in his hand put a bright point of light in the band of metal. "This I could see faintly shining as I lowered and raised my cigarette, and at each whiff, the inside of my hand was lit up, and became for a moment the highest light on the landscape."

Stevenson later looked back at this moment as one of almost mystical significance. He was utterly alone and quiet and self-contained, deliberately cut off from his friends, his family, his fellow-men, as isolated as any monk, but also perfectly free, perched on a high hill under the stars, attuned to the faintest stirrings of the natural world. But at the same time the bright point of light on the silver ring, glowing and fading in time with his own breath, indicated the true centre of his thoughts and being: the band of human love.

The following morning, at dawn, as Modestine munched a new supply of black bread and the first sunlight caught the upper clouds above the Pic, Stevenson sat by his streamlet chewing chocolate and jotting a long, eloquent entry in his journal:

In the whole of my life I have never tasted a more perfect hour of life . . . O sancta Solitudo! I was such a world away from the roaring streets, the delivery of cruel letters, and the saloons where people love to talk, that it seemed to me as if life had begun again afresh, and I knew no one in all the universe but the almighty maker. I promised myself, as Jacob set up an altar, that I should never again sleep under a roof when I could help it, so gentle, so cool, so singularly peaceful and large, were my sensations.

The religious tone of this—the reference is to Genesis 28, "surely the Lord is in this place, and I knew it not"—a sort of dreamy pantheism, seemed to me to arise quite naturally from his circumstances, a sudden release from his moments of "black care" and physical exhaustion.

But it was the immediate qualification of this state of sublime content that struck me as so decisive. Stevenson wrote on:

> And yet even as I thought the words, I was aware of a strange lack. I could have wished for a companion, to be near me in the starlight, silent and not moving if you like, but ever near and within touch. For there is, after all, a sort of fellowship more quiet even than solitude, and which, rightly understood, is solitude made perfect.

Then at last he becomes explicit:

> The woman whom a man has learned to love wholly, in and out, with utter comprehension, is no longer another person in the troublous sense. What there is of exacting in other companionship has disappeared; there is no need to speak; a look or a word stand for such a world of feeling; and where the two watches go so nicely together, beat for beat, thought for thought, there is no call to conform the minute hands and make an eternal trifling compromise of life.

It was, in effect, a proposal of marriage to Fanny Osbourne.

For me this passage came to represent the central experience of Stevenson's Cévennes journey. Against it, in his notebook, he wrote in French "*à développer*", to be filled out—which in a sense he did for the rest of his life.

Yet in the published text of the *Travels* he added only one further ringing sentence: "And to live out of doors with the woman a man loves is of all lives the most complete and free"—which points directly to his honeymoon with Fanny in 1880, as the pair of "Silverado Squatters" in California. Far from developing the rest of the entry, he cut it back to a few lines, omitting both the religious and the amorous meanderings of his thoughts and replacing them with a brisk, even somewhat self-mocking observation. "I thought I had rediscovered one of those truths which are revealed to savages and hid from political economists: at the least I had discovered a new pleasure for myself."

Once again I glimpsed Stevenson deliberately covering his

tracks. The truth of the Pic de Finiels experience lay in its exposed, sweeping emotions. The toning down, the correcting and balancing, hid exactly that boyish hope and mysticism which finally rushed out towards the figure of Fanny, the ideal "companion" of Stevenson's future adventuring, and which was indeed made permanent reality in the exotic, open-air and strongly matriarchal last encampment of the Vailima house, in Samoa, with its sprawling airy verandahs, its alfresco feasts, its native ceremonials and expeditions. The sacred "green dell of turf" on Finiels, for ever withdrawn from ordinary society—focused, as it were, on the possibilities of starlight—was a real found place in Stevenson's heart. That he later hid it from his reading public gave me some measure of the gap between the social and the private self, even in supposedly "autobiographical" writing.

Stevenson crossed the Lozère on Sunday, 29 September into a new land of blue, tumbled hills, and plunging down a breakneck slope turning "like a corkscrew" descended into the valley of the River Tarn. "All the time," he wrote, "I had this feeling of the Sabbath strong upon my soul; and heard in spirit the church bells clamouring all over Christendom, and the psalms of a thousand churches."

Part of that feeling came, I knew, from the very sensation of being so high up in that country, that you feel you can see and hear for a hundred, a thousand miles, and that the wind will bring you news from everywhere. It is a mad, visionary sensation, and is partly a product of sheer physical exertion, a sort of oxygen "high". But Stevenson's mind was still running much on religious matters, and the thought of bells always turned him towards home.

At Le Pont de Montvert, with its fine stone bridge, the first thing he noticed was the Protestant temple; but the second thing was the perfume of French Sunday *déjeuner* at the inn, and "we must have been nearly a score of us at dinner by eleven before noon". This clubbable note of good food and good company came as quite a shock to me after the high-flown solitary meditations of the night before. But Stevenson's appreciation of the "roaring *table-d'hôte*" is typical of his quicksilver changes of mood, and the grave or sacred note is never long sustained even on the harshest parts of this last leg of his journey.

Indeed, after all those night declarations of ideal love, he promptly set up a comic flirtation with the serving-girl at the inn, a slow heavy blonde girl called Clarisse, which caused much amusement among his fellow-diners. Stevenson is rude about her, in a teasing amorous way, and I did not find it hard to read some sexual interest in this bantering account:

> What shall I say of Clarisse? She waited the table with a heavy, placable nonchalance, like an educated cow; but her huge grey eyes were steeped in a sort of amorous languor; her features, although they were fleshy, were carefully designed; her mouth had a curl, her nostril was a personal nostril that belonged to herself and not to all the world, her cheek fell into strange and interesting lines. It was a face capable of strong emotion and, with training, it offered a promise of delicate sentiments. It seemed to me pitiful that so good a model should be left to country admirers and a country way of thought . . . Before I left, I assured Clarisse of my hearty admiration; she took it like milk, without embarrassment or surprise, merely looking at me steadily with her great eyes; and I felt glad I was going away. If Clarisse could read English, I should not dare to add that her figure was unworthy of her face; hers was a case for stays; but that will grow better as she gets up in life.

The ribbing tone is worthy of Bob Stevenson—it is suddenly the philandering bohemian painter's voice, an echo of the laughter at Grez, with its talk of "model", "lines", and "flesh" and its knowing wink: if he had remained, who knows, he might have made a casual conquest. Nor did Stevenson suppress any of this in the *Travels*; even the remark about stays for Clarisse's bovine haunches remains. For this was acceptable Victorian smoking-room bavardage about buxom serving-wenches and perky laundry-girls, which goes back in the travellers' tradition beyond Byron's Swiss chambermaids to Sterne's supple French milliners in *A Sentimental Journey*. Stevenson manages it with a flourish, and yet the effect is not wholly happy or convincing. There is something a little awkward and defensive about the episode, and I think this was because Stevenson was no longer one of the boys in the usual sense. In particular the undertone of class superiority comes uneasily from him, and is not at all in keeping with the rest of the journal, or with the man who was to travel steerage to New York in the *Amateur Emigrant*. What Clarisse really brought out in him, I think, was his intense sexual loneliness and longing for Fanny Osbourne.

At all events, Stevenson did not remain at Le Pont de Montvert, but hurried on down the steep, twisting road through the Gorges du Tarn towards Florac, and spent one of his worst nights camped on the steep chestnut terraces which shelve out above the river. The place was so narrow that he had to lay his sack on a little plateau formed by the roots of a tree, while tethering Modestine several yards higher up on another shelf. The position was unpleasantly exposed to the road, the air heavy with the noise of frogs and mosquitos, the ground alive with ants, and the fallen chestnut leaves full of inexplicable sounds and scurryings which he afterwards put down to rats. For the first time during his journey Stevenson admits that he was frightened—"profoundly shaken"—and unable to sleep. He fingered his pistol and tossed uneasily, listening to the river running below in the darkness: "I perspired by fits, my limbs trembled, fever got into my mind and prevented all continuous and happy thinking; I was only conscious of broken, vanishing thoughts travelling through my mind as if upon a whirlwind . . ."

Nothing ill occurred, except in the morning he was surprised in the act of packing by two labourers come to prune the trees. One of the men demanded in unfriendly tones why Stevenson had slept there. "My faith," said Stevenson pulling on his gaiters and trying to hide his pistol, "I was tired." They watched, swinging their pruning knives at the next tree but one, until Stevenson and Modestine had stumbled back down on to the road.

I had a sort of superstitious fear of this same night, and it was the one time I looked for company. Le Brun picked out a rather jaunting *chapeau de paille* leaning over the bridge at Montvert; it belonged to a tall smiling chap carrying a backpack and old painter's case with brass locks. We went to the café and discussed local wine ("*le rouge de Cahors est tellement fort . . .*"), Cézanne, Swiss army penknives, the Beatles, and of course English girls. Later we camped down by the Tarn, made a fire, and got gently drunk. Le Paille admitted he wanted to be a great painter, and Le Brun muttered most strangely about being a great poet. "*C'est égal,*" said Le Paille, "*on le fera.*" I forgot all about Stevenson and slept like a log

In the dawn, over bread and black coffee, somewhat penitential, I explained about Stevenson's travels and Modestine. Le Paille regarded me indulgently: "*Mais vraiment tu es plus fou que moi. Il faut vivre ta propre vie à toi. Sinon . . .*" We parted cheerfully, with mock flourishes of the hats, repeated at several turns in the road, as we moved off in opposite directions. *Bonjour Monsieur Courbet. Bonjour Monsieur Steamson.* But I have often thought of that "*sinon . . .*" since.

On the road to Florac, pensive after his bad night, Stevenson was rewarded by his last significant encounter of the route. As it stands in his journal it has an almost proverbial quality. He fell in with an old man in a brown nightcap—"clear-eyed, weather-beaten, with an excited smile"—who was driving two sheep and a goat to market, accompanied by a little girl, his grand-daughter.

"*Connaissez-vous le Seigneur?*" the old man began briskly, and started to question Stevenson about his faith. This strange figure, whom Stevenson later described as "my mountain Plymouth Brother", turned out to be a member of an obscure but genial Protestant sect, and for some reason took the Scotsman to be of the same persuasion. Far from embarrassing him, their halting, somewhat inspired conversation served to confirm Stevenson in his pantheistic beliefs and in the principle of tolerance which he had been meditating on ever since La Trappe. The old man also seemed to appreciate the saving grace of a life lived in the open, free from formalities and conventional creeds.

I could not help thinking that Stevenson, for all his troubles, had brought down from the high hills a transcendental glow. "The old man cried out, when I told him I sometimes preferred sleeping under the stars to a close and noisy alehouse, 'Now I see you know the Lord!' " It struck me that their conversation along the winding road was ideally the kind of talk that Stevenson, in other circumstances, would have liked to have had with his father. He felt there was no real dishonesty in sliding over their differences and trying to keep to common ground: "I declare myself a Morave, with this Moravian, just as I tried to persuade the priest at Our Lady of the Snows that I was, in essential things, a Catholic; it is not my fault if they put me out, I continue to knock at the door, I will be in; there is no sect in the world I do not count mine."

Adding to this in the *Travels*, Stevenson drew the lesson more explicitly, giving the incident a weight and universality that he associated with Bunyan's *Pilgrim's Progress*, one of the models for his own book:

> For charity begins blindfold: and only through a series of similar misapprehensions rises at length into a settled principle of love and patience, and a firm belief in all our fellow men. If I deceived the good old man, in the like manner I would willingly go on to deceive others. And if ever at length, out of our separate and sad ways, we should all come together into one common house, I have a hope, to which I cling dearly, that my mountain Plymouth Brother will hasten to shake hands with me again. Thus, talking like Christian and Faithful by the way, he and I came down upon a hamlet on the Tarn.

This I suppose is the most public meaning of the *Travels*, its formal declaration of informality in faith, with the stress on charity and good fellowship as the most profound virtues for the journey of life. In a sense it is a quite deliberate contradiction of his stiff Presbyterian upbringing, and it was not without irony that Stevenson remarks: "I scarcely knew I was so good a preacher." And is the "good old man" his father (in the journal he addresses him as "*mon père*")?

Perhaps: it is particularly difficult to appreciate the degree to which religious differences could rend an otherwise close and loving family a hundred years ago. Differences of politics, morality, even career ambition—yes, these can still be felt from the inside; but differences of creed, these are almost lost to us. Unless of course you happen like me to have been brought up within a powerful "sect" like Catholicism and know from within the struggle and sense of guilt involved in breaking away. It did not surprise me to discover that when Stevenson first announced his agnosticism (although a very Christian form of it) to his father the latter wrote bleakly: "You have rendered my whole life a failure."

Their interview in Paris in February 1878 had much improved this situation. But Stevenson still felt the need for some kind of intermediary figure, like the old Plymouth Brother; and in this sense, while much of the *Travels* is "mere protestations" to Fanny, so much else in the book is still the appeal of a wayward son, "mere protestations" to Thomas Stevenson. As he put it in the journal: "'My father,' said I, 'it is not easy to say who knows the Lord, and it is none of our business. Protestants and Catholics and even people who worship stones, may know Him and be known by Him, for He has made us all.'"

At Florac Stevenson again lunched at the inn, where he was received as something of a portent. "My knife, my cane, my sack, all my arrangements were cordially admired." The village schoolmaster came in to question him, and the young innkeeper—unmarried, living with his sister—struck an amusing note: "'*Tout ce que vous avez est joli*,' said the young man, '*et vous l'êtes*'"—which Stevenson let pass with a smile. But again I sensed his hurry: he pressed on down the road towards Cassagnas—overtaken by that "black care" on his knapsack—and once again the dusk found him groping for a camp in the valley of the Mimente: "I slipped down to the river, which looked very black among its rocks to fill my can; and then I dined with good appetite in the dark, for I scrupled to light my lantern in the near neighbourhood of a house . . . All night, a strong wind blew up the valley and the acorns fell pattering over me from the oak."

This was his penultimate night on the road—and peace fell from the stars, he says, on to his spirit "like a dew". But he was much disturbed by the barking of a watch-dog from that nearby house, and the first hints of returning civilisation were upon him. "To a tramp like myself," he noted, "the dog represents the sedentary and respectable world in its most hostile form. There is something of the clergyman or the lawyer in the engaging animal."

I made a little fire among the rocks by the river, and slept in the doorway of an isolated barn. My diary notes "a solitary star below the door-lintel, a little rain, and an occasional blink of lightning over the oak trees".

The same dog, the messenger of civilisation, woke Stevenson early on the morning of Wednesday, 2 October, and already beginning to think of the letters awaiting him at Alais he was packed and on the road for Cassagnas before the sun had slid into the valley. It was one of his longest day's walks, he was clearly close to exhaustion—like Modestine—and his final journal entries are desultory.

At Cassagnas, "a black village on the mountainside"—again that note of drained colour—he dined with the local gendarme and a travelling merchant at the inn. There was some gossip of a renegade Catholic curé, who had given up his ministry and "taken to his bosom" the local schoolmistress; the villagers, though almost all Protestant, showed little sympathy for the man's predicament, despite the fact that their own Protestant priests were allowed and indeed encouraged to marry. The general sentiment seemed to be that "it is a bad idea for a man to go back on his engagements" —even if it was such an unnatural one as Catholic celibacy. Stevenson remarks wryly that "perhaps the bad idea was to enter into them at the first" and continues with a brief, rather hazy passage about the "holy simplicity" of physical desires and needs. "The world gives liberally of things to eat; it is all over spouting fountains; and a man need not travel very far ere he finds a woman to whom his soul can cling. If he can but lay aside some dismal ascetic standards, and a few hollow aspirations . . ."

But he was pleased to find that both the policeman and the merchant were more than a little shocked to discover that he had been sleeping in the open. There was talk of wolves and thieves— "the English always have long purses"—and general head-shaking. To all Stevenson's smiling and shrugging—"'God,' said I, 'is everywhere'"—the merchant replied in grave, flattering disapproval: "*Cependant, coucher dehors!*" and finally asked for one of Stevenson's visiting cards, saying that "it would be something to talk about in the future, this donkey-driving, English amateur vagrant." Stevenson was charmed to comply.

Without further delay, he then crossed back over the Mimente to the southern side of the valley and began to climb the ragged path that leads steeply up through "sliding stone and heather tufts" to the huge, long escarpment known as Mont Mars. It took him nearly all afternoon to get over the crest and discover the astonishing panorama of hills on the other side, dominated by the Plan de Fontmort where the Camisards fought their last, bloody and suicidal battle.

To me this was the single most impressive view of the entire journey. I scrawled wildly in my diary:

> Like gasping for breath in a rolling blue sea of hills going southwards as far as the sky and further—being washed entirely away by it all—exalted and lonely as hell—stood on a rock of the heathery col drinking toast to RLS—tin cup held up to horizon— somewhere he must have heard—black cicadas exploding all round with shiny red wings in the sunlight.

Obscurely I felt that the whole trip "made sense beyond metaphor of explanation", in that high, bright, windy place of the Cévennes. I lay for hours on my back in the heather watching the clouds troop endlessly and majestically overhead in the blue. If you were dead and buried, I thought, that is how life would go on around you; that is how Stevenson would see it. And of course I recited his epitaph, known by heart, to generations of English children like me:

> Here he lies where he longed to be;
> Home is the sailor, home from the sea,
> And the hunter home from the hill.

Stevenson arrived on the edge of Mont Mars when it was already late in the afternoon. He was deeply moved too by the realisation that his journey must be near its end; he could not continue it much longer. "It was perhaps the wildest view of my journey; peak upon peak, chain upon chain of hills ran surging southward, channelled and guttered by winter streams, feathered from head to foot with chestnuts and here and there breaking out into a coronal of cliffs." The sun was setting behind the Plan de Fontmort and the darkness was filling up the valleys. "Away across the highest peaks, to the south-west, lay Alais, my destination." An old shepherd hobbling on a pair of sticks and wearing a black cap of liberty, "as if in honour of his neighbourhood to the grave", directed him to the road for St Germain-de-Calberte.

Here Stevenson was to spend his final night, and his journal ends with a description of the long descent to the village, through high terraces of chestnut trees, as the dusk fell and the moon came up. The road glimmered white, "carpeted with noiseless dust", and Stevenson drank mouthfuls of Volnay wine until he was no longer conscious of his limbs. He arrived just as the landlady of the inn was putting her chickens to bed. "The fire was already out and had, not without grumbling, to be rekindled; quarter of an hour later and I must have gone supperless to roost."

He met no one on this last, light-headed stretch; but he heard a voice, the voice of a woman singing, somewhere below him through the rustling chestnut trees. In a sense, of course, it was Fanny's voice, and he wished he could have responded. "I could barely catch the words, but there was something about a *bel amoureux*, a handsome lover. I wished I could take up the strain and answer her, as I went on my invisible woodland way. If a traveller could only sing, he would pay his way literally, it seems to me."

In the *Travels* Stevenson gently elaborates on this last encounter, describing the song as "some sad, old, endless ballad" (was he thinking of Wordsworth's "solitary highland lass" heard singing in the fields?) and wondering what he might have said to her: "Little enough; and yet all the heart requires. How the world gives and takes away, and brings sweethearts near only to separate them again into distant and strange lands; but to love is the great amulet which makes the world a garden; and 'hope, which comes to all', outwears the accidents of life . . ."

The following day, Thursday, 3 October, he took the carriage road over the Col de St Pierre to St Jean-du-Gard. Here Modestine was declared unfit to travel by the farrier, and Stevenson found his journey had come abruptly to an end. His relief is evident. He sold his "lady friend" for thirty-five francs, boxed up his belongings and caught the afternoon diligence—"now eager to reach Alais for my letters". His envoi is light-hearted: "It was not until I was fairly seated by the driver, and rattling through a rocky valley with dwarf olives, that I became aware of my bereavement. I had lost Modestine. Up to that moment I had thought I hated her; but now she was gone—'And oh! The difference to me!'" This time the reference is explicit, to Wordsworth's *Lucy* poems. Stevenson adds mockingly that "being alone with a stage-driver" and four or five other passengers he wept openly for his loss.

I spent my last night under one of those huge spreading chestnut trees, off the old coaching road—now no more than a track—beyond St Germain-de-Calberte. I had walked along for an hour in the moonlight, after supper at the *auberge*, listening for the sounds of singing. I was tired and slept well, to be woken after six by a red squirrel skittering in the branches overhead. I immediately felt alone: Stevenson had departed. I cooked my last coffee with strange sensations of mixed relief and abandonment. Then as I packed up my rucksack a wild happiness filled me, and a sense of achievement. I had done it, I had followed him, I had made a mark. Very deliberately and self-consciously I stuck my bone-handled sheath-knife deep into the bark of the old chestnut, and left it there like a trophy.

I walked over the Col de St Pierre in six hours, and came down to St Jean-du-Gard, a modern market town on the high road between Alès and Millau, no longer in the magic *département* of Lozère. Suddenly I was back in civilisation. I had two beers at a café, one for Stevenson and one for Modestine, and seeing my silver ring and long hair the *garçon* addressed me charmingly throughout as "Monsieur Clochard". Indeed I was no longer quite sure *who* I was, except a stranger back in the modern world like Rip van Winkle.

The sense of having been away, somewhere quite else, was extraordinarily strong: my first experience of biographer's "time-warp". I hitch-hiked home to my vine-farmers, in the south-east beyond Nîmes, riding in the open back of a big lorry carrying red Calor-gas cans. Facing backwards, my pack swaying at my feet, the cans clanging like sea-buoys, the wind plucking at Le Brun, I watched the dark-brown line of the Cévennes drop below the north-west horizon like "a sea-coast in Bohemia". My head was full of poems I would write.

5

Stevenson published his *Travels with a Donkey* some six months later, in the spring of 1879. He spent several weeks working on it during the autumn, in Cambridge, at Sidney Colvin's rooms in Trinity; and then, over Christmas, at home in Edinburgh. All this time he had no news of Fanny in San Francisco. His aim was to expand his original journal from some twenty thousand words to a small volume of about double that length. To this purpose he filled in topographical details from guide-books and added the Camisard history from Napoléon Peyrat and other sources; he carefully rewrote his religious reflections (partly so as not to shock his father) and rehandled the encounters with the monks and the priest at La Trappe, and the old Plymouth Brother at Florac; finally, he deleted or generalised the amorous reflections that were originally written with Fanny in mind—so effectively that even a recent modern biographer has concluded that "there is only one passage in which we are made aware of the fact that he was missing Fanny intensely".

The book was dedicated to Sidney Colvin, in one of those warm, enigmatic public letters of introduction that Stevenson could write so well, hinting at Romantic mysteries and philosophies but leaving everything half-explained, half in shadow:

> The journey which this little book is to describe was very agreeable and fortunate for me. After an uncouth beginning, I had the best of luck in the end. But we are all travellers in what John Bunyan calls this wilderness of the world—all, too, travellers with a donkey: and the best that we can find in our travels is an honest friend . . . Every book is, in an intimate sense, a circular letter to the friends of him who writes it. They alone take his meaning; they find private messages, assurances of love, and expressions of gratitude, dropped at every corner. The public is but a generous patron who defrays the postage . . .

In private Stevenson was much more explicit, writing to cousin Bob in June 1879, in his downright and devil-take-it style. He makes no pretences as to who is at the centre of the work:

> My book is through the press. It has good passages, I can say no more. A chapter called 'The Monks', and then 'A Camp in the Dark', a third, 'A Night in the Pines'. Each of these has I think some stuff in the way of writing. But lots of it is mere protestations to F., most of which I think you will understand. That is to me the main thread of interest. Whether the damned public—But that's all one. I've got 30 quid for it, and should have had 50.

His preoccupation with money had a simple explanation. For he had at last secretly determined to rejoin Fanny in San Francisco, and once her divorce from Sam Osbourne was through to marry her. Two months later, on 7 August 1879, he bought a second-cabin steerage ticket to New York for eight guineas, and without telling his parents embarked on his second pilgrimage: the greatest adventure of his life.

For the "damned public" the book has remained essentially an exercise in style, "agreeably mannered", and a model of polite essay-writing for generations of English and Scottish schoolchildren. My own little brown-backed copy, printed in 1936, still gives as likely essay-subjects, in an appendix after the text, such lines of enquiry as: "What are the respective advantages of a walking, cycling, motoring, and caravaning tour?" And, "What is Stevenson's religious position, and can a charge of affectation be made against it?" However, I do like one suggestion: "Put yourself in Modestine's place, and write a character study of your Master." It might lead on to deeper matters.

For Stevenson himself there remains no doubt now in my own mind that the whole Cévennes experience was a kind of initiation ceremony: a grappling with physical hardships, loneliness, religious doubts, the influence of his parents, and the overwhelming question of whether he should take the enormous risk of travelling to America and throwing his life in with Fanny's—"for richer, for poorer; in sickness and in health". In the desperate summer months of 1879, immediately prior to his departure for New York, the memory of the trip was obviously much in his mind. He wrote to a friend: "I can do no work. It all lies aside. I want—I want—a holiday; I want to be happy; I want the moon or the sun or something. I want the object of my affections badly anyway; and a big forest; fine, breathing, sweating, sunny walks; and the trees all crying aloud in the summer wind and a camp under the stars."

So the pilgrimage begun at Le Monastier ended six thousand miles away in a honeymoon on the wooded hills of the Pacific coast of California. But that is another story, as eventually told in *The Silverado Squatters*.

For me, the Cévennes was a different initiation. I embarked on it, and finished it, in all innocence from a literary point of view. It never crossed my mind that I might write about Stevenson; or that my diary should be anything more than a "route-journal", a record of my road and camps. If I wrote anything at all, I thought, it would be poems about walking, swimming, climbing hills and sleeping under the stars. But what happened was something quite other, something almost entirely unexpected. Instead of writing poems I wrote prose meditations. These concerned not so much the outward physical experiences of my travels but inward mental ones that were often profoundly upsetting. The full record of my black depressions, intense almost disabling moments of despair, and childish weeping fits, still seems inexplicable and embarrassing. The corresponding moments of intoxication and mad delight are still vivid to me twenty years afterwards, so that my pulse-rate increases when I write about them, even now. But all these inward emotions were concentrated and focused on one totally unforeseen thing: the growth of a friendship with Stevenson, which is to say, the growth of an imaginary relationship with a non-existent person, or at least a dead one.

In this sense, what I experienced and recorded in the Cévennes in the summer of 1964 was a haunting. Nothing of course that would make a Gothic story, or interest the Society for Psychical Research; but an act of deliberate psychological trespass, an invasion or encroachment of the present upon the past, and in some sense the past upon the present. And in this experience of haunting I first encountered—without then realising it—what I now think of as the essential process of biography.

As far as I can tell, this process has two main elements, or closely entwined strands. The first is the gathering of factual materials, the assembling in chronological order of a man's "journey" through the world—the actions, the words, the recorded thoughts, the places and faces through which he moved: the "life and letters". The second is the creation of a fictional or imaginary relationship between the biographer and his subject; not merely a "point of view" or an "interpretation", but a continuous living dialogue between the two as they move over the same historical ground, the same trail of events. There is between them a ceaseless discussion, a reviewing and questioning of motives and actions and consequences, a steady if subliminal exchange of attitudes, judgments and conclusions. It is fictional, imaginary, because of course the subject cannot really, literally, talk back; but the biographer must come to act and think of his subject as if he can.

The first stage of such a living, fictional relationship is in my experience a degree of more or less conscious identification with the subject. More or less, because the real elements of self-identification are often much more subtle and subliminal than one originally thinks. This, strictly speaking, is pre-biographic: it is a primitive form, a type of hero- or heroine-worship, which easily develops into a kind of love affair. Looking back at the Cévennes, I can now see that I went straight into that phase with Stevenson, passionately identifying with what I saw as his love of bohemian adventuring, getting out "on the road", and sharing with him his delight in all things French, original, eccentric. I saw him, naïvely, as a direct predecessor of figures like Jack Kerouac—though the European Kerouac, the Kerouac of *Lonesome Traveller*, a bit lost and a bit uncertain of himself, not the roaring American romantic of *On the Road*. The Kerouac who, at the very end of his drunken career, comes back to France looking for his lost family roots in Brittany, searching for the Lebris de Kéroack in *Satori in Paris*.

My real reasons for self-identification I now see as rather different: they involved the confrontation with religious upbringing and lost faith, Stevenson's Calvinism having some equivalence to my Catholicism. They also involved a natural struggle to free myself from parental influences—benign ones, but nevertheless encroaching. Hence I suspect the powerful note struck by Stevenson's exploration of the "dream childhood" theme, the poetry of homesickness—of travelling far away over blue hills and brown rivers, only to find yourself once more back on the final wooded ridge above the natal valley, the small boy wanting to come home.

This form of identification or self-projection is pre-biographic and in a sense pre-literate: but it is an essential motive for following in the footsteps, for attempting to re-create the pathway, the journey, of someone else's life through the physical past. If you are not in love with them you will not follow them—not very far, anyway. But the true biographic process begins precisely at the moment, at the places, where this naïve form of love and identification breaks down. The moment of personal disillusion is the moment of impersonal, objective re-creation. For me, almost the earliest occasion was that bridge at Langogne, the old broken bridge that I could not cross, and the sudden physical sense that the past was indeed "another country".

The past does retain a physical presence for the biographer—in landscapes, buildings, photographs, and above all the actual trace of handwriting on original letters or journals. Anything a hand has touched is for some reason peculiarly charged with personality—Thomas Hardy's simple steel-tipped pens, each carved with a novel's name; Shelley's guitar, presented to Jane Williams; Balzac's blue china coffee-pot, with its spirit-heater, used through the long nights of *Le Père Goriot* and *Les Illusions Perdues*; other writers' signet rings, worn walking-sticks, Coleridge's annotated books, Stevenson's flageolet and tortoise-shell "Tusitala" ring. It is as if the act of repeated touching, especially in the process of daily work or creation, imparts a personal "virtue" to an inanimate object, gives it a fetichistic power in the anthropological sense, which is peculiarly impervious to the passage of time. Gautier wrote in a story that the most powerful images of past life in the whole of Pompeii were the brown, circular prints left by drinkers' glasses on the marble slabs of the second-century taverna.

But this physical presence is none the less extremely deceptive. The material surfaces of life are continually breaking down, sloughing off, changing, almost as fast as human skin. A building is restored, a bridge is rebuilt or replaced, a road is widened or rerouted, a forest is cut down, a wooded hill is built over, a village green becomes a town centre. Stevenson's La Trappe had been burnt down, redesigned and rebuilt; many of his donkey-tracks had become tarred roads; his wild upland heaths had been planted over; and even his terraces of deep chestnut trees had been replaced by the commercial foresting of young pines.

The well-meaning attempt to conserve or recover the past can be more subtly destructive. Since the centenary of Stevenson's *Travels* I am told the whole route has been marked out, by the local Syndicats d'Initiative, with a series of blazed stakes which lead the pilgrim from one picturesque *point de vue* to the next, and bring him safely down each evening to some recommended hotel, Carte Touristique, hot bath, and Souvenirs Cévenols. I have not had the heart to go back and see.

Beyond this sense of physical presences growing upon the biographer—which includes the whole aura of personal body influence, the sound of Stevenson's voice, his particular loose-limbed gait, his mixture of frail boniness and hectic energy, the large mobile brown eyes, the quick thin wrists and ankles, the smell of tobacco and cognac and cologne and sweaty Scottish tweed mixed with the rank odour of Modestine—there is the growing awareness of psychological complication.

This is the second factor that awakens the necessary objectivity of the biographer. My gradual discovery of Fanny Osbourne, and her hidden importance in Stevenson's journey, made me realise how Stevenson fitted into the enormously intricate emotional web of other people's lives. The single subject of biography is in this sense a chimera, almost as much as the Noble Savage of Jean-Jacques Rousseau, living in splendid asocial isolation. The truth is almost the reverse: that Stevenson existed very largely in, and through, his contact with other people: his books are written for his public; his letters for his friends; even his private journal is a way of giving social expression—externalising—his otherwise inarticulated thoughts. It is in this sense that all real biographical evidence is "third party" evidence; evidence that is witnessed. Just as the biographer cannot make up dialogue, if he is to avoid fiction; so he cannot really say that his subject "thought" or "felt" a particular thing. When he uses these forms of narration it is actually a type of agreed shorthand, which must mean—if it means anything factual —that "there is evidence from his letters or journals or reported conversations that he thought, or that he felt, such-and-such a thing at this time . . ." In this way the biographer is continually being excluded from, or thrown out of, the fictional rapport he has established with his subject. He is like the news reporter who is told something in confidence, "off the record", and then can do nothing about it until he has found independent evidence from other sources. His lips are sealed, his hands tied. Otherwise he is dishonourable and prosecutable, not only in the courts of Justice, but in the courts of Truth as well.

My final lesson from the Cévennes is as much metaphysical as literary. It is the paradox that the more closely and scrupulously you follow someone's footsteps through the past the more conscious do you become that they never existed wholly in any one place along the recorded path. You cannot freeze them, you cannot pinpoint them, at any particular turn in the road, bend of the river, view from the window. They are always in motion, carrying their past lives over into the future. It is like the sub-atomic particle in nuclear physics that can be defined only in terms of a wave-motion. If I try to fix Stevenson in his green magic dell in the Lozère, or his whitewashed cell at La Trappe, or under his chestnut tree below Mont Mars; if I try to say—this man, thinking and feeling these things, was at this place, at this moment—then at once I have to go backwards and forwards, tracing him at other and corresponding places and times—his childhood bedroom at No 17 Heriot Row, Edinburgh, or his honeymoon ranch at Silverado, California.

So without knowing it, my youthful journey through the Cévennes led me over the hills and far away into the undiscovered land of other men's and women's lives. It led me towards biography.

TWO

1968 : Revolutions

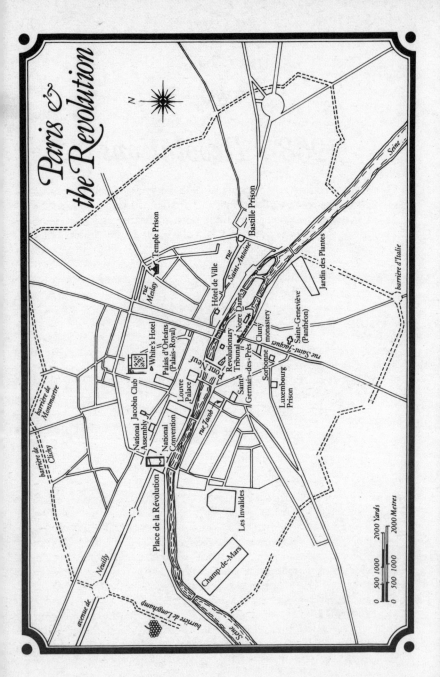

Paris & the Revolution

N

Temple Prison

Bastille Prison

rue Meslay

rue Saint-Antoine

Hôtel de Ville

Jardin des Plantes

Seine

barrière d'Italie

White's Hotel

Palais d'Orléans
(Palais-Royal)

National Jacobin Club

National
Assembly

National
Convention

Louvre
Palace

Pont Neuf

Notre Dame

Revolutionary
Tribunal

Cluny

Saint-Geneviève
(Panthéon)

Saint-Germain-des-Prés

Sorbonne

rue Saint-Jacques

monastery

Luxembourg
Prison

barrière de Montmartre

barrière de Clichy

rue Jacob

Place de la Révolution

Les Invalides

Champ-de-Mars

Seine

avenue de Neuilly

barrière de Longchamp

0   500 1000   2000 Yards
0   500 1000   2000 Metres

1

One sultry evening in the spring of 1968, standing at the window of a small upper room in Paddington, I first heard the sounds of the new French Revolution. I had not been to France for four years, and the idea of biography had lain dormant in my mind. After taking a degree at Cambridge I had come down to London and found a temporary job compiling the political register for Westminster City Council. It brought me to the hundreds of poor flats and bedsits in Victoria and Pimlico, the depressed area of South London by the Thames. I sat discussing paintwork, plumbing and social security benefits in endless sad kitchens, sipping tepid tea or sweet sherry. Powerless to act on the petty injustices and miseries I saw, I learned at least how to listen to other people, and observe some of the forces that shaped their lives. I expressed my anger in poems, written with the clumsy literalness of pop-songs, but could find no real outlet for my deeper feelings.

The five-storey house in which I had my garret was almost entirely let to other young people and students, and in keeping with the times we became a kind of commune, busy with macrobiotic food and anti-Vietnam marches and geodesic domes.

The ground-floor was occupied by the consulting rooms of a lady psychiatrist, specialising in drug-addicts and other youthful breakdowns, many of them gifted drop-outs from universities, unmarried mothers trying to find their feet, or young painters and musicians who'd temporarily blown their minds. I sketched a story-essay, which eventually became an impressionistic study of the poet Thomas Chatterton, a precursor of Romanticism, who came to London at the age of seventeen, took opium and committed suicide by mistaken overdose—or "OD", as it was succinctly called on the ground-floor. Chatterton lived at the end of the eighteenth century, but I had a strange feeling that I was writing about someone in the same house.

It was a restless time. The window of my attic room overlooked the shunting yards of Paddington station, and my dreams were shaken by the whistle and roar of departing trains. The sense of movement and change was everywhere. News of disturbances in Paris had been reported piecemeal in the English papers for weeks, but largely in terms of isolated disruptions by students at Nanterre, or *syndicalistes* at Renault. Then I began to get letters from friends already in the city, speaking in confused, rapturous terms of the long "sit-ins", the great marches and demonstrations, people coming from all over Europe—Berlin, Rome, Amsterdam—to celebrate the new spirit of *Liberté*, and take part in some huge, undefined *événement*. It was a carnival, they wrote, and a revolution too. The world would never be the same again, the authorities were cracking, the old order was in retreat.

A letter from Françoise, a girl I'd met after the Cévennes journey, now a student in Paris, reached me; it was carried over by a lorry-driver as the French post had gone on strike:

> Across the boulevard a dark-blue Peugeot was lying on its side burning. Its wheels in the air meant the whole city had turned upside down. The pavements glittered with broken glass, and the flames shone on our posters flyleaved up the trees. The night stank of riot gas, and my eyes ran with tears—of happiness! At the bottom of the rue des Ecoles the wall below the barred windows of the Medical Faculty was painted with enormous graffiti in red—*Imagination au Pouvoir* . . . The CRS surged by in their black boiler suits and visored helmets, swinging their long batons like madmen who didn't understand our sanity. I saw a little old lady with a Samaritaine carrier-bag walk straight through them untouched . . . Everyone in the café was cheering and embracing each other, bringing in the latest news. It is like a dream come true!

I read this with mixed feelings, half-excited and half-sceptical. Then, one evening at my window, staring out into the quiet English night and hearing the distant clankings, I tuned my radio to Luxembourg and heard with astonishment that they were trying to burn down the Bourse. It was a live report—French state radio had been forbidden live coverage—and the noises seemed to fill my room. I could hear the huge crowds shouting, the crack of CRS gas-canisters, the brittle, thrilling sound of breaking glass, the sudden ragged bursts of cheering. And suddenly the idea of "the Revolution" came to life in my head, and I knew that it was something I had to write about. It was not the destruction that excited me but the sense of something utterly new coming into being, some fresh, immense possibility of political life, a new community of hope, and above all the strangely inspired note—like a new language—that sounded in the voices of those who were witnessing it. It was a glimpse of "the dream come true", the golden age, the promised land.

Moreover, I identified it—immediately, naïvely—with that first French Revolution as seen by the English Romantics some hundred and eighty years before. The gap in time, the great and complex historical differences, for a moment meant nothing to me. For what I was feeling, what my friends were feeling, seemed to be expressed perfectly by the Romantics, and by no one else.

> 'Twas a time when Europe was rejoiced,
> France standing at the top of golden hours
> And human nature seeming born again.

So William Wordsworth had written, when in July 1790 he set off to walk through France on the first anniversary of the fall of the Bastille.

There were moments when the student barricades round the Sorbonne and in parts of the Latin Quarter really did seem to be re-enacting the events of 1789–94 (though no Robespierre arrived and no Terror began). The huge open debates in the courtyard of the Sorbonne and in Paris theatres like the Odéon seemed to be emulating, if not the great ideological discussions of the first Assemblée Nationale—in many ways the climax of the entire eighteenth-century Enlightenment—at least the more fervid and impassioned meetings of the Cordeliers and the Club des Jacobins. If there was no Robespierre there were many who looked and sounded like the young, handsome, long-haired and insolent Saint-Just.

When on 27 May de Gaulle took mysterious flight from Paris to an unknown destination (actually he went by helicopter to consult with General Massu at an army base in Germany), many people drew the parallel with Louis XVI's fatal flight to Varennes of autumn 1792. If history was not exactly repeating itself then at the least it was in a strange state of theatrical *correspondence*. It was a replay, a rerun, a harmonic echo across nearly two centuries.

The whole ethos of the Sixties—that youthful explosion of idealism, colour, music, sex, hallucinogenic states, hyperbolic language and easy money ("the counter-culture", as the sociologists called it)—was based on a profoundly romantic rejection of conventional society, the old order, the establishment, the classical, the square (and also, in fact, austerity).

> Bliss was it in that dawn to be alive,
> But to be young was very heaven!

Many of the catchwords and concepts of the Sixties, indeed the very idea of "revolution" itself as a flamboyant act of self-assertion—"the language of personal rights"—found either inspiration or confirmation in the generation of the 1790s. Coleridge and Southey's plan to found a commune on the banks of the Susquehanna river; Blake's poetry of visions and defiance ("The Tigers of Wrath are Wiser than the Horses of Instruction", from *The Proverbs of Hell*, was one of the most popular graffiti); Shelley's notions of free love and passive resistance, understood as an early form of Flower Power, "Make Love Not War"; Coleridge's and later Thomas de Quincey's interest in drugs and dream-states; Mary Wollstonecraft's championship of the rights of women—all these spoke directly to the generation of May '68.

Above all, there was the challenge to the conventions and structures of authority, the whole tone of confrontation, which took place daily, whether in the matter of clothes, art, sexual morality, religious piety or politics. Such confrontation was international: the counter-culture took to the road and passed all frontiers, entered all cities; just as the first Romantics had set out on their wanderings to Wales, France, Germany, Italy, Greece or the Levant—only "the Orient" now meant India rather than Arabia.

What William Hazlitt wrote of the face of the young Southey before he cut his hair and settled down with his extended family in the Lake District, could have been written of many of the young bearded and Christ-like faces on the barricades of '68. These in turn unconsciously reflected the revolutionary features of the young Cuban, Che Guevara, whose image hung like an icon in a million bedsits, *aparts*, pads and communal kitchens, in London, New York, Hamburg, Paris and Rome. Hazlitt described this revolutionary and utopian archetype, as it first made its appearance in the 1790s:

Mr Southey, as we formerly remember to have seen him, had a hectic flush upon his cheek, a roving fire in his eye, a falcon glance, a look at once aspiring and dejected. It was the look that had been impressed upon his face by the events that marked the outset of his life. It was the dawn of Liberty that still tingled his cheek . . .

While he supposed it possible that a better form of society could be introduced than any other that had hitherto existed, while the light of the French Revolution beamed into his soul —while he had this hope, this faith in man left, he cherished it with a childlike simplicity, he clung to it with the fondness of a lover. He was an enthusiast, a fanatic, a leveller; he stuck at nothing that he thought would banish all pain and misery from the world; in his impatience at the smallest error or injustice, he would have sacrificed himself and the existing generation (a holocaust) to his devotion to the right cause.

Hazlitt was himself one of these young radical enthusiasts, and had visited Paris as an art student during the Peace of Amiens in 1802. In *The Spirit of the Age*, his portrait of the leading writers and politicians of his generation, written twenty years after, he continued to judge men like Southey, Coleridge, Wordsworth and Godwin by the yardstick of their first revolutionary ideals, and in that dawn light of the French Revolution. It was a light that most of them, he felt, had gone on to deny or betray, and there is a mixed tone of cynicism and elegy—the "hectic flush" and the "falcon glance"—to many of these portraits, which the witnesses and survivors of May '68 will instantly recognise as part of their own experience. As Hazlitt wrote mockingly of Southey: "He wooed Liberty as a youthful lover, but it was perhaps more as a mistress than a bride; and he has since wedded with an elderly and not very reputable lady, called Legitimacy."

For the sense of disillusion set in quickly after May '68. This was also something about which I wanted to write. Contemporary historians now describe it in terms of the Arab oil crisis, the economic depression in Europe, the rise of right-wing governments and the advent of the first mass unemployment since the 1930s. We saw it in more immediate and human terms: communes that went broke, free unions that became bad marriages, university faculties that became hotbeds of rivalry and fruitless dispute, artistic spirits who became addicts and breakdowns, travellers who came home sick and sorry, women who became exhausted, one-parent families, a world of little presses and alternative newspapers that dropped into oblivion, and a Paris where the Bourse remained and Les Halles was destroyed.

How to make sense of all this? And how not to betray the light? As Hazlitt, once more, wrote of William Godwin, the author of *Political Justice* (1793), the most radical of all the English revolutionary tracts:

Fatal reverse! Is truth then so variable? Is it one thing at twenty and another at forty? Is it at a burning heat in 1793, and below *zero* in 1814? . . . Were we fools then, or are we dishonest now? Or was the impulse of the mind less likely to be true and sound

when it arose from high thought at warm feeling, than afterwards, when it was warped and debased by the example, the
vices, and follies of the world?

I was soon in France again myself. For a moment I saw fragments
of the great *événements*, though already the carnival was in chaos and
the millennial hopes in retreat, the visions of those banners against
the blue spring sky, those great roaring crowds, those nightly
barricades, scattered by violence and confusion and confrontations
with intense personal fear.

One night, coming out of the place de la Sorbonne on to the boul'
Mich, my hands full of books and papers, I was caught up in a
sudden CRS sweep. It was raining lightly, a sweet-scented summer
rain, and the CRS coaches—dark-green, with grilled windows, and
rows of doors opening simultaneously, like a train pulling into a
rush-hour station—came skidding up on to the pavements, lights
flashing and klaxons blaring. A few yards away a girl in blue lycée
overalls, painted with Maoist signs, was knocked to the ground and a
mass of leaflets spilled out of her canvas shoulder-bag. Hesitatingly,
I took a step towards her, and found myself jammed against the
iron fence that runs along the site of the old Cluny monastery,
where Peter Abelard used to lecture before he met Héloïse. The
pressure on my chest was from the barrel of an automatic rifle.

I was looking into the face of a CRS trooper. He was slightly
smaller than myself, with a dark complexion—a man from the
Midi, or Corsica perhaps. He had an expression of intense bore-
dom, and the drops of rain glittered on his visor. I felt lonely,
unheroic and unrevolutionary, and never wanted to see a British
policeman so much in my life. It was time for a clear, unequivocal
statement of ideological loyalty.

My mouth was dry, and for a moment no sound came out. Then
I heard myself saying in a thin voice: "*Je suis anglais.*" There was a
pause, in which nothing much happened in the world, and then I
began to add: "*J'avais peur que mademoiselle là-bas . . .*"

The visor moved impatiently, the rifle barrel dropped to my
stomach, and began to prod—quite gently. "*Alors, espèce d'Anglais*"
—with each word a prod—"*occupe-toi de tes affaires*"—prod—"*rentre
chez toi*"—prod—and with a final roar—"*FOUS-MOI LA PAIX!*"

I crept away, but did not take his advice till much later.

I thought about this incident a good deal, however. It contained
a real challenge, and it was this that made me begin to explore "the
Revolution" in a different way. If I were English, why indeed
didn't I mind my own business and go home? I was a foreigner, an

outsider. The Revolution was a French affair, and perhaps it had always been so. What had happened to the English in 1790? Had they too been told to go home and leave everyone in peace? And if they had stayed on, beyond the September Massacres of 1792, or beyond the execution of the King in 1793, or right on into the Terror of 1794 . . . what had happened to them? What had they made of their experiences?

I began my investigations with Wordsworth, who had written so well in *The Prelude* about the intoxicating atmosphere of the times. He was an undergraduate at St John's College, Cambridge, when he made that first summer visit to France, walking three hundred miles in two weeks through Artois and Burgundy, with his friend Robert Jones. Though they did not visit Paris the excitement of the Revolution was evident in every country town and village through which they passed. At Calais, the celebrations of Bastille Day, "the great federal day", were still in progress, and the entire population had taken to the streets in rejoicing. Going southwards through Arras (Robespierre's birthplace) and Troyes, towards Chalon-sur-Saône, they found each hamlet "gaudy with reliques of that festival, flowers left to wither on triumphal arcs, and window-garlands". The French were open and welcoming, full of hope and enthusiasm for the future, with "benevolence and blessedness spread like a fragrance everywhere, when spring has left no corner of the land untouched".

On the public boat from Chalon to Lyons they met delegates from Paris eager to talk with them, and Fédéré soldiers with muskets draped with flowers, some flourishing their swords "as if to fight the saucy air". Stopping off by the banks of the Rhône in the evenings, they were invited to open-air banquets provided free by the Communes. They drank at long wooden tables under the summer stars of the Midi and danced with the peasant-girls, radiant with ribbons fluttering in their hair and tricolour scarves tied tightly round their waists. It was an experience of the early, fraternal days of the Revolution that Wordsworth never forgot, politics and romance perfectly entwined, as they danced hand in hand, "at signal given", round and round the little dusty squares. "All hearts were open, every tongue was loud with amity and glee; we bore a name honoured in France, the name of Englishmen."

The following year Wordsworth abandoned his studies in Hebrew and Oriental languages (intended to qualify him for a post as a clergyman) and went directly to Paris. He arrived in December 1791, armed with a letter of introduction to Helen Maria Williams, poetess and francophile, to whom his first published poem had been dedicated in rapturous terms. He attended the debates in the

National Assembly at the Louvre Palace, and in the noisy Jacobin Club nearby: "In both her clamorous Halls, the National Synod and Jacobins, I saw the Revolutionary power toss like a ship at anchor, rocked by storms."

He quartered the city from one end to the other in a series of long hiking expeditions, as if he were still in his native Cumberland. From west to east, from the Champ-de-Mars to the boulevard Saint-Antoine (where Dickens later placed Madame Defarge's wine-shop); and from north to south, descending the slopes of Montmartre, still covered with vines, crossing over the Seine and the Île de la Cité, to climb again up the long rue Saint-Jacques to the "dome of Geneviève" on the hill where the Pantheon now stands. He patrolled the arcades of the Palais-Royal (then the Palais d'Orléans) fascinated by the mercurial crowds: soldiers, hawkers, ballad-mongers, prostitutes, soapbox "haranguers"— including a feminist club—and local demagogues, "a hubbub wild!" He noted the mixture of respectable bookshops, taverns, brothels and gaming houses (Balzac describes them, still there a generation later, in *La Peau de Chagrin*), and was struck by the way that political talk had become common currency in the streets, so that everywhere he was surrounded by "hissing Factionists with ardent eyes, in knots, or pairs, or single ant-like swarms of builders and subverters, every face that hope or apprehension could put on . . ."

He went to the ruined site of the Bastille prison, at the north-east corner of the city wall. Until the coming of the Terror, this remained the joyful symbol of the Revolution, the *ancien régime* torn apart brick by brick; then it was replaced by the symbol of the guillotine, set up on the place de la Révolution (now Concorde). Bastille keys were carried across Europe as the insignia of liberation; Chateaubriand even took one to the Governor of Newfoundland, while another reached Jefferson's house in Virginia. Tourists and sympathisers like Wordsworth eagerly picked up pieces of stone from the prison rubble to bequeath to their children. Wordsworth described emotionally how he watched the west wind, the zephyr (later to be Shelley's "destroyer and preserver"), whipping through the debris and "sporting with the dust" of the ruins. He sat "in the open sun and pocketed a relic, in the guise of an enthusiast".

But this phrase brought me up short. Why only "in the guise" of an enthusiast? Was this a kind of political retraction—he was writing ten years after the events he describes? Or was it that same odd sense of alienation, the feeling that it was somehow "not his business" either, that revolution was something for the French alone?

His responses were complicated: he was looking for "something I could not find"; for an uplifting wave of revolutionary joy which did not quite touch him; in "honest truth" he was "affecting more emotion" than he felt. His reflections on this "strange indifference", in *The Prelude*, brought him suddenly close to me, and made me want to enter more deeply into the personal reactions of those few and scattered English witnesses. I wanted to know more about their hesitations and their innermost thoughts. What I needed, once again, was their biography. I pressed more closely on Wordsworth's poem, but without realising it I was beginning to ask questions that such a literary and public text could not answer.

Wordsworth said that in going to witness the Revolution he had passed too abruptly "into a theatre, of which the stage was busy with an action far advanced". Though he had prepared himself by reading "the master pamphlets of the day" and endless discussions with his friends, his understanding was too intellectual, too rational perhaps. Real events lacked a "living form and body" in his mind; they had not fully entered his imagination. "All things were to me loose and disjointed, and the affections left without a vital interest." His heart was "all given to the people, and my love was theirs"; yet it was precisely from these ordinary people—*les citoyens*—that he was most cut off. He had no friends in Paris, and he could not experience directly how the Revolution had shaken and transformed their lives. He was the outsider, the observer. He describes this in a passage that uses no revolutionary symbols at all, but reverts instead to the familiar imagery of his childhood in the Lakes—to the images of plants and weather, presenting the French Revolution in terms, of all things, of an English greenhouse:

> . . . I scarcely felt
> The shock of these concussions, unconcerned,
> Tranquil almost, and careless as a flower
> Glassed in a green house, or a parlour shrub
> When every bush and tree, the country through,
> Is shaking to the roots . . .

It was almost as if the great revolutionary wind, the shaking of the foundations, had still not touched anything deep or permanent within him.

What changed Wordsworth happened not in Paris that winter, but in Orléans and Blois, where he went to study French throughout the spring and summer of 1792. It was here that his affair with Annette Vallon, his teacher, took place, which resulted in a child born in December 1792; and here that his great friendship with

Capitaine Michel Beaupuy, a cavalry officer and passionate sympathiser with the revolutionary cause, was formed.

Wordsworth tells the story, partially in disguised form, in Books IX and X of *The Prelude*; and later added that Beaupuy had more influence on his thinking than any other man except Coleridge. He describes how in his conversations with Beaupuy a "hatred of absolute rule" daily laid a stronger and stronger hold upon his feelings, "mixed with pity too, and love" for the poor and abject people of France.

One day, as he was walking with Beaupuy in the country lanes near the Loire, there occurred one of those quintessentially Wordsworthian incidents—a meeting with one of the lonely outcasts of society, like the Cumberland beggar of later years—which seemed to crystallise everything that he had believed intellectually, and give it decisive human shape and conviction. It was for Wordsworth a form of conversion-experience, in which revolutionary theory was suddenly flooded by a personal truth.

The meeting was simplicity itself. A poor farm-girl, thin, weary and "hunger-bitten", was leading a heifer along the lane by a cord. The heifer nibbled hungrily at the wild berries in the hedgerows, and the girl, too exhausted and depressed to lead it on, "crept" by its side distractedly knitting, "in a heartless mood of solitude". Neither man spoke, but when they had passed by Beaupuy broke out in extreme agitation and anger: "'Tis against *that* which we are fighting'" and Wordsworth instantly felt that "a spirit was abroad" in France which would destroy such poverty for ever, and

> . . . Should see the people having a strong hand
> In making their own laws; whence better days
> To all mankind.

At the end of October, "inflamed with hope", Wordsworth was back in Paris to see this spirit at work. But what he found appalled and shook him: the King was imprisoned, the September Massacres had taken place, the guillotine had been set up in the place de la Révolution, and Robespierre was in the process of seizing dictatorial power in the National Convention. It was one of the great spiritual crises of Wordsworth's life: where did his true loyalties now lie? Should he stay in France, ally himself to the Girondist cause, throw in his lot with the other English and Americans in Paris—Tom Paine, Helen Maria Williams, the Barlows, the Christies? Above all, should he remain with Annette to give her what protection he could, and to make their love-child legitimate? Or should he flee back to England and safety, because in the end none of all this was "his business"; because he was an English poet who had had an adventure, who had gathered his "copy", and who owed it to his family—and his poetry—to scramble back home and begin to write about what he had seen and experienced? I was gripped by his dilemma. I entered into it, suspending history, seeing obscurely so many of the problems of my own generation expressed in a new and vivid way; seeing the vague excitements and cloudy enthusiasms focused down to an intense burning point of a single life: seeing, in fact, the biographical process become an instrument of moral precision and analysis—a way of making sense of my own world. And, of course, I passionately wanted Wordsworth to stay.

Well, he did stay: for approximately five weeks, in the tiny fifth-floor garret room—*une chambre de bonne*—of an unknown hotel on the Left Bank, ranging "more eagerly" through the city than he had done before, walking beneath the high walls of the Temple prison where the King and his family were incarcerated and crossing the pont du Carrousel to stand in the grim, deserted square in front of the Louvre—"a black and empty area then"—where the Swiss Guards had opened fire on the mob as it stormed the Louvre Palace. The scarred trees and the stained gravel bore witness to the struggle, and his mind dwelt on the heaps of dead and dying.

He went again to the arcades of the Palais-Royal, tasting its new atmosphere of rumour and political fear: a hawker thrust into his hand a copy of the pamphlet entitled "Denunciations of the Crimes of Maximilien Robespierre"—the text of Louvet's famous attack on Robespierre in the Convention, which failed to rally support, and ultimately sealed the fate of the Girondists the following summer. Wordsworth began to see with his "proper eyes" how the great questions of Liberty, Life and Death would be settled—not, as he had imagined, by some great common impulse of the people, some invincible natural force like a storm sweeping all before it, "the spirit of the age"; but rather by the personal struggles and "arbitrement" of those who ruled in the capital city. In the crucible of power the conflict of individual men would be decisive. His idealism was chastened; yet his response was the reverse of cynical. He says that he almost prayed that the Revolution would now draw in only the men worthy of Liberty, "matured to live in plainness and in truth", and that men like this might arrive, with the gift of tongues,

> . . . From the four quarters of the winds to do
> For France, what without help she could not do,
> A work of honour . . .

I remembered our talk of friends flying in to Paris in May from all the capitals of Europe.

It was clear that Wordsworth realised the Revolution had reached a critical stage. But what did he think of his own situation within it? It was here that I came up against the biographer's dependence on the survival of personal papers. No letters or journals of Wordsworth are known for this period, and the touching letters of Annette Vallon, discovered over a hundred years later in the municipal archives (they were detained by the French political censor), threw no light on Wordsworth's time in Paris. I had to make what I could of the 1805 text of *The Prelude*.

Up to a point, it is remarkably frank and revealing. He describes the nights he used to lie awake in his little hotel room, reading with "unextinguished taper", and how—thinking of the violence of the mob, a violence like nothing he had ever remotely experienced in his life before—"the fear gone by pressed on me almost like a fear to come."

> I thought of those September massacres,
> Divided from me by a little month,
> And felt and touched them, a substantial dread . . .

He could not sleep, and his imagination "wrought upon" him until he felt he could hear a voice crying through the whole city, "Sleep no more." He tried to calm himself with rational thoughts in the long hours before the winter dawn, but he could not recover his sense of "full security", and gradually a deep and almost nightmarish terror of Paris possessed him:

> . . . At the best it seemed a place of fear
> Unfit for the repose of night
> Defenceless as a wood where tigers roam.

Finally, in the third week of December 1792, Wordsworth took the diligence to Calais and "reluctantly" returned to England. In *The Prelude* he says the decisive reason was "absolute want of funds for my support"—and also, one may suppose, for the support of Annette, whose baby had just been born. Fear for his personal safety was not the conscious motive, for he says in a crucial passage that he had considered sacrificing himself to the revolutionary Girondist cause, though "no better than an alien in the land". What he says is convincing—there is every evidence that the young Wordsworth was a brave and adventurous man. Moreover, it

shows how deeply he had pledged himself to the Revolution as he
understood it, even though he saw realistically that his contribution
"must be of small worth". Had he had means, had he been free, he
says,

> I doubtless should have made a common cause
> With some who perished; haply perished, too,
> A poor mistaken and bewildered offering—
> Should to the breast of Nature have gone back,
> With all my resolutions, all my hopes,
> A Poet only to myself, to men
> Useless . . .

Of course, it is in retrospect—after some ten years—that he regards
such a sacrifice as "useless" and "mistaken". At the time it must
have been an agonising decision to take, and there is no doubt that
in making the sensible choice to go home he felt he had betrayed
some ideal deep within himself—had in fact abandoned most of
what both Beaupuy and Annette represented: his youthful hopes of
life, his revolutionary spirit. In the long term, and from the literary
point of view, he was right, and justified: he was destined to be a
great poet, not a political martyr. But the months of depression and
uncertainty he suffered after this at Racedown with Dorothy, before
being reanimated by his meeting with Coleridge (the "Friend" to
whom all this part of *The Prelude* is addressed), show what the
decision cost him.

In one of the most moving passages of Book X, speaking directly
to Coleridge the bare truth "as if to thee alone in private talk", he
says that "through months, through years" he was haunted by
what he had left behind in France. His daytime thoughts were
melancholic, his dreams miserable. Even long after the atrocities of
the Terror were over he scarcely had "one night of quiet sleep",
and he was filled with visions of despair. Most striking of all, he
dreamed continually of being back in Paris and being hauled before
one of the revolutionary courts, accused of some nameless act of
treachery. Hopelessly and desperately he would try to defend
himself by

> . . . Long orations which in dreams I pleaded
> Before unjust tribunals,—with a voice
> Labouring, a brain confounded, and a sense
> Of treachery and desertion in the place
> The holiest that I knew of, my own soul.

Nothing could be more frank, no confession more heartfelt, than this admission of the revolutionary who—for the best of reasons, perhaps—had in 1792 abandoned the cause.

Here my own investigations were also brought up short again. Wordsworth had left Paris in December 1792, along with so many others who saw the radical direction in which Robespierre was steering the Revolution. Were any writers bold enough to remain? The history of the so-called White's Hotel group of expatriates had never been written, though the individual stories—of largely political figures like Tom Paine, who was elected Deputy for the Pas de Calais, fell foul of Robespierre in 1793 and missed the guillotine only by the mistaken marking of his cell door—were comparatively well known. There were also minor celebrities like Helen Maria Williams, who survived the Revolution, and several weeks of imprisonment with her mother and sister in the Luxembourg, to write such highly coloured accounts as her *Memories of the Reign of Robespierre* (1795). The description of her midnight arrest, by the head of her local Paris *section*, a mixture of curious gallantry and ruthless revolutionary police work, is one of the few memorable and convincing passages; though there is also a fine black-comic episode in which she explains the enormous value of her English tea-kettle in keeping up the morale of those in the condemned cells.

But none of these memoirs provided the day-to-day authenticity, the biographical intensity, the quality of first-hand witness to a decisive experience which I wanted to supply some mirror to the events of 1968. Moreover, I had already glimpsed, through Wordsworth, the shadow of a philosophical problem—though was it philosophical or psychological?—which seemed to lie behind the English experience of revolution. It was not so much the alienation of the English witness from the events he observed, though this was obviously important; more the enormous gap that was revealed between his *rational* expectations of the Revolution, the whole atmosphere of progressive eighteenth-century Enlightenment—and its *imaginative* impact upon him as an individual, a wild mixture of hope and terror and desperation, the sense of life being radically altered in a way that broke every form and convention that had been previously held. It was also the sense of personal demands made, of a sudden need for sacrifice and risk—Wordsworth's choice to go or stay—which might never be encountered in ordinary life in such an absolute form. I wanted to discover someone who had met all this head-on; and I wanted to know in detail how they had, quite simply, made out.

2

The gap between rational expectation and imaginative impact or, to put it in its classical form, between Reason and Imagination, was something that became progressively more significant as the heady excitements of 1968 drained away into the anxious and cynical 1970s. "Imagination" had been one of the watchwords of the Paris students, conjuring up a whole new world of brilliant, creative, unauthoritarian (another key notion) solutions to society's problems. But what did it mean? It was of course taken from nineteenth-century Romantic vocabulary—it assumed the rebellious idealism and individualism of Blake and Baudelaire, Shelley and Bakunin, Trotsky and Lautréamont. But still, what did it actually *mean*?

In the famous poster stuck to the bolted door of the Sorbonne on the night of 13 May 1968—like Luther's declaration on the door of Wittenberg Cathedral—it was used in a curious way. Posters are not intended to be philosophical statements, but this one indicated a particular way of thinking. It read: "The revolution which is beginning will call into question not only capitalist society but industrial society. The consumer society must perish of a violent death. The society of alienation must disappear from history. We are inventing a new and original world—*Imagination au Pouvoir!*"

"Imagination" is an instrument both of creation and of destruction. It is a way of wiping the slate clean, of achieving a gleaming tabula rasa. The attempt to oppose it to existing society in all its corrupt forms—capitalist, industrial, consumer, and alienated—evokes not so much Marx as Jean-Jacques Rousseau. "Imagination" is a way of purifying society from all corruption or organisation; a way of starting again from the individual goodness of man, unfettered by prejudice or convention. Indeed, it slowly dawned on me, "Imagination" is here used in the opposite sense to what one might expect: it means precisely the "Pure Reason"—the "Godlike Reason"—the "Progressive Reason"—of the eighteenth-century Enlightenment. Like the early idealist revolutionaries of the 1790s, the students had been intoxicated by supremely rational expectations. They had wanted to change a whole world—or re-invent it—without having the faintest notion of the impact this would have. They had been led on, not as they thought by their warm hearts (and they *were* warm), but by the wonderful ice-palaces in their heads. They hadn't imagined anything in the *constructive* sense at all. They were utopian speculators whose Brave New World lay in their minds alone, a bundle of slogans, images, dream-words and seed-ideas.

That, at any rate, seemed one way of looking at it; and of accounting for the lack of political consequences to 1968, which began to make my comparison with the earlier Revolution seem superficial. One of the most influential. French commentators, Edgar Morin, writing in *Le Monde* at the end of May of that year, already drew the distinction along similar lines: between a political and a cultural revolution, in which "Imagination" had played a role more educative than socially revolutionary. He wrote:

Marx once said that the French Revolution was a classic revolution because it developed the characteristics upon which all succeeding bourgeois revolutions were modelled. Perhaps, in a similar way, the Paris Student Commune will become the classic model for all future transformations in Western societies. The destruction of the University Bastille drew together all types of young people in much the same way as the destruction of that other Bastille united the Three Orders in 1789. The transformation of the Sorbonne into a forum-cum-festival-cum-laboratory of ideas created the image of an open society and an open university where imagination reigns in the place of a dismal bureaucracy; where education is available to all; and where economic exploitation and domination have been eradicated . . . Precisely *because* it has been utopian rather than constructive it has been able to envisage a future that embraces the whole of society.

Pondering on these various interpretations, I continued to search among the scant records of the White's Hotel group. I located the actual site of the hotel, strategically placed in the passage des Petits-Pères, between the King's prison in the Temple and the arcades of the Palais-Royal. It is a tiny side-street, next to the old church of Notre Dame des Victoires which was pillaged in 1794 and which became the official Bourse des Valeurs between 1796 and 1809. The present hotel building is largely occupied by the local Commissariat de Police, who knew nothing of its historic associations; which was perhaps just as well.

The existence of the White's Hotel group became best known in England in 1792, when the *Annual Register* carried a report of the notorious banquet held there by the Friends of the Rights of Man, on 18 November—just after Wordsworth had gone back to Paris. The banquet was attended by some fifty ardent francophiles—English, Irish and American—among whom were Tom Paine, who was currently being burnt in effigy in England; and Lord Edward Fitzgerald, who was to be killed in Dublin before the rising of the United Irishmen in 1798.

Forty "treasonous toasts", as the *Register* reported, were drunk —to the National Convention, to the French armies, and to the "speedy abolition of all hereditary titles and feudal distinctions" —and a revolutionary verse by Helen Maria Williams was recited. A wealthy banker, Sir Robert Smythe, formally renounced his title, to prolonged applause. An American poet, Joel Barlow, presented a "Letter to the National Convention in France" which earned him, along with Thomas Christie and John Horne Tooke, the title of "Citoyen". Barlow's works had been printed in London by Joseph Johnson, a radical publisher of St Paul's Churchyard, who was also to print the early work of Wordsworth and Blake. Yet within three months this whole ebullient group was to be scattered, and my researches led mournfully to a history of arrests, trials, recantations or executions: either at the hands of Pitt's Government in England for treason (especially during the great Treason Trials of 1794), or at the hands of Robespierre's Committee of Public Safety for being aliens and spies.

For the White's Hotel group were caught between the two fires of revolution and reaction. Among their most tragic stories was that of the Rev William Jackson, who was arrested on a mission between Paris and Dublin, and tried for High Treason in November 1794. While waiting for the capital sentence to be passed, his wife brought him a strong brew of tea in the cells below the dock. On his own instructions it had been heavily laced with whisky—and "metallic poisoning"—and in a few minutes he was convulsed in agony. The court, outraged at this gesture of revolutionary suicide, demanded that Jackson be dragged back up to the dock to hear his sentence. But one of the jury, an apothecary, mercifully intervened: "I think him verging to eternity; he has every symptom of death upon him . . . I do not think he can hear his judgement." So the enthusiast of Liberty died in the cells in his wife's arms, leaving no record of his life but a bare court transcript.

From White's Hotel in Paris I myself moved back to Joseph Johnson's publishing house in London, determined to pursue my enquiries from the other direction, among the circle of radical writers in London who sympathised with events in France. I searched among the names of those who had dined at Johnson's table—Blake, William Godwin, Joel and Ruth Barlow—and then, many months later, I came across a letter written to one of Johnson's little-known friends, William Roscoe, a liberal attorney, in Liverpool. This letter is still kept in the Central Library at Liverpool, among a mass of minor papers. But to me it was one of the most exciting documents I had ever read. It was dated London, 12 November 1792—exactly six days before the banquet at White's—and contained the following paragraph:

> I have determined to set out for Paris in the course of a fortnight or three weeks; and I shall not now halt at Dover, I promise you; for I go alone—neck or nothing is the word. During my stay I shall not forget my friends; but I will tell you so when I am really there. Meantime let me beg you not to mix with the shallow herd who throw an odium on immutable principles, because some of the mere instruments of the Revolution were too sharp.—Children of any growth will do mischief when they meddle with edged tools.

The voice broke in on me like a new sound, a new dimension: brisk, cheerful, daring, strangely modern. Paris, alone, neck or nothing! It was like that moment in a Shakespearian play when, after the muffled scene-setting dialogue of the minor characters, the hero abruptly enters from an unexpected angle in the wings, speaking with the sudden clarity and assurance that a major actor brings to his part. The whole theatre instinctively stiffens to attention. Yet in this case it was not a hero but a heroine. For the author of the letter to Roscoe was Mary Wollstonecraft. It was she who was setting out for Paris, quite alone, and airily referring to the September Massacres as "meddling with edged tools". I had found my exemplar, and my guide.

3

In November 1792 Mary Wollstonecraft was thirty-three years old, unmarried, and that rarest of things in eighteenth-century England, a woman freelance reviewer and writer, living entirely by her own pen. She had published, as well as a mass of occasional journalism, four books: a critique of teaching methods, *Thoughts on the Education of Daughters* (1786); a semi-autobiographical novel, *Mary* (1788); a collection of tales for children, *Original Stories* (1788); and a classic first statement of British feminism, *A Vindication of the Rights of Woman with Strictures on Political and Moral Subjects* (1792). This last work, attacking male attitudes to education, marriage and the Rousseauistic "romanticising" of women's subservient role in conventional society, was dedicated to the French statesman Talleyrand. The dedication closed with a characteristically cool but insistent demand that the revolutionaries should turn their legislative attention to the claims of women everywhere: "I wish, sir, to set some investigations of this kind afloat in France; and should they lead to a confirmation of my principles when your Constitution is revised, the Rights of Women may be respected, if it be fully proved that reason calls for this respect, and loudly demands JUSTICE for one-half of the human race."

Characteristic, too, that her claims were based on "Reason"—not on "Imagination", a word she was still inclined to associate with what was fanciful and frivolous.

All Mary Wollstonecraft's works had been published by Joseph Johnson, and he was the linchpin of her professional career. She had led a penurious early life as a schoolteacher at Newington Green, in North London, and as governess to the aristocratic Kingsborough family in Ireland (a job she detested) before he encouraged her to return and settle in the capital in 1787. He took lodgings for her in Blackfriars, and she began to mix with his circle of radical intellectuals and religious nonconformists. While working on her books she supported herself by translating and writing essays and reviews on the books and topics of the day for Johnson's newly founded magazine, the *Analytical Review*. Johnson found in her a person of exceptional intelligence and forceful views, who could write with great speed and fluency—though not always elegantly—and argue in mixed company without reserve or embarrassment.

A harsh and unhappy childhood, dominated by an unstable and drunken father whom she never respected, had given Mary Wollstonecraft an unusual sense of her own independence and reliance in her own judgment; and a corresponding lack of respect for all kinds of male authority that she did not feel had been genuinely earned, whether in life or in literature. At the same time this passionate, ebullient and frequently opinionated woman was given to terrible swings of mood, from hectic noisy enthusiasm to almost suicidal depression and a sense of futility and loneliness.

It was typical of her that after a violent disagreement with Johnson one evening she should flash round a note of hand the next morning which said simply:

You made me very low-spirited last night, by your manner of talking.—You are my only friend—the only person I am intimate with.—I never had a father, or a brother—you have been both to me, ever since I knew you—yet I have sometimes been very petulant.—I have been thinking of those instances of ill-humour and quickness, and they appeared like crimes.

Yours sincerely, Mary.

It was this spontaneous warmth of heart and feeling, this direct touch upon the chords of life, that seems to have captivated almost everyone, man or woman, who got to know her well. Although among those who only knew her public persona as a feminist author, she frequently excited scorn and even hatred. Horace Walpole, the friend of the poet Gray, and the kindly eccentric of Strawberry Hill, called her a "hyena in petticoats". The philosopher William Godwin, a man of almost studied calm and self-control, came home in a fever of irritation from a dinner at Johnson's in 1791 where he had hoped to be introduced to Tom Paine. The fourth member of the dinner-party had not allowed him to get a word in edgeways with the author of *The Rights of Man* before he decamped to France. The vexatious person who had dominated the conversation was the author of *The Rights of Woman*. She was also to be, six years later, Godwin's wife. He called her a "sort of female Werther"—after Goethe's popular novel of the new, "emotional" sensibility.

Certainly the fact that she was still unmarried in her early thirties excited considerable speculation. She was a large, handsome woman with a striking pair of brown eyes, an unruly mass of chestnut hair and long expressive hands—not the trim, dowdy blue-stocking of eighteenth-century convention. She had noticeable dress sense, and each of the half-dozen different portraits I found of her in the 1790s showed a different fashion of clothes and a completely different hairstyle.

The portrait of late 1791, especially commissioned by her friend Roscoe to celebrate the publication of her *Rights of Woman*, showed her in her Amazonian phase: lean-featured, with the severe dark dress and high white stock of the nonconformist intellectual, her carefully curled and powdered hair brushed back from her brow and shoulders. She looks like a formidable young headmistress. Yet some two years later an engraving shows her as a thoroughly romantic *femme de trente*, wearing the loose white gown of the progressive woman, with high waist and low décolletage, her chestnut hair falling in a mass of wild tresses over her forehead and shoulders, uncombed and unpowdered, and her head crowned with a sort of half-stovepipe riding hat, a racy Parisian affair, with a velvet band and curved brim.

These outward changes of style give some clue to her mercurial and passionate temperament, and certainly belie any suggestion of mannish coldness or lesbian hauteur. In fact, in 1792, gossip not surprisingly gave her a romantic connection with her publisher, which she laughingly denied in her letters to Roscoe, while trailing her petticoat in a most unhyena-like manner: "Our friend Johnson is well—I am told the world, to talk big, married me to him while we were away; but you know that I am still a spinster on the wing. At Paris, indeed, I might take a husband for the time being, and get divorced when my truant heart longed again to nestle with its old friends; but this speculation has not yet entered into my plan."

This talk of a husband was actually bravado, or at least putting a brave face on matters. For the truth was that Mary Wollstonecraft had passed the summer of 1792 in the agonies of an unrequited love affair with another of Johnson's friends, the gifted and highly unstable painter Henri Fuseli. Mary had insisted that her passion was platonic, or anyway based on a marriage of true minds. But Fuseli's wife had not been of the same opinion, especially when Mary suggested a trip to Paris with Fuseli and Johnson; and, when this fell through, planned a ménage à trois with Fuseli in London. That September a domestic row ensued, and Fuseli's door was for ever closed to Mary—the abrupt but inevitable termination of what she had described, curiously, as "a rational desire". This story—largely based on the hearsay of friends, for Mary's letters to Fuseli were destroyed—gave me a further clue to Mary's character: headstrong, entirely impatient with conventions (though the ménage à trois was, a generation later, to be a typical Romantic solution to the "problem" of marriage), and yet with an odd kind of sexual innocence. For there can be no doubt, from later events, that Mary Wollstonecraft was still a virgin at this time.

She had, moreover, fallen for a perhaps unexpected kind of man. Fuseli was brilliantly imaginative to the point of neurosis, philandering, foreign (he was Swiss by birth) and extremely demanding. Many of these qualities are summed up in his most famous painting, the disturbing and sexually symbolic picture *The Nightmare*—with its abandoned female sleeper flung back across a bed, while a hideous incubus crouches on her breast. That this man should have been Mary's type made me think that any simple interpretation of her emotional character—a frustrated spinster intellectual (as she jokingly implied) or a hungry, dominating, even man-hating woman—would be rather short of the mark.

Moreover, Mary had not led an emotionally sheltered life, hidden away in books or schools. As a child she had protected her mother physically from the assaults of her drunken father; and when her mother was dying in 1782 it was Mary—aged twenty-three—who came home to nurse her. When her younger sister Eliza lapsed into depression after the birth of her first child, it was Mary who spirited her away in a carriage and insisted on a separation from her bullying husband. It was Mary, too, who set up the school in Newington Green where her other sister, Evarina, taught; and where her greatest friend, Fanny Blood, found independence. Most indicative of all, when Fanny Blood married and went away with her husband to Portugal, it was Mary who answered the call to attend her in childbirth, in November 1785, sailing to Lisbon alone to do so. Mary's feelings for Fanny were the most important thing in her early life, and showed both her loyalty to those she loved and her powerful organising and maternal instinct, at its best in a crisis.

When Fanny, too, died in her arms after giving birth, Mary's profound sense of vocation to speak for the plight of women crystallised. Two years later she was beginning to write for Johnson, and with her intensive reading and her eager pursuit of the intellectual debate aroused by the Revolution in France—most especially by the work of Tom Paine and Condorcet—the intense awareness of women's *plight* leapt forward into the powerful and socially revolutionary concept of women's *right*.

A journey to Paris was, on the face of it, not such a mad adventure for a woman who had already travelled to Dublin and to Lisbon. Besides, Mary Wollstonecraft, whatever her private uncertainties, was now a writer with a growing public reputation both in England and France. She had met Talleyrand in London—he remarked on her insouciant manner of serving tea out of unmatched cups and saucers. Her book had been widely reviewed, and attacked, in the English press; and a translation of it had rapidly appeared in Paris, under the title *Une Défense des Droits des Femmes*. There it had attracted the attention of the Girondists, the moderate party opposed to Robespierre's Jacobins. They already had close contacts with Johnson through White's Hotel and specifically through Citoyen and Député Tom Paine. The Girondists' group were particularly interested in social and educational reform, and the *Rights of Woman* was a *carte de visite* to Madame Roland's salon and those leading deputies who met there, like Brissot, Condorcet, Pétion and Vergniaud. It also gave Mary great standing among the more eccentric and active feminist campaigners, like the flamboyant Olympe de Gouges (originally an actress called Marie Gouze) and the glamorous Madame Stéphanie de Genlis, author of several polemical works on women's rights, who always wore a polished piece of Bastille stone on a gold chain in her plunging cleavage, to the confusion of her male colleagues—an early case of radical chic.

Yet Mary Wollstonecraft's decision to go alone to Paris was a brave one. On the eve of her departure in mid-December she wrote frankly to her sister Evarina that she was struggling with "vapourish fears". She was alarmed by the increasingly hostile attitude to the Revolution that was becoming apparent even in liberal circles in London, ever since the arrest of the King. Had she not already booked and paid for her place in the Dover mail she says she would "have put off the journey again on account of the present posture of affairs at home". In his *Memoir* of her, Godwin later said that she would not have gone at all had it not been for her anxiety to forget Fuseli, and there may be much truth in this. However, her practical arrangements show that the expedition was well thought out, and only intended to last about six weeks. She had kept on the small apartment she now rented at Store Street behind the British Museum (on the present site of the University gardens east of Bedford Square) and left her cat with a neighbour. She had arranged to draw money through Johnson's publishing contacts in Paris, and accepted a commission from him to write a series of "Letters from the Revolution", with a Paris dateline in the best tradition of the foreign correspondent.

Like Wordsworth, she appears to have had notes of introduction to Helen Williams, and probably also to Madame Roland. She had wisely arranged to stay with private friends in the rue Meslay in the third arrondissement—a quiet street in the north-east corner of the city, off the boulevard Saint-Martin and near the present place de la République. The large house at No 22 was owned by a well-to-do French merchant, Monsieur Fillietaz, who had married Aline Bregantz—one of Mary's friends from her teaching days. So familiar faces, as she supposed, awaited her in Paris. What she did not realise was that the Fillietaz family had left for the country, and that the rue Meslay stood within five minutes of the King's prison at the Temple.

Mary Wollstonecraft finally arrived in Paris on about 12 or

13 December 1792—almost the exact day that Wordsworth was leaving the city. She carried the obligatory tricolour cockade in her hatband (these were forced on prudent travellers at Calais, at exorbitant prices), and also caught a heavy head cold on the three-day diligence. For three weeks Johnson and her friends in London heard nothing: Mary had disappeared into the heart of the Revolution.

Once again I followed her, wandering up and down the narrow, rising thoroughfare, the home of cheap china and plumbing shops which is the modern rue Meslay, trying to make sense of her extraordinary story, to catch the echoes of her voice and the glimpses of what she had witnessed.

The broad outline of her adventure soon became clear enough. Mary's journalistic expedition of six weeks prolonged itself into a sojourn of two years, the most transforming and probably the most crucial years of her life. She remained in France during the trial and execution of Louis XVI and his family; during the declaration of war against England and her continental allies who aligned themselves against the Revolution; during the struggle for power which led to the execution of all the leading Girondists; during Robespierre's Terror and the arrest of all the English; during the wartime famine, and the terrible dictatorship of the Committee of Public Safety, and the guillotining of Danton, Desmoulins and all the original heroes of the Convention; and at last into the relatively tranquil period following Thermidor—the execution of Robespierre and Saint-Just on 29 July 1794—and the repeal of the dreaded Maximum Laws.

During these hectic months she was, successively, in Paris, then at Neuilly, then at Le Havre, and finally back in Paris again for the winter of 1794–5. She wrote fifty-two extant letters, one long journalistic article for Johnson—the first of the "Letters from the Revolution", laconically entitled "On the Present Character of the French Nation"—and the first volume of a projected *Historical and Moral View of the French Revolution*, which was published by Johnson in late 1794. But much more important than all this—and to me the biographical fact that transformed my conception of the inner nature of the revolutionary experience—she fell violently in love with a fellow-enthusiast of the French cause, and had an illegitimate child. Like Annette Vallon (though far more tragically) she was abandoned by the child's father in circumstances that led to her almost despairing of everything she believed in and had struggled to achieve. This story is now much better known, through the fine modern biography by Claire Tomalin (1974); but at the time, as I pieced it together in the retreating hopes of "*Imagination au Pouvoir*", it came to grip my mind like one of those recurrent dreams—half mysterious symbol and half fretful nightmare—that seize on our unconscious with inexplicable power and authority during times of confused action and ill-defined aims in life. Oddly, I associated Mary's whole story with an isolated line of Wordsworth's which had nothing at all to do with Paris: "The sounding Cataract haunted me like a passion." There was something, I suppose, like a wild waterfall in the headlong, broken, plunging quality of Mary's life. I stood and gazed at it roaring through the streets of Paris, visible only to me.

4

What were Mary Wollstonecraft's initial impressions of Paris, the first liberated city of Europe? I expected a paean of praise and excitement; a wild traveller's letter full of the crowds, the Fédéré soldiers, the tricolour flags and the wall-posters, impressions of the cafés and arcades, and news of the Convention. Thomas Carlyle, in his great pageant-history of the Revolution, described the English sympathisers arriving with "hot unutterabilities in their hearts" and, having felt something of the same myself, I thought Mary would express no less.

What she actually wrote, on 24 December, was a hurried note to Evarina, saying that Madame Fillietaz was away, the servants were largely incomprehensible, she went to bed every night with a headache, and she had still "seen very little of Paris, the streets are so dirty". The one introduction she had used was that to Helen Williams, whom she described as affected in manner but with a "simple goodness of her heart" that continually broke through the varnish. "She has behaved very civilly to me and I shall visit her frequently, because I *rather* like her, and I meet French company at her house." There was only one brief observation that gave any clue to how she was really reacting. It referred to the forthcoming trial: "The day after tomorrow I expect to see the King at the bar—and the consequences that will follow I am almost afraid to anticipate."

It gradually dawned on me that Mary, for all her genuine revolutionary enthusiasm, was frightened and isolated; but being Mary, she was not going to show it—at least to her sister.

Writing much later in her *History of the Revolution*, she put some of the ambiguity of her first feelings into the description of the King being brought by the mob from Versailles to the Tuileries. She describes how he would have been struck, as he rode down the Champs-Elysées, by the "charming boulevards, the lofty trees, the alleys and the noble buildings"; and by the way the ordinary people "walk and laugh with an easy gaiety peculiar to their nation". But then his gaze—which was really her gaze—would have rested on the great barrier towers and walls of the city, originally built in 1784 by the Fermiers-Généraux for tax collection purposes, but now producing a terrible effect of "concentration"—an ominous word to use—and so "cutting off the possibility of innocent victims escaping from the fury, or the mistake of the moment". The barrier wall was built of stone, about twelve feet high, and enclosing a perimeter of twenty-three kilometres round the whole city along the line of the boulevards from the present place Charles de Gaulle, place Clichy, and place de la Nation on the Right Bank, to the place Denfert-Rochereau and the place d'Italie on the Left Bank. This formidable wall was guarded by sixty barrier towers, each enclosing a narrow iron gateway, controlled and guarded by troops and customs officers, and bolted for the curfew at dusk. Thus Mary felt these "magnificent porticoes", instead of being the great welcoming gateways into a new paradise, seemed insensibly to reverse their roles, and to threaten to become "gates to a great Prison", preventing anyone getting out.

It was a sharp reminder to me of the nature of eighteenth-century Paris. It was still a walled, semi-medieval, fortified city-state. The Revolution took place within a physically contained area—all exits guarded by their barrier towers—which could build up the kind of psychological pressures (rumours, mob scares, as well as the intoxications of a great carnival) impossible to imagine in a modern city, with its immense networks of roads, railways, airports and information services, constantly open to the outside world. The only modern comparison I could think of was West Berlin. The Parisians themselves invented a popular saying about the barrier wall: "*Le mur murant Paris rend Paris murmurant.*"

Moreover, just as Mary was struggling with a new language (like so many English people, she could translate fluently on the page, but became completely tongue-tied in real life—"how awkwardly I behaved, unable to utter a word and almost stunned by the flying sounds"), she was also struggling with a new language of objects. For in the revolutionary city the significance of everything external —the buildings, the behaviour of the people—depends completely on one's own degree of sympathy with the cause that they express. What is beautiful can become terrible, what is elegant something mocking and sinister. Like the barrier towers, the meaning of every-thing can suddenly become ambiguous, or actually be reversed. The friendly crowd becomes a mob; the fine palace a grim prison. The pavement may open up, the front door may shut on a cell, the trusted shopkeeper *du coin* may become the *section* secret policeman.

Again, Mary put this perception in her *History*:

But how quickly vanishes the prospect of delights, of delights such as man ought to taste! . . . The cavalcade of death moves along, shedding mildew over all the beauties of the scene, and blasting every joy! The elegance of the palaces and buildings is revolting when they are viewed as prisons; and the sprightliness of the people disgusting, when they are hastening to view the operation of the guillotine, or carelessly passing over the earth stained with blood.

These of course were early impressions viewed with the bitterness of hindsight. Yet Mary saw something even in those first days that she recorded at the time, and which clearly shook her deeply. It was the sight of the King being driven in cortège from his prison in the Temple (on the site of the present square du Temple) to his trial at the Convention.

Here arose a small but significant biographical puzzle. Mary says she saw the procession from her window in the rue Meslay. Yet the King's route on that morning of 26 December lay up the rue du Temple, and then westwards along the boulevard Saint-Martin towards the Tuileries, and I did not understand how she could have witnessed this without leaving the house and walking down to the end of the street and turning up on to the boulevard itself (which runs parallel with the rue Meslay). Yet she clearly says the King passed by her window. Surely she was not romanc-ing? Because if she was it would be quite out of character (as I had begun to understand hers), and besides it would cast doubt on other things she said in her letters.

The solution became clear the moment I walked over the same ground. No 22 rue Meslay stands on a rising piece of land — it is, so to speak, the crown of the street — and the *back top* windows of the house have an unobstructed view clear across the rooftops to the north, commanding the whole panorama of the boulevard beyond them, from the present place de la République to what was then, and still is, the archway of the porte Saint-Martin. So Mary had, in effect, a view from the grandstand. This also, incidentally, told me that Madame Fillietaz's servants had bundled the strange

Englishwoman to an obscure apartment at the back of the house, rather than give her one of the lavish guest-rooms with balcony at the front. This helps to explain what Mary subsequently says about feeling lost at the far end of a labyrinth of corridors.

Mary's description of the procession is given in her first letter to Joseph Johnson that same evening. Unlike her note to Evarina, it contains no domestic trivialities—not even a mention of Christmas Day—but goes straight into the historic scene, merely saying that she would have written earlier, but she "wished to wait till I could tell you that this day was not stained with blood" thanks to the prudent precautions taken by the National Convention "to prevent a tumult". With this slightly ominous preface, she plunges into the following remarkable account of what she saw, and how she felt:

> About nine o'clock this morning, the King passed by my window, moving silently along (except now and then a few strokes on the drum, which rendered the stillness more aweful) through empty streets, surrounded by the national guards, who, clustering around the carriage, seemed to deserve their name. The inhabitants flocked to their windows, but the casements were all shut, not a voice was heard, nor did I see any thing like an insulting gesture.—For the first time since I entered France, I bowed to the majesty of the people, and respected the propriety of behaviour so perfectly in unison with my own feelings. I can scarcely tell you why, but an association of ideas made the tears flow from my eyes, when I saw Louis sitting, with more dignity than I expected from his character, in a hackney coach going to meet his death . . .

The cinematic immediacy of this thrilled me: one could see the rows of faces behind those closed casements, looking down, like something out of a piece of early silent newsreel. Yet at the same time I was surprised and touched by Mary's tears, the last thing one might have expected from her, a good republican. She saw the whole order of power and authority stood on its head—the "majesty of the *people*". In theory she approved, but in practice she was also shocked. Here at once was that divide between Reason and Imagination; and most of her fellow-revolutionaries from England felt the same. Even Tom Paine, the most vociferous of all king-haters, was soon to go to the bar of the National Convention to plead for "Citizen Capet's" life—thereby earning Robespierre's permanent distrust.

But Mary goes much further than describing a mere political

event. She senses in herself a profound disturbance at what she had witnessed, a threat to the whole notion of personal order and safety, and this too she attempted to describe to her old friend Johnson. It is an almost unique passage in her letters, an admission of vulnerability very rare, yet done with her same matter-of-fact style and the same little gleams of self-mockery that she habitually employed. Yet it is, unmistakably, the same kind of experience that Wordsworth described in his hotel garret room. It has the same quality of confusion between reality and dream, and it even has the same candle burning symbolically on the bedside table. Again I thought of Fuseli's picture *The Nightmare*, and wondered if there were some hitherto unexplained connection between the fear of revolutionary violence erupting in the daytime and the fear of psychic violence—a disordering of the personality, as well as the society—erupting from the unconscious mind in the dark. Did the Revolution open one to both kinds of disorder?

Mary begins by explaining to Johnson that she had spent the rest of the day in the house at rue Meslay alone, and as the night came on she found the images of the procession coming back to haunt her—to possess her imagination—with increasing menace. She felt alone and isolated, and—now she says it explicitly—very frightened indeed:

> . . . Though my mind is calm, I cannot dismiss the lively images that have filled my imagination all the day.—Nay, do not smile, but pity me; for, once or twice, lifting my eyes from the paper, I have seen eyes glare through a glass-door opposite my chair, and bloody hands shook at me. Not the distant sound of a footstep can I hear. My apartments are remote from those of the servants, the only persons who sleep with me in an immense hotel, one folding door opening after another—I wish I had even the cat with me!—I want to see something alive; death in so many frightful shapes has taken hold of my fancy.—I am going to bed—and, for the first time in my life, I cannot put out the candle.

How much of this was real—the glaring eyes, the bloody hands—and how much of it was Mary's imaginary identification with the doomed King? She does not say, she does not even seem to care much, so anxious is she to impress Johnson with the power of what she has experienced. Even the company of her little Store Street cat would have made her feel less isolated from normal life. Instead there is just the image of those folding doors—one opening on to the next, endlessly, like a looking-glass maze—to give me a new idea of what her lonely journey into the Terror involved. Receiving this letter, Johnson must have prepared himself for Mary Wollstonecraft's imminent return to London.

But Mary did not return; her natural courage and tenacity—and her belief in the Revolution—sustained her. In January 1793 the Fillietaz family returned to Paris, and she dug herself in, working hard at her spoken French, cultivating the circle round Helen Williams, and making contact with the prominent Girondists through Madame Roland. Godwin later said that she became friendly with many of the Girondist leaders in the Convention—Roland himself, Brissot, Pétion (all of whom were to be executed)—and became a popular figure in the "international brigade" of revolutionary sympathisers. He mentions a Swiss couple, Jean-Gaspard and Madeleine Schweizer; a romantically minded Polish aristocrat, Count Gustav von Schlabrendorf, who afterwards claimed he had been in love with her; and the Americans Joel and Ruth Barlow. Ruth, whom she had already met in London, became Mary's special confidante. There were also several hot-headed young adventurers who attached themselves to Helen Williams, including another American, Gilbert Imlay, and an Englishman, John Hurford Stone (who left his own wife and became Helen's lover and subsequently her husband).

In the excited and dangerous atmosphere it is clear that romantic unions flourished, as in wartime, and Mary was the object of much gallantry: a provokingly unattached woman, and a famous author as well. She seems to have liked this, but maintained her detachment, remarking somewhat archly in a letter to her other sister, Eliza, that "those who wish to live for themselves without close friendship, or warm affection, ought to live in Paris for they have the pleasantest way of whiling away time."

Some of the men were tiresome, however; particularly the tall, rangy American Imlay, whom she met at the house of Paine's friend, John Christie. He was a protégé of the Barlows', and with his knowledge of Kentucky was working on a somewhat madcap scheme with the Girondist Brissot to foment a pro-French uprising against Spanish colonial rule in the southern territories of Louisiana. He was regarded as an expert on the question, as a result of his book *A Topographical Description of the Western Territory of America*; but also fancied himself as a romantic novelist, having just published in London a saga of backwoods Kentucky life—told in letters—entitled *The Emigrants*. The book extolled the simple pioneer life, and had a liberated heroine, whom Imlay seems subsequently to have likened to Mary herself. Mary clearly thought him bumptious, while he found her unaccountably frosty. Besides, the gossip among the international set said that Imlay stayed overnight with Helen Williams. Anyway, Mary was busy with more important matters. Condorcet, who had been appointed to the special Girondist Committee on Public Instruction, had commissioned her to draw up a paper on female education: at last she seemed to be becoming directly involved with the shaping of the Revolution itself.

Yet the progress of public affairs was increasingly alarming. Possibly because of the tightening political censorship, only two letters from Mary reached England between January and June 1793, and during this time the whole aspect of the Revolution altered. On 21 January the King was executed; on 1 February England declared war on France, and a series of laws against "enemy aliens" were promulgated in Paris, beginning with special registration and passport requirements; on 25 February there were food riots in Paris, and three weeks later the first loyalist rising in the Vendée began. Finally, with growing fears of enemies both abroad and at home, on 15 April 1793 the Committee of Public Safety was instituted. From now on Mary was living in a Revolution threatened by both war and civil war.

Once again, the question arose whether Mary would now go back to London. On the declaration of war many English sympathisers followed the example of the English Ambassador and headed rapidly for the Channel ports, showing their freshly stamped passport papers at the barrier towers as they departed. The White's Hotel group effectively disbanded, and Helen Williams stopped writing special reports for *The Times*.

Mary, who had already stayed in France for more than her planned six weeks, debated with herself about her next move. During this uncertain time she wrote the essay, "On the Present Character of the French Nation", which she had originally promised Johnson, dating it 15 February. Her general thesis was not optimistic: she argued that the great and universal political ideals of the Revolution, especially as expressed by the National Assembly of 1789–91, were in the process of being betrayed by the weakness of the French as a people. Their natural volatility, their tendency to extremism, their moral shallowness, and above all the years they had spent as a subject nation beneath the authoritarian rule of the French kings completely unfitted them to act responsibly in their new historic role as revolutionary liberators. (I could not help thinking that Mary felt that the English, with their tradition of constitutional monarchy, would have handled the whole thing much better.)

The French, in other words, lacked revolutionary *virtue*, and this would lead them away from the Paradise on Earth which all the radicals of the 1790s believed in. Mary wrote mournfully:

> Before I came to France, I cherished, you know, an opinion that strong virtues might exist with the polished manners produced by the progress of civilisation; and I even anticipated the epoch, when, in the course of improvement, men would labour to become virtuous, without being goaded on by misery. But now, the perspective of the Golden Age, fading before the attentive eye of observation, almost eludes my sight . . .

Mary's stress on revolutionary, or republican "virtue" was in fact a commonplace among radicals of every type at this time: it is found equally in the writings of William Godwin on political justice or the speeches of Robespierre on the loyalty or otherwise of the French army—though Robespierre would soon shift to the far more alarming term, "purity". What struck me was how alien this demanding concept of moral virtue in public affairs was to the attitudes of 1968. I was moving further and further away into a wholly different world-view of what a revolution required of its participants. Virtue, duty, labour . . . these were what Mary Wollstonecraft saw as essential to the new world.

Mary's apparent disillusion with the course the Revolution was now taking, together with the increasing personal restrictions applied to "aliens", suggest that this was the sensible moment to go home. Besides, in a letter to Ruth Barlow (still at this time in London, though Joel was in Paris) she says she continued to feel tired and ill, the weather was extremely bad, and she "half-ruined" herself in coach-hire. On 14 February someone in the White's Hotel group offered her a place in his private carriage which was departing for Calais: it was the moment to decide. But once again she decided to stay.

Why was this? In her letter to Ruth she is wonderfully offhand about it. She says in effect that she cannot bear to give up learning French just as she is beginning to master the language, and besides she has not finished her paper for Condorcet:

> Yesterday a Gentleman offered me a place in his carriage to return to England and I knew not how to say no, yet I think it would be very foolish to return when I have been at so much

trouble to master a difficulty, when I am just turning the corner, and I am, besides, writing a plan of education for the Committee appointed to consider the subject.

Of other reasons she says nothing, though there is just a hint that the company of her fellow-expatriates was increasingly agreeable and even exciting: "I am almost overwhelmed with civility here, and have even met with more than civility . . ." Reading between the lines I could see Mary being steadily drawn into the heady, dangerous but immensely stimulating atmosphere of the city. The excitement and uncertainty obviously suited her: there was no time to be depressed as in the grey, safe and reactionary world of literary London. The more she complained about the foul Parisian streets, the insolent crowd, the "fatiguing" vivacity, the more she obviously revelled in them. However carefully she stated her theoretical objections to the Revolution it is clear that emotionally she was more and more committed to it: she knew that this was the great historical moment, and that Paris was the focus—the burning-glass—of European consciousness.

Indeed, it must have felt like the centre of the universe. Good and evil forces were inextricably mixed, as she now realised; this was not yet the Golden Age. But what was taking place was an event of historic proportions, and universal significance for later generations, and she intended not only to witness it but to take part in it if she could. As she later wrote, with extraordinary restraint and judgment at the very height of the Terror:

> All Europe saw, and all good men saw it with dread, that the French had undertaken to support a Cause, which they had neither sufficient purity of heart nor maturity of judgement, to conduct with moderation and prudence . . . [But] malevolence has been gratified by the errors they have committed, attributing that imperfection to the Theory they adopted, which was applicable only to the folly of their practice. However, Frenchmen have reason to rejoice, and posterity will be grateful, for what was done by the Assembly.

There was one other reason why Mary stayed: Gilbert Imlay, the man who was so tiresome. As the doubters fled to safety and those who remained drew closer together, meeting more frequently at Helen Williams's house or Madame Roland's salon new qualities emerged from behind formal exteriors. The brash backwoodsman turned out to have certain depths and a good deal of charm. Imlay was from New Jersey, and had served with some distinction during the American War of Independence. As the political situation in Paris became more dangerous he became resolutely more sanguine. A friend described him as "very cheerful and high-spirited". He left off his airs of an author, and began to tease Mary with boyish good-humour. Slowly she responded, her formidable, assertive manner becoming lighter, even girlish. There is an anecdote about her bad French which she told to Ruth Barlow, and which almost certainly refers to one of Imlay's meaningful jokes: "A Gentleman the other day, to whom I frequently replied, —*oui, oui*—when my thoughts were far away, told me that I was acquiring in France a bad custom, for that I might chance to say *oui*, when I did not intend it, *par habitude*."

That she might one day say *yes*, without thinking: the joke has a faint but distinct sexual suggestion. Mary later said she was disarmed by Imlay's sudden, tender smile: it had the vulnerable look of a child who had somehow got into mischief.

It is not clear exactly how their liaison now developed (what of Imlay's supposed *faiblesse* for Helen Williams?) but it is evident that the helter-skelter pace of political events contributed a good deal. In May the first Maximum Law was passed, controlling food prices with ferocious punishments for black marketeers, and making daily life difficult and unpleasant—long queues outside the shops, shortages, curfews, sudden scares and casual violence in the streets. All householders had to post the names of their occupants on their front doors, and the whereabouts of foreigners was known and marked. The Fillietaz family began to think of leaving permanently for the country; Mary's position became awkward. She applied for a travel document to get her through the barrier, but it was not immediately granted. Then, at the end of May, Robespierre unleashed his attack on the Girondists in the Convention. Within two weeks the Rolands, Pétion, Brissot—all had been arrested, while Condorcet had escaped and was in hiding, later to commit suicide. Quite apart from the terrible shock this gave to the international group, it meant the collapse of both Mary's involvement with the Committee for Public Instruction and Imlay's Louisiana scheme with Brissot. They were effectively isolated, though Imlay, like Paine and Barlow, was protected by his American citizenship, as the national of a friendly power. Mary was not.

In the midst of this maelstrom Mary suddenly sent a rapturously happy letter to Eliza, dated 13 June, from outside Paris, but without further address or postmark. (It was almost certainly carried in the private baggage of one of Barlow's American business contacts who still moved freely between Paris and London.) Of political affairs she says precisely, and very carefully, nothing: "I write with *reserve* because all letters are opened." But of her own situation she is radiantly yet mysteriously optimistic:

> I will venture to *promise* that brighter days are in store for you. I cannot explain myself excepting just to tell you that I have a plan in my head, it may prove abortive, in which you and Evarina are included, if you find it good, that I contemplate with pleasure as a mode of bringing us all together again. I have been endeavouring to obtain a passport a long time and did not get it till after I had determined to take a lodging in the country—for I could not think of staying any longer at Madame F's. I am now at the house of an old Gardener writing a great book; and in better health and spirits than I ever enjoyed since I came to France . . .

Mary's secret, what she could not explain, was that she and Imlay had become lovers. They were already planning—after the Revolution, should they survive it—to go to America together and seek the Golden Age there, perhaps on a farm in some far western territory. Meanwhile Mary had contrived, with the help of the Fillietaz family, to cross the barrier at Longchamp (between the present place Charles de Gaulle and the place du Trocadéro), and take rooms in an idyllic little country house at Neuilly, hidden in its own grounds, and looked after by the Fillietaz's faithful old gardener. She had brought her books and papers with her, and was embarking on her *History of the Revolution*—her "great book".

The gardener kept house for her, and brought her fruit and vegetables, especially a particular kind of grape which she adored. The old man, she later told Godwin, grew wonderfully fond and protective, "contending for the honour" of making her bed, warning her against walking alone in the woods by the Seine, and making solemn difficulties about the grapes "when she had any person with her as a visitor". Her most frequent visitor was of course Imlay, whom she would go to meet at the barrier in the summer evenings. Long after she would recall with delight the smiling, expectant look of his "barrier face".

Mary remained in her retreat at Neuilly for four months, until September 1793. It was a magical time—perhaps the happiest of her whole life. Within the turmoil of the Revolution she had unexpectedly discovered what came to seem like her own private Garden of Eden. She was writing hard, and at the same time successfully sharing her life with someone she deeply loved. Intellectually Imlay was a stimulating companion, and constantly brought her the latest news of events in Paris, which they would discuss long into the night. Physically the relationship—which had begun, like so many others, in a small hotel in Saint-Germain—was an immense success on both sides. Indeed, from what Mary later told Godwin, it was a completely transforming experience: a revolution within her own being. "She entered into that species of connection for which her heart secretly panted . . . Now, for the first time in her life, she gave a loose to all the sensibilities of her nature." In his *Memoir*, Godwin described her sense of well-being, her excitement, her radiant glow of sheer animal exhilaration, in beautiful pre-Freudian imagery, and without a trace of jealousy:

> She was like a serpent on a rock, that casts its slough and appears again with the brilliancy, the sleekness, and the elastic activity of its happiest age. She was playful, full of confidence, kindness and sympathy. Her eyes assumed new lustre, and her cheeks new colour and smoothness. Her voice became cheerful; her temper overflowing with universal kindness; and that smile of bewitching tenderness from day to day illuminated her countenance, which all who knew her will so well recollect and which won, both heart and soul, the affection of almost everyone that beheld it.

Or, in the expressive French phrase, *Mlle Wollstonecraft était bien dans sa peau.*

No trace now remains of Mary's magic house and garden, though I long searched for it. In those days Neuilly was a country village, surrounded by woods, allotments and a network of little lanes leading down to the Seine. Now, on one side, lie the elegant parklands and shaded rides of the Bois de Boulogne; on the other, the bleak windy skyscrapers of La Défense. The sole remaining evidence of the place lies in two of her little love-notes scrawled to Imlay; the one regretting a "snug dinner" she had missed with him, but leaving the key in the door; the other begging him to cherish her, "and your own dear girl will try to keep under a quickness of feeling, that has sometimes given you pain". Though Imlay's side of the correspondence has not survived it is impossible to doubt that they were both very much in love, and constantly anxious to be with each other. One of the notes, written at two in the morning in late July, ends:

> But good-night!—God bless you! Sterne says, that is equal to a kiss—yet I would rather give you the kiss into the bargain, glowing with gratitude to heaven, and affection to you. I like the word affection, because it signifies something habitual; and we are soon to meet, to try whether we have mind enough to keep our hearts warm.—Mary. I will be at the barrier a little after ten o'clock tomorrow.

5

Mary's love affair with Imlay was to dominate her remaining year and a half in France. Public events, and even her "great book", took second place to it; indeed, I came to feel that her deepest understanding of what the Revolution meant was produced by the emotional changes in the "little kingdom" of her own heart. She gave an entirely new importance to instinctive feeling, and sincerity of emotions.

In fact I found her to be exemplary in a more profound, indeed spiritual way than I had supposed when I first set out looking for a simple witness to events. The Revolution was, in a sense, internalised in her own biography: from the clever rational feminist to the suffering and loving woman writer with a deep understanding of her fellow-beings she had passed through a revolution of sensibility. It was only towards the end of the affair, in her *Letters Written in Sweden*—her least-known book—that she was able to write about human relationships with the tenderness and insight of the following passage:

> Friendship and domestic happiness are continually praised; yet how little is there of either in the world, because it requires more cultivation of mind to awake affection, even in our own hearts, than the common run of people suppose. Besides, few like to be seen as they really are; and a degree of simplicity, and undisguised confidence, which, to uninterested observers, would almost border on weakness, is the charm, nay the essence of love or friendship: all the bewitching graces of childhood again appearing . . . I therefore like to see people together who have affection for each other; every turn of their features touches me.

It was perhaps that ability to be touched, never to be the "uninterested observer", that Mary learned from her time with Imlay.

Poor Gilbert Imlay! Subsequent biographers of Mary, mostly feminist writers, have torn him limb from limb. Taking their cue from Virginia Woolf, who irresistibly described his courtship of Mary as "tickling minnows" and hooking "a dolphin", they have condemned him for shallowness, bad faith, bad manners. But it never seemed like that to me.

In the first place, there is the evident and extraordinary change that he produced in Mary as a writer. In the second, there is the biographical fact—or rather lack of fact—that his side of the correspondence, and therefore his side of the story, has not survived; Imlay therefore stands undefended before the bar of history. In the third place, there is what Godwin himself described in his *Memoir*, with pointed emphasis, as Mary's own attitude long after the affair was over. "Be it observed, by the way, and I may be supposed best to have known the real state of the case, she never spoke of Mr Imlay with acrimony, and was displeased when any person, in her hearing, expressed contempt of him." Fourthly there is Mary's own noticeably difficult personality, independent and powerful and assertive, and her compensating need for demanding and equally difficult men—as her pursuit of Fuseli had shown. Finally, there was the simple truth that Imlay, in the autumn of 1793, certainly saved Mary from arrest, and possibly from execution on the grounds of her being in possession of incriminating papers—those pertaining to the Girondists, and to her *History of the Revolution*. She later said that Helen Williams had strongly advised her to burn the whole manuscript, "and to tell you the truth—my life would not have been worth much, had it been found".

To understand the critical nature of Mary's position one has to look outside the little garden at Neuilly and return to events within the barrier of Paris. The Committee of Public Safety, waging a fierce war on the eastern borders of France, had become obsessed with its own security at home. On 10 July Danton was removed from the Committee after an internal power struggle with Robespierre, and three days later Marat was assassinated in his bath by Charlotte Corday (an act which, incidentally, completely undermined the position of the remaining French feminists—Olympe de Gouges was at once arrested). Throughout September the Committee tightened its hold on the Parisian population, adopting a series of emergency powers—the Law of Suspects, the Law of 40 Sous (restricting *section* or neighbourhood meetings), the Law of General Maximum and finally, on 10 October, suspending the entire Constitution in favour of what was in effect a military dictatorship directed by Robespierre and Saint-Just.

The revolutionary Terror was now absolute, and guillotinings took place daily. Almost the first act of the Committee within its new powers was to order the arrest of all British citizens, and on the night of 9–10 October, with ruthless efficiency, some four hundred people (the bulk of these being nuns and clergymen who had stayed in the English convents and communities in Paris) were picked up in closed carriages and taken to a special prison established at the Luxembourg. No one seems to have escaped the police sweep, organised by the notorious Fouquier-Tinville. Helen Williams, together with her sister and mother, was arrested shortly after midnight; Tom Paine—with the proofs of *The Age of Reason* in his pocket—was brought in by dawn; even Joel Barlow, vigorously protesting American citizenship (with more success than Paine), was temporarily arrested as a precautionary measure. But Mary Wollstonecraft escaped, and this was thanks to Imlay.

For in French law she was now his wife. Mary had discovered in early autumn that she was pregnant, and had insisted on leaving the safety of Neuilly to come to live with Imlay at his hotel in Saint-Germain. Seeing the inevitable course of the Committee, Imlay had taken her to the American Embassy and overriding her protests (for she still in theory regarded matrimony as bondage) he registered her as his wife and obtained for her papers of American citizenship. So when the terrible blow fell in October Mary was immune, and indeed with characteristic courage she used her papers to visit Helen and other friends in the Luxembourg. Once again, no record of this appears in her letters—the reminiscences of Godwin and Helen Williams were my source—for political censorship made it more than ever perilous to make the least reference to public affairs. What does appear in the letters is Mary's anxiety about her new responsibility, and the strain now imposed on a relationship that had begun in such freedom and high hope. How were they to domesticate a free union within the heart of a Revolution run mad, apparently intent on consuming even its most passionate supporters?

Imlay's position must have been very difficult. In saving Mary he had of course taken on responsibility for a family. Since the collapse of the Louisiana scheme he had been trying to work out with Barlow the basis of a trading company, to bring much needed imports of raw materials into France—running the blockade—from the free port of Hamburg, and through Scandinavian contacts. It was now more than ever vital that this business succeed financially, and that terrifying brushes with the Committee of Public Safety (like Barlow's temporary incarceration) be avoided. Imlay had chosen brave and gifted people to work with, all of them natural survivors. Barlow would eventually be appointed, in 1811, Special American Envoy to Napoleon; while their Scandinavian contact, Elias Backman, was to become in 1799 the first American Consul in Sweden. But it was hectic and uncertain work, involving sudden trips out of Paris—notably to his base port at Le Havre-Marat (recently renamed). Inevitably Mary was left frequently alone. How he must have wished that she had remained in the relative safety of Neuilly! Moreover, Mary now revealed a growing distaste for his commercial projects, and far from sharing his interests began to mock him for his "business-face", openly wondering if "these continual separations" were necessary to warm his affection for her. "Of late," she wrote in October, "we are always separating.—Crack!—crack!—and away you go. This joke wears the sallow cast of thought." Imlay cannot have appreciated the sexual allusion here; or even the mocking quotation from *Hamlet*.

By the end of the year—and it was indeed a terrible one, for all the Girondists had now been executed, including Madame Roland, and the whole of Europe was now at war with France—Mary had fallen back into her old state of depression, doubting everything, from the historical outcome of the Revolution to their personal future together. Imlay must have been shaken by her bitterness.

"I hate commerce," she wrote to him in Le Havre-Marat, "how differently must [Ruth Barlow's] head and heart be organised from mine! You will tell me, that exertions are necessary: I am weary of them! The face of things, public and private, vexes me. The 'peace' and clemency which seemed to be dawning a few days ago, disappear again. 'I am fallen,' as Milton says, 'on evil days'; for I really believe that Europe will be in a state of convulsion, during half a century at least. Life is but a labour of patience: it is always rolling a great stone up a hill . . ."

If he did not come back soon, she threatened, she would throw his slippers out of the window, "and be off—nobody knows where."

But nor indeed did she. There is no indication that Mary ever seriously considered abandoning France, even at this low point. There was something tenacious and irrepressible in her spirit, stronger even than her depressions, and she seems to have got over her physical fears of the Parisian streets. One particular story about her became famous in expatriate circles at this time: crossing the place de la Révolution one morning, she slipped on a patch of wet earth, and looking down saw that the wetness was blood from the previous day's victims. She exclaimed out loud at the horror—the injustice—of it all, and started to create a scene (I could by now vividly imagine a Wollstonecraft scene). It was only when a friendly *citoyen* drew her aside by the arm, and in a low urgent voice explained that she was attracting the attention of nearby soldiers (her French was by now excellent), that she realised her danger and hurried indignantly away. This incident was later put into a novel by Amelia Opie, *A Wife's Duty*, and became a symbol of Mary's courage during the Terror.

Besides, reading the mass of little notes she fired off to the absent Imlay in December and January, it became clear to me that the relationship, though stormy, was still very passionate. Mary's depressions were matched only by her sudden bursts of renewed high spirits. "A man is a tyrant!"—she would exclaim at one moment; and then at the next, "I do not want to be loved like a goddess; but I wish to be necessary to you. God bless you!" She would mock his "money-getting face", then suddenly picture his "honest countenance" relaxed by tenderness: "a little—little wounded by my whims; and thy eyes glistening with sympathy.—Thy lips feel softer than soft—and I rest my cheek on thine, forgetting all the world."

Whenever he came back to Paris all was well; and even his letters could have a transforming effect on her. She wrote on the night of 6 January:

> I have just received your kind and rational letter, and would fain hide my face, glowing with shame for my folly.—I would hide it in your bosom, if you would again open it to me, and nestle closely till you bade my fluttering heart be still, by saying you forgave me . . . Do not turn from me, for indeed I love you fondly, and have been very wretched, since the night I was so cruelly hurt by thinking that you had no confidence in me . . . You perceive that I am already smiling through my tears—You have lightened my heart, and my frozen spirits are melting into playfulness.

Throughout this I could see also that Mary was coming to have a much better understanding of her own nature than before: she refers to her tendency to quarrel, to be low-spirited, and the "whole torrent of emotions" that she was continually struggling to keep under control. People had thought of her as cold and intellectual, and perhaps she had sometimes thought of herself like that too: now she realised the truth was the contrary.

But what of the baby, due in May 1794, a true child of the Revolution? Understandably, Mary was anxious to rejoin Imlay on some more permanent basis well before the birth, so she suggested that she might follow him to the port and settle in a house at Le Havre-Marat. His response seems to have amused and delighted her: "What a picture you sketched of our fire-side!" she wrote on 11 January. "Yes, my love, my fancy was instantly at work, and I found my head on your shoulder, whilst my eyes were fixed on the little creatures that were clinging about your knees. I did not absolutely determine that there should be six—if you have not set your heart on this round number."

So it was that Mary Wollstonecraft, five months pregnant and with half her "great book" written, finally passed through the barrier gates of Paris at the end of January 1794, heading for the coast. She had obtained her passport with unexpected ease, and once again she felt that she was "on the wing". How much had happened to her in the last thirteen months! And how surprised was I, her following shadow, to find that in this final stage of her journey through the Revolution almost all my own thoughts of public affairs had been banished by this affair of the heart. The natural focusing effect of biography had, in a sense, reduced the entire outcome of the Revolution to the success or failure of a single relationship, and to what occurred within "one little room".

Mary herself now felt, and admitted openly, the transforming nature of her relationship with Imlay. She who had prided herself, for half a lifetime, on her independence, her vocation as a writer, her revolutionary duty to her fellow-women, was now committed to achieving and sharing domestic happiness of the most traditional kind. "You have, by your tenderness and worth," she wrote to Imlay on the eve of her departure, "twisted yourself more artfully round my heart, than I supposed possible.—Let me indulge the thought, that I have thrown out some tendrils to cling to the elm by which I wish to be supported.—This is talking a new language for me!—But, knowing that I am not a parasitic-plant, I am willing to receive the proofs of affection, that every pulse replies to, when I think of being once more in the same house with you. God bless you! Yours truly, Mary."

6

Mary Wollstonecraft was to remain in Le Havre-Marat for the next seven months, until the autumn of 1794. Imlay had found a delightful town house, "pleasantly situated" down by the harbour in the section des Sans-Culottes, rented from one of the flourishing English traders there, a Mr John Wheatcroft, purveyor of soap and alum. In this bustling provincial port, with a solid bourgeois tradition of Anglo-French commerce, the pressures of the Revolution seemed far away. Businessmen with American passports still moved easily across the Channel to Brighton and Newhaven (which almost had neutral status), and eastwards to the Dutch, German and Scandinavian ports. Correspondence became much easier, carried unofficially among commercial documents and not having to pass the strict customs and censorship formalities of the Parisian barrier. Imlay laughed at the idea that Mary might be able to have her books shipped down from Saint-Germain, but Ruth Barlow arranged for copies of the *Journal des Débats* and other Government decrees to be posted down from Paris on the diligence, so Mary could continue the documentation for her *History of the Revolution*.

Indeed, the main censorship danger was now on the other side, from the British Postmaster, for as it afterwards emerged in the Treason Trials of Horne Tooke, Tom Hardy and Stone's brother, William, suspicious letters from France were being carefully intercepted and copied in London, and Mary's and Helen Williams's names frequently appeared in the transcripts of cross-examinations conducted at the Old Bailey in the autumn and winter of 1794.

Mary's sense of comparative safety was increased not only by Imlay's constant presence but by the news that nearly all the English had now been released from the Luxembourg prison. Indeed most of her close friends had been freed by Christmas 1793—otherwise she might have stayed on in Paris despite everything. Tom Paine alone remained languishing in a condemned cell, slowly becoming alcoholic under the terrible tension of waiting for Robespierre's final decision on his fate, and soon to be suffering from a jail fever that threatened to anticipate the work of the guillotine.

I had to admit that I was disappointed, in a way, that Mary was no longer in the eye of the revolutionary storm. It was a cruelty, a hunger for dramatic action, that came easily to a biographer learning his métier; and formed one layer of that slight but complex sense of guilt which shadows the vicarious element in historical research into individual lives. Sometimes even I would imagine myself, like a character out of Baroness Orczy, committing Mary to some fatal escapade in the Luxembourg prison, then personally intervening to save her, with the elegant flourish of a Scarlet Pimpernel—"Your faithful biographer, Ma'am, come to extricate you in the next paragraph, which has a secret trapdoor . . ."

Had she stayed in Paris, how I would have loved to have read her piercing comments on the female divinities Robespierre recruited, in his madness for revolutionary purity, to perform the vestal roles in his Festival of the Supreme Being, staged on the Champ-de-Mars on 8 June. But Mary's letters from Le Havre-Marat, speaking their "new language" of emotional self-discovery, were now turned upon her private situation, and slowly, almost reluctantly at first, I obeyed the fundamental dictate of biography, and followed where the materials led, to that deeper revolution of the human heart which I had not even conceived—or done more than half-glimpsed—when I first set out in the euphoria of 1968.

On 10 March, some six weeks after installing herself with Imlay, Mary wrote the first surviving letter to Evarina for over a year. Though she says nothing of the expected child—due in two months—she describes her companion with obvious affection and pride (is there even a hint that *she* had made something of a fine, wild catch?):

> If any, of the many letters that I have written, have come to your hands or Eliza's, you know that I am safe, through the protection of an American. A most worthy man, who joins to uncommon tenderness of heart and quickness of feeling, a soundness of understanding, and reasonableness of temper, rarely to be met with.—Having also been brought up in the interior parts of America, he is a most natural, unaffected creature. I am with him now at Le Havre, and shall remain there, till circumstances point out what it is necessary for me to do.

There is an odd note here too: is it faintly patronising—"a natural unaffected creature" (a noble savage)? Or is it just the old Wollstonecraft pride and self-sufficiency which makes her say, "what is necessary for *me* [not *us*] to do"? Or just a certain stiffness before her younger sister? A mixture of all these, perhaps—though it is surprising not to find a hint of what Imlay looked like: his lean dark features and the boyish smile which so enchanted her.

The immunity from censorship encouraged Mary to give Evarina her first freely expressed thoughts on the political situation, and all she had been through in Paris. It is still phrased in generalities—it was perilous to mention any public figure by more than an initial—but it shows the weight of her experiences and strikes a new, elegiac note. She speaks indeed like someone who has come through fire; like a combat veteran returning from a war that cannot really be explained to those who have remained, safe in their beds at home. She no longer thinks of herself as an adventurer, but as a survivor:

> It is impossible for you to have any idea of the impressions the sad scenes I have been a witness to have left on my mind. The climate of France is uncommonly fine, the country pleasant, and there is a degree of ease, and even simplicity, in the manners of the common people, which attaches me to them. — Still death and misery, in every shape of terror, haunts this devoted country. — I certainly am glad that I came to France, because I never could have had else a just opinion of the most extraordinary event that has ever been recorded. — And I have met with some uncommon instances of friendship, which my heart will ever grately store up, and call to mind when the remembrance is keen of the anguish it has endured for its fellow creatures, at large: — for the unfortunate beings cut off around me — and the still more unfortunate survivors.

There is no mistaking the literal horror of that "cut off"; and no more airy talk of "meddling with edged tools". Her voice has lost much of its matter-of-factness, it is sorrowful and more than a little bewildered.

Throughout March and April Mary quietly laboured away at her book, went for walks by the sea and thought about her baby. News of the Terror filtered down from Paris, like a distant rumbling storm, in letters from Ruth Barlow and Helen Williams. On 5 April, Helen saw Danton and Desmoulins taken in a cart to the guillotine, but her account is curiously unfeeling: perhaps she was too stunned by it all: "I saw them pass — they seemed indifferent to their fate. I think I never saw such an assemblage of people. I was in a carriage going to the rue Saint-Honoré, but the coachman could not possibly pass the pont Neuf — I wonder criminals are not allowed to be executed in a more private manner."

What a wonderfully absurd remark — as if it were nothing more than a traffic hold-up. Unlike Mary's letters, it is also inaccurate: we know from other witnesses that poor Desmoulins wept and raged till the last, begging to see his young wife. I imagined Helen sitting well back in her coach with her eyes shut.

On 16 April all foreigners were finally ordered out of Paris by the Committee, on pain of death. Helen went to Marly, with Stone, then on to Switzerland; Ruth joined her husband Joel in Hamburg;

Paine remained in his feverish cell. Mary was anxious whenever Imlay was away, and wrote more fondly than ever:

> I could not sleep. — I turned to your side of the bed, and tried to make the most of the comfort of the pillow, which you used to tell me I was churlish about; but all would not do. — I took neverthe-less my walk before breakfast, though the weather was not very inviting — and here I am, wishing you a finer day, and seeing you peep over my shoulder, as I write, with one of your kindest looks — when your eyes glisten, and a suffusion creeps over your elaxing features.

She took on a maid to help her in the house, and ordered white calico gowns for the baby and linen shirts for Imlay. Writing to Ruth, she began to talk of "us" and "we", remarking in a deliber-ate parody of her own feminist manner: "You perceive that I am acquiring the matrimonial phraseology without having clogged my soul by promising obedience etc etc."

By the end of April the first volume of the *History* was finished, and the manuscript sent over to Johnson in London; a great relief to her. There is some evidence that she had become bored with it: reviewers were to say that it consisted largely in copying out official documents. It is certainly her dullest work, and Johnson himself must have been disappointed that it broke off with the trial of the King in 1792 — thus leaving out everything that she had witnessed in Paris thereafter. I came to think that Mary simply could not face writing publicly about what she had seen; it is only in her *Letters Written in Sweden* that she begins to reflect openly on some of the experiences she had undergone — and then only in brief asides. Writing, for example, of the vaunted patriotism of the Norwegians, she remarks: "They love their country, but have not much public spirit. Their exertions are, generally speaking, only for their families; which I conceive will always be the case, till politics, becoming a subject of general discussion, enlarges the heart by opening the understanding. The French Revolution will have this effect."

But she also says, in another place, looking at the magnificent landscapes of fjords and mountains, that for the first time "I forgot the horrors I had witnessed in France, which had cast a gloom over all nature . . ."

Mary Wollstonecraft's baby, a little girl, was born at Le Havre-Marat on 14 May 1794; or, as the birth certificate stated, on the 25th day of Floreal in the Second Year of the Republic.

The Register was witnessed by "*citoyen Gilbert Imlay, négociant américain*"; and the child christened Fanny Imlay—the forename standing as a touching memorial to Mary's soul-sister, Fanny Blood. The French midwife observed proudly that Madame had treated the labour so lightly that she "ought to make children for the Republic". Mary naturally broke the bourgeois convention and breast-fed Fanny herself; at which Imlay teased her—as she told Ruth: "My little Girl begins to suck so *manfully* that her father reckons saucily on her writing the second part of *The Rights of Woman*." He showed her "constant tenderness" and affection—despite all the "continual hinderances" in his business affairs and the "whipping embargoes" on his ships—and she felt great pleasure at being a mother.

Indeed the Revolution had brought her a happiness she had never expected. For the next three months there was almost complete domestic silence from the little household. In Paris the guillotine rose and fell with increasing regularity, moving ever closer to Robespierre himself, and a single cry of anguish escaped Mary, writing to Ruth on 8 July: "The French will carry all before them—but, my God, how many victims fall beneath the sword and the Guillotine! My blood runs cold, and I sicken at thoughts of a Revolution which costs so much blood and bitter tears."

But for the rest it was wordless tranquillity, their backs stubbornly turned against a world of horrors, their hopes concentrated in a little smiling face, oblivious to all but milk and love.

This odd, slightly overwritten last phrase of mine stayed in my head for many months. It was only slowly that I came to realise its oddness was important, that it signified something I could not really express. It was not so much fulsome and sentimental as hollow and empty of sentiment. It covered, in fact, a biographical gap. It was the substitute for a kind of information to which, as a biographer, I simply could not get access. To begin with I thought of this material as something slightly abstruse and poetic. In Mary's happiness as a mother, in her act of breast-feeding, I felt sure there was a way of drawing some contrast between the milk of her maternity and the blood of the Revolution. She had come out to France to witness the "blood of freedom", as it were, but what she had actually discovered was something even more fundamental, "the milk of human kindness". I saw that contrast between milk and blood strongly in her letters, and I wanted some way of showing that she had grown conscious of it. I wanted in fact to make her something that she wasn't—a poet. Whereas what I really needed to show was something much simpler, but in the end more

119

remarkable: that this extraordinary and exceptional woman had become a mother—just like any other.

But that ordinariness, and that family intimacy, is the very thing that the biographer—as opposed to the novelist—cannot share or re-create. Tolstoy in the opening of *Anna Karenina* writes that all happy families are happy in the same way; he might have added, that they leave little record of that happiness, even though it is the stuff of life. The very closeness of husbands and wives precludes letters between them, and often the keeping of journals (unless one party is secretly unhappy). The private, domestic world closes in on itself, and the biographer is shut out. It is only when arguments occur, separations, confrontations, crises—or the sudden revelation in a letter to a friend, or a melancholy diary-entry—that the biographer's trail warms up again.

I found something sad and unbalanced in this, almost as if the biographer were doomed to feed upon other people's struggles and miseries; like a doctor, he rarely seemed to see his patients in the bloom of health and contentment. I have since come to believe that the re-creation of the daily, ordinary texture of an individual life—full of the mundane, trivial, funny and humdrum goings-on of a single loving relationship—in a word, the re-creation of *intimacy*—is almost the hardest thing in biography; and, when achieved, the most triumphant.

I seemed to have no hope of discovering this intimacy between Mary and Imlay and their child at Le Havre-Marat; yet without it an important element in Mary's story, and the nature of her experience in France, was missing. For the story itself was nearly over: in the autumn of 1794 Imlay was to leave for London, and in the spring of the following year Mary would follow him. A different and better-known chapter of her life would begin: quarrels, separations, suicide attempts, the journey to Scandinavia and the liaison with William Godwin, her second husband.

Eventually I had one small stroke of luck which led me to a tiny fragment of material that no previous biographer seems to have considered. In the British Library there is a rare four-volume edition of Mary's *Posthumous Works*, edited by Godwin and published by the ever-faithful Joseph Johnson in 1798, one year after her death. Volume Two contains her last, unfinished novel, *The Wrongs of Women, or, Maria*, and bound into the back—but not mentioned in the contents list—are a dozen fragmentary pages entitled "Lessons for Children".

Mary's note from the manuscript says that it was the first part of a series, "which I intended to have written for my unfortunate girl"; while Godwin's editorial preface adds that it was probably "written in a period of desperation in the month of October 1795". But what was important to me was that in drafting these fourteen "Lessons"—teaching her child early vocabulary, simple guides to conduct and ways of learning to appreciate and understand the people and animals around her—Mary had drawn on her own secret memories of the time of family happiness that had existed in the first few months after Fanny's birth. In other words, it gave me a small but precious glimpse into that lost world of intimacy.

Strictly speaking, the "Lessons" recall a time when Fanny was beginning to crawl and talk, so they cannot refer to events in the household much before the winter of 1794 (though there is mention of weaning). However, the picture they give is somehow timeless, or outside time. I was tempted to think of domestic events as operating on a different timescale from that of the external, historical time of the Revolution; a slower rhythm altogether, more like the rhythm of plants or animals; so that it did not seem false to build this into my picture of Mary and Imlay together at this point, before their final separation in France. Indeed, in her memories I think Mary actually pushed them back to the time of their first happiness together, for the "Papa" figure of the "Lessons" is a radiant, smiling presence, only a little anxious or tired sometimes from overwork.

The first three Lessons present a child's basic vocabulary, and the natural order of things in and around their house. "The bird sings. The fire burns. The cat jumps. The dog runs. The cow lies down. The man laughs. The child cries." It seems somehow inevitable that the man should be laughing—his birthright. We also see Mary's instinctive combination of discipline and love in dealing with Fanny. "Hide your face. Wipe your nose. Wash your hands. Dirty mouth. Why do you cry? A clean mouth. Shake hands. I love you. Kiss me now. Good girl." Was it only my imagination that brought the little scene alive with Mary's suddenly tender voice?

In Lesson Seven there is a discussion of crying, and how we all have to accept being hurt, and from that a memory of weaning:

At ten months you had four pretty white teeth, and you used to bite me. Poor Mamma! Still I did not cry, because I am not a child, but you hurt me very much. So I said to Papa, it is time the little girl should eat . . . Yes, says Papa, and he tapped you on the cheek, you are old enough to learn to eat? Come to me, and I will teach you, my little dear, for you must not hurt poor Mamma, who has given you her milk, when you could not take anything else.

In Lesson Eight there is a vivid picture of Fanny getting Papa to play with her. Mary reminds Fanny that she could still only crawl, and her "running" across the room was "quick, quick, on your hands and feet like a dog". Then she describes the scene, with deft and simple touches and explanations, which catch the charm of family life better than anything I ever found in her novels:

> Away you ran to Papa, and putting both your arms round his leg, for your hands were not big enough, you looked up at him, and laughed. What did this laugh say, when you could not speak? Cannot you guess by what you now say to Papa?—Ah! it was, Play with me, Papa!—play with me! Papa began to smile, and you knew that smile was always—Yes. So you got a ball, and Papa threw it along the floor—roll, roll, roll; and you ran after it again—and again. How pleased you were!

Nothing could be more simple, yet Mary's delight in the love between father and child is perfectly eloquent.

In Lesson Nine there is a list of Fanny's accomplishments, which includes a momentary glimpse of the Fédéré soldiers: "You can trundle a hoop, you say; and jump over a stick. O, I forgot!—and march like the men in the red coats, when Papa plays a pretty tune on the fiddle."

It is nice to think of Imlay playing the violin, Kentucky-style perhaps, while Fanny pranced like a conquering hero.

Finally, in Lesson Fourteen, there is a glimpse into what must have been the growing tensions in the household, and for the first and only time we see "Papa" distracted by outside affairs and business. Mary is teaching Fanny about what she calls "thinking". Mary's "thinking" has nothing to do with schoolroom learning—in fact, all the Lessons are free from any hint of formal teaching. Thinking means *imagining* how someone else feels, and what effect your behaviour will have on them. (Indeed, it is very close to loving.) She begins the lesson by recalling how once, when Mary had a headache, Fanny made a noise and Papa had to tell her to be quiet; and how Fanny learned from this. Mary explains it all with quick intuitive humour—itself a beautiful demonstration of the imagination at work on her little child's mind:

> You say that you do not know how to think. Yes, you do a little. The other day Papa was tired; he had been walking about all the morning. After dinner he fell asleep on the sofa. I did not bid you be quiet; but you thought of what Papa said to you when *my* head

ached. This made you think that you ought not to make a noise, when Papa was resting himself. So you came to me, and said to me, very softly—Pray reach me my ball, and I will go and play in the garden, till Papa wakes. You were going out, but thinking again, you came back to me on your tiptoes. Whisper—whisper! Pray Mama, call me, when Papa wakes; for I shall be afraid to open the door to see, lest I should disturb him. Away you went. Creep—creep—and shut the door as softly as I could have done myself. That was thinking.

Again, it is completely simple—one moment of domestic intimacy seen through the eyes of a child. (Was Imlay often tired now, did he get irritable more often, was his cheerfulness disappearing? Perhaps.) But to me, in the midst of all the public drama of Mary's life, it gave a sense of the new emotional centre that had been created in Mary's world, and the change that this must have produced in her whole outlook. It altered everything.

7

The moment of intimacy was soon over. On 26 July 1794 the opposition to Robespierre finally asserted itself in the Convention, and within three days he and Saint-Just were executed and the extreme wing of the Jacobins in Paris was destroyed in the coup d'état of Thermidor.

Almost at once Imlay set out for Paris, determined to exploit the commercial opportunities of the liberalised régime, and Mary's letters begin again in August. Soon it appears she is worried and discontented, and deeply uncertain about their future. Without Imlay life in Le Havre-Marat is boring—full of "fat-bottomed" nymphs and cupids on the mantelpiece, and the dull faces of "square-headed money-getters". Moreover they disagree about each other's attitudes. Imlay says Mary lacks judgment, Mary that Imlay lacks feeling.

"I will allow you to cultivate my judgment," she writes, "if you will permit me to keep alive the sentiments in your heart, which may be termed romantic, because, the offspring of the senses and the imagination, they resemble the mother more than the father, when they produce the suffusion I admire.—In spite of icy age, I hope still to see it, if you have not determined only to eat and drink, and be stupidly useful to the stupid."

The sarcasm in Mary's tone hardly requires comment, and it is repeated in the other letters of August. Clearly all was not well, and I suspected that Imlay's reasons for going to Paris so precipitously were not entirely commercial: Mary was proving a demanding wife with whom to live.

But there was another side to these letters, softer and more affectionate, which showed the transformation in Mary's outlook in an almost philosophical way. It appears in the wholly new emphasis she gave to human affections and the faculty of the imagination in forming them.

Writing on 19 August of the growth of her feelings for her child—"my affections grow on me, till they become too strong for my peace"—she expressed it quite simply in the capacity to love. Her attitude towards their little girl was "at first very reasonable —more the effect of reason, a sense of duty, than feeling—now, she has got into my heart and imagination, and when I walk out without her, her little figure is ever dancing before me." The same thing had happened to her feelings for Imlay—she does not know how—but he possesses her even in his absence. "You too have somehow clung round my heart—I found I could not eat my dinner in the great room—and, when I took up the large knife to carve for myself, tears rushed into my eyes. Do not however suppose that I am melancholy—for, when you are from me, I not only wonder how I can find fault with you—but how I can doubt your affection."

But of course Mary did not intend to accept that absence for long. In early September, growing impatient with his explanations, she suddenly closed up the house at Le Havre-Marat and took the diligence for Paris. It appears to have been a nightmare journey. Fanny was teething and had only recently recovered from smallpox; the maid had announced that she was pregnant, and naturally Mary would not abandon her; while the coach, overladen and badly driven (a metaphor of the present chaos in France), overturned no less than four times. Imlay seems to have taken rooms for them all in one of their old hotels in Saint-Germain, but the reunion was ominously brief. Within a few days urgent business called him away—this time to London.

Now at last Mary really did begin to feel abandoned: she was not to see her husband again for six months. All that was left to her were the few remaining members of the expatriate circle—the Schweizers, Count von Schlabrendorf and a new recruit, Archie Hamilton-Rowan, a genial Irish lawyer and active member of the United Irishmen, who had already been prosecuted in Dublin for sedition.

Rowan vividly recalled his first sight of Mary, as she walked into one of their soirées, defiantly accompanied by little Fanny. "[A friend] whispered to me that she was the author of the *Rights of Woman*. I started. 'What!' I said within myself, 'this is Miss Mary Wollstonecraft parading about with a child at her heels, with as little ceremony as if it were a watch she had just bought at the jeweller's. So much for the rights of women,' thought I."

In fact Rowan quickly became a close friend of Mary's, frequently took "a dish of tea" and some good conversation with her, and when finally Mary left France her last letters were to him, affectionately recalling his help and support—one more conversion to the cause.

Writing to Evarina at the end of September, Mary tried to put the best face on things, describing Imlay as "a brother you would love and respect—I hope the time is not very distant when we shall all meet", and endearingly singing the praises of her child. "I want you to see my little girl, who is more like a boy—She is ready to fly away with spirits—and has eloquent health in her cheeks and eyes—She does not promise to be a beauty, but appears *wonderfully* intelligent; and, though I am sure she has her father's quick temper and feelings, her good humour runs away with all the credit of my good nursing . . ."

But in her many letters to Imlay in London—there are sixteen of them between September 1794 and April 1795—she runs the gamut of emotions, from tearful melancholy despair to sudden, high-spirited teasing; from bitter, depressed reflections on the Revolution to jaunty headstrong thoughts about the future that Liberty may eventually bring them all. Sometimes she makes Paris catch something of the glamour of their earliest days together:

I am making a progress in the language among other things. I have also made some new acquaintance. I have almost *charmed* a judge of the tribunal, R---, who, though I should not have thought it possible, has humanity, if not *beaucoup d'esprit*. But let me tell you, if you do not make haste to come back, I shall be half in love with the author of the "Marseillaise", who is a handsome man, a little too broad-faced or so, and plays sweetly on the violin.

No doubt little Fanny also liked the violin of Rouget de l'Isle, a forty-year-old army officer, as well as the musical hero of the Republic: it would have reminded her of Papa.

In other letters, however, Mary is overwhelmingly bitter, and obviously suspects Imlay's sexual fidelity. Indeed, in the spring, it is known that he took up with a young actress in London.

> I consider fidelity and constancy as two distinct things; yet the former is necessary, to give life to the other . . . You know my opinion of men in general; you know that I think them systematic tyrants, and that it is the rarest thing in the world, to meet with a man with sufficient delicacy of feeling to govern desire. When I am thus sad, I lament that my little darling, fondly as I doat on her, is a girl.—I am sorry to have a tie to a world that for me is ever sown with thorns.

Without Imlay's side of the correspondence, it remains difficult to judge fairly between them. All we know is that he continued to write regularly ("your hasty *notes*"); continued to support Mary and Fanny financially (volume II of the *History of the Revolution* was not being written, and Mary could expect no further advances from Johnson); and continued to talk of the "permanent views and future comfort" of their life together. Yet when he wrote that "our being together is paramount to every other consideration", Mary regarded his declaration as a cheat and an insult; and surely she was right to do so. None the less it was Imlay who finally persuaded Mary to return to England in April 1795—something that the most dangerous moments of the Revolution had not succeeded in doing.

There is one passage in this increasingly tragic exchange of letters which stands out with a kind of magnificence, far beyond the immediate clash of personalities, and which places Mary on a philosophical high ground above the immediate experience of the Revolution and her revolutionary love affair. It concerns the powers of the Imagination in the human heart, and it looks forward with prophetic insight to the major creative work of the next generation of the Romantics—to Coleridge's *Biographia Literaria* (1817), and to Shelley's *Prometheus Unbound* (1820). In the latter case I was to discover a connection that was indeed a direct and touching one. For when in July 1814 the young Shelley eloped to France with Mary Godwin, Mary brought with her a special travelling box, containing all her mother's works including the *Letters to Imlay* which Godwin had edited. Their shared journal records that they opened this box on their first night together in Paris, at the Hotel de Vienne. So, in an odd way, the circle was completed: or rather—for me—it was started up once more.

Mary first recalls to Imlay their early happiness together, during the Neuilly days: "There is nothing picturesque in your present pursuits; my imagination then rather chooses to ramble back to the barrier with you, or to see you coming to meet me, and my basket of grapes.—With what pleasure do I recollect your looks and words, when I have been sitting on the window, regarding the waving corn!"

In a way this says everything about their love: how excitingly it had been launched amid the storm and danger of the Terror —which brought out the best in both of them—and then ran aground and wrecked in the calmer and safer months that followed. It was essentially a "barrier affair", one of those thousands of relationships, passionate and spontaneous, that so often start up in times of war or crisis—the fire of life burning more brightly in the mouth of destruction—but which rarely survive a time of peace and security. What use are recriminations in such matters?

Mary then goes on, in her best style, half-mocking at first, but gradually gathering passion and seriousness to produce what is in effect a hymn to the Imagination—and what was, for me, a new definition, in a new language, of *Imagination au Pouvoir*:

> Believe me, sage sir, you have not sufficient respect for the Imagination.—I could prove to you in a trice that it is the mother of sentiment, the great distinction of our nature, the only purifier of the passions.—Animals have a portion of Reason, and equal, if not more exquisite, senses; but no trace of Imagination, or her offspring Taste, appears in any of their actions. The impulse of the senses,—passions if you will—and the conclusions of Reason, draw men together; but the Imagination is the true fire, stolen from heaven, to animate this cold creature of clay—producing all those fine sympathies that lead to rapture, rendering men social by expanding their hearts, instead of leaving them leisure to calculate how many comforts society affords.

"Imagination is the true fire, stolen from heaven": here at last the cool, rationalist Mary was speaking like a full-blooded Romantic, seeing man's finest aspect in the rebellious, Promethean element in his character which will never settle for "the conclusions of Reason" or the "comforts" of society. It is what he is capable of imagining which alone "expands his heart" and makes him truly —and in a rapturous, revolutionary sense—"social".

But what did this mean in terms of Mary's original hopes of the French Revolution, her glimpse of the Golden Age? In one sense it is clearly a retreat, a revulsion even from the extreme calculating

127

rationalism of the Jacobins, and a rejection of public revolutionary action in favour of the more inward, enduring truths of the heart. Mary's glimpse of the Golden Age was not in the National Convention, or on the boulevards of Paris, but in the friendly salons of the Girondists and in the lovers' garden at Neuilly with its prospect of the corn harvest.

Yet Mary Wollstonecraft did not simply retreat into a sentimental, conservative, "feminine" view of family life and the sacredness of personal relationships. Far from it—she remained a social rebel to the end. To her critique of the French as a nation historically unprepared for revolution, she added a much broader understanding of the human qualities required to make a transformation in public affairs. She pointed, as I saw it, precisely to the Romantic revolution—that "expansion of the heart"—which would be needed to make real and enduring social progress in the coming age. Central to this perception remained the concept of "rights"—the rights of woman and the rights of man—and the pre-eminent need for feeling and imagination to shape and reform the entire social fabric, and the institutions which governed it. This it seemed to me was the essential inheritance which she left to the next generation, and beyond.

In practical terms, Mary's loyalty to France and the sufferings of her people remained unshaken to the end. In October 1794 she had already seen that the Terror would never return: "The liberty of the press will produce a great effect here. — *The cry of blood will not be in vain!*—Some more monsters will perish—and the Jacobins are conquered."

Yet the winter of 1794–5 was extremely harsh. Though the Maximum Laws were repealed there were something like famine conditions within the barrier, the weather was bitterly cold and Mary took turns with her maidservant queuing for food and wood. She caught a violent chest cold and a hacking cough, which by February convinced her that she had "a galloping consumption". She gave up the Saint-Germain hotel and moved in with a German couple, who had a child the same age as Fanny, and who were living "just above poverty". She sank her own griefs in those around her, writing on 10 February: "This has been such a period of barbarity and misery, I ought not to complain of having my share. I wish one moment that I had never heard of the cruelties that have been practised here, and the next envy the mothers who have been killed with their children."

She felt bitterly the humiliation of having to apply for money from Imlay, through the American business agent he had left in the city. "I have gone half a dozen times to the house to ask for it, and come away without speaking—you may guess why." Yet when, at the end of February, Imlay began to insist that she return to London—evidently worried about her health, and that of the child —she expressed horror at the idea of England, adding that she did not believe anyway that he would stay with her, but would embark on another project in Germany or Scandinavia:

> What! is our life then only to be made up of separations? am I only to return to a country that has not merely lost all charms for me, but for which I feel a repugnance that almost amounts to horror, only to be left there a prey to it! Why is it so necessary that I should return?—brought up here, my girl would be freer. Indeed, expecting you to join us, I had formed some plans of usefulness that have now vanished with my hopes of happiness.

What plans of "usefulness" these were we do not know—did Mary have ideas perhaps for an English-speaking school in Paris, or publication of her paper on female education? Her attitude shows that she was far from disenchanted with France, even now.

None the less, at the beginning of April, yielding to Imlay's entreaties, she passed through the barrier for the last time, packed into the coach with Fanny, her new maid Marguerite, her salvaged books and papers and the few bits of clothing and crockery she still owned. The great towers of the Paris barriers, with their bitter, ambiguous memories, dropped behind her on the road and they travelled down to Le Havre where they stopped at Wheatcroft's house for the final few days. On 7 April Mary wrote to Imlay saying that she was "on the wing" towards him—the same phrase that she had used thirty long months ago before leaving London. She was so full of conflicting emotions—sadness and yet relief at leaving; hope and yet fear for the future—that she sat on the harbour wall, gazing blankly at the choppy spring waters of the Channel:

> I sit, lost in thought, looking at the sea—and tears rush into my eyes when I find that I am cherishing any fond expectations. I have indeed been so unhappy this winter, I find it as difficult to acquire fresh hopes, as to regain tranquillity.—Enough of this —Lie still, foolish heart!—But for the little girl, I could almost wish that it should cease to beat, to be no more alive to the anguish of disappointment.

Her last act on French soil was characteristically practical. She arranged for a "little store of provisions" to be locked in a closet in a kitchen of the house, so that should Archie Hamilton-Rowan or any other member of the United Irishmen come through Le Havre-Marat (there was talk of Wolfe Tone's associate Thomas Russell fleeing from Dublin), there would at least be food for them. "Pray take care of yourself," she scrawled to Rowan, "direct to me at Mr Johnson's, St Paul's Churchyard, London, and wherever I may be the letter will not fail to reach me . . . I neither like to say, or write, *adieu.*"

So, on 9 April 1795, Mary Wollstonecraft finally left France. Instead of the tricolour cockade she now carried a small child wearing the bright red sash she had bought for her at one of the republican fêtes in Paris. Here was the only symbol of hope left to her.

In a way, I think I never really came to a conclusion about Mary's experiences in the Revolution. In one sense, what happened to her was a personal tragedy, and this aspect is emphasised by much of what she suffered subsequently. Putting it in its barest, harshest form, it was this: in April 1795 she found Imlay was living with another woman in London, and tried to commit suicide by an overdose of laudanum; between June and August she travelled on business for him in Scandinavia; in September she returned to London, and on the night of 10 October 1795 tried to drown herself by jumping off Putney Bridge. The following year she published her *Letters Written in Sweden*, and began her affair with William Godwin. But on 10 September 1797, eleven days after giving birth to her second daughter, Mary, she died from septicaemia. This sequence of catastrophes only reached its end in 1816, when Fanny Imlay, then aged twenty, herself committed suicide by an overdose of opium at a lonely inn in South Wales. It is a tale of such unhappiness it is easy to draw the moral that Mary should never have gone to Paris in the first place.

But of course biography, as I slowly came to realise, does not draw this kind of moral. It sees a more complicated and subtle pattern. Even out of worldly "failure" and personal suffering (indeed perhaps especially from these) it finds creative force and human nobility—and what are more important values than these? Mary's story in France astonished me: her courage and tenacity, as well as her marvellous honesty as a witness to her own revolutionary experiences, made her a woman in a million. She was exemplary in a way that completely altered my conception of what "the Revolution" was about. Most important of all, she directed me away from any cynical or over-hasty reaction to 1968 and made me realise that conclusions lie in the long term, in the next generation, in the "seeds of time".

For the real impact of the French Revolution, as far as the English were concerned, lay in the thirty years after Mary's death: in the generation of Byron, Shelley, Hazlitt, Keats, Mary Shelley— one of the most brilliant literary circles that has ever existed —all of whom returned to Europe, regarding it as deeply and truly "their business". To them, and most especially to the Shelleys, Mary Wollstonecraft was a bright star, permanently on the horizon. When, in the spring of 1814, Shelley and Mary pledged their love on Mary Wollstonecraft's tombstone in Old St Pancras Churchyard, the flame was consciously carried forward; and I went with it. (I am happy to see that the church is still illuminated by Camden Council every evening until after midnight.)

Moreover, even in Mary Wollstonecraft's final years there was a sense in which her tragedy became a triumph. Her love for William Godwin healed many of the wounds that Gilbert Imlay had caused, and it is one of the most intriguing of all biographical footnotes that in her last months Mary decided to write a stage play about her experiences in Paris. It is only a footnote because Godwin subsequently burnt the manuscript; but he tells us one wonderfully provoking fact about the play. It was a *comedy*. The accusers of Imlay should think hard about that.

The last of the many portraits of Mary was painted by John Opie (husband of the novelist Amelia) in 1797, probably when she was pregnant with her second child, the future Mary Shelley. Once again she has undergone a transformation. Her face is softer and more open, her thick chestnut hair tucked casually up under a green velvet cap, and her loose white linen dress falling in relaxed folds. She looks more confident in the world than ever before, and if there is something sad and thoughtful in those large eyes of hers it gives her a romantic presence, a contained power and an imaginative force which is new and impressive. It is this portrait that now hangs in the National Portrait Gallery in London, properly among her peers, a celebrity.

I do not think Mary ever solved the conflict between Reason and Imagination. But equally I cannot think that she ever quite gave up her vision of the Golden Age. In her *Letters Written in Sweden*, the last published and best written of all her books (Godwin said it was the kind of book that made you immediately fall in love with its author), she made many reflections on her time in France, and the hopes and ideals that were still vital to her. In her thirteenth letter, written while crossing one August morning into Norway, she was told of the brave independent life led by the inland farmers of the far north, and finding some secret spring touched off inside her she wrote the following passage:

> The description I received of them carried me back to the fables of the Golden Age: independence and virtue; affluence without vice; cultivation of mind without depravity of heart;—with "ever-smiling liberty" the nymph of the mountain. I want faith! My imagination hurries me forward to seek an asylum in such a retreat from all the disappointments I am threatened with; but reason drags me back, whispering that the world is still the world, and man the same compound of weakness and folly, who must occasionally excite love and disgust, admiration and contempt.

It was this dilemma that I carried with me, into the next generation of writers, poets and witnesses. My pursuit had begun.

THREE

1972 : Exiles

1

It was the late autumn of 1972 when I came down to the Gulf of Spézia. By then I had been filling notebooks about Shelley for nearly three years, and was possessed by him, and the voices of his family and friends.

My pursuit of his restless journeyings had taken me from his birthplace in Sussex through an ever-widening circuit of exile. From the heartlands of Oxfordshire and the Thames Valley I had moved outwards to the West Country, to North Wales, to the Lakes, to Scotland and Ireland, and then to France, Switzerland and finally Italy. Nothing else seemed quite so real. I supported myself with freelance journalism, and I had a contract for a book. But I mark my beginning as a professional biographer from the day when my bank bounced a cheque because it was inadvertently dated 1772.

Now the inner, growing and imagining part of my life seemed completely bound up with the fate of this small Romantic circle, the post-revolutionary generation, who were trying to turn the principles of the 1790s—republicanism, atheism, free love and the shared commune of "like spirits"—into a form of daily existence, an experiment in living, which would sustain themselves, their children and their writing in a new creative harmony of which the cold, disillusioned world had barely dreamed.

It would end in disaster, I knew that already. But I suspended belief, knowing that the history of what the world calls failure is often more important, humanly speaking, than any other: for it tells those who come after what remains to be tried. It is, as I later found myself writing, more a haunting than a history: it is peculiarly alive and potent, like all those slumbering winged seeds and disembodied spirits and ambiguous, shadowy monsters that fill the best of Shelley's poetry.

The biographer often has to work, not with a tabula rasa, but with a powerfully received image of his subject, already unconsciously formed from the mass of previous work in the same field. I feared this so strongly that I never completely read—and still have not read—the accepted authority on the subject, a detailed American biography by Newman Ivey White, published in two volumes in 1940. With my sense of meeting Shelley afresh, of approaching him from the inside, I felt I could not afford to open myself to the shaping interpretation of a previous generation. My urge was to go directly to the original materials—and most especially to the *places* —for myself, and risk the numerous details that I might consequently (and did on occasions) get wrong. I journeyed, in every sense, alone.

In Italy my outward life took on a curious thinness and unreality that I find difficult to describe. It was almost at times as if I was physically transparent, even invisible. I drifted without contact through the tourist crowds of the cities, and among the sleepy inhabitants of remote villages where the Shelleys had stayed a hundred and fifty years before. Except for the two hefty red volumes of Shelley's letters and the journals of his wife Mary and her stepsister Claire Clairmont (the child of Godwin's second wife), I was travelling light with the single rucksack of my Cévennes days. I hitch-hiked or took the local buses and little two-carriage branch-line trains that wound slowly through the foothills of the Tuscan Apennines. My tiny radio, a last link with the outside world, had been stolen weeks before when I slept on a sandy beach outside Livorno. I had left a girl I met in Florence in front of a picture in the Casa Dante, a smiling sensible girl with fine dark hair, because she wanted to go to Siena – and Siena did not lie on Shelley's itinerary. In little hotel rooms in Venice, in Rome, in Pisa, I read and reread Shelley's poetry and letters and got quietly drunk in the evenings because I felt so solitary and yet so tense with the voices in my head. I gazed into mirrors above small washbasins with no plugs and did not see myself properly.

In the endless art galleries I saw nothing but Shelley's favourite pictures and statues, the *Medusa*, the grotesque *Laocoön*, the lovely *Venus Anadyomene* with her armbands, the strange sprawled erotic shape of the *Hermaphrodite*, all of which thrilled and disturbed me, so I carried round photographs of them, as another man might carry round intimate pictures of his wife or mistress. I frequented cheap cafés and tavernas, municipal gardens, deserted formal parks, dusty riverside walks and hot back-street piazzas with their dancing washing-lines and pattering fountains. Occasionally I fell in with tramps, odd expatriate couples, or bleached hippies washed up from the shores of Greece and North Africa, the flotsam of the Sixties, an army in retreat talking softly of the great times past, the trips and the highs, the lost islands and the beautiful, broken communes in the sun. I listened, nodded and questioned, and slipped away again with my own demons. On the left-hand pages of my notebooks I put fragments of my own travels, on the right-hand pages I put Shelley's; the former became scattered and disjointed, the latter ever more intricate and detailed and dark.

The bus from La Spézia to Lérici was full of Italian school-children, brown knees below blue worsted skirts and shorts, busily eating *gelati* and chanting Beach Boys songs, down the long rocky road to the sea. I sat with my pack between my plimsolls, sunk in thought. The afternoon sun, already low, glinted across the water, far to the west, through outcrops of umbrella-pines. The road ran down to sea-level and followed the curve of the bay along a thin stone promenade. Round the beach, a mile or so away, the cluster of masts and sails in Lérici harbour flashed and shone, as they appeared and disappeared beyond the promontories and cliffs that indent the bay. So here, at last, it was: the furthest point, the edge of my story.

"You Americano?" said a voice at my shoulder. She was leaning over from the seat behind, gazing at the picture of Claire Clairmont in the journal on my knee, the same dark long hair.

"No, *Inglese*."

She was disappointed: "Oh, Beatles, Lordo Byron." She offered me a stick of violent-green chewing-gum, to make up for it, I think.

"You don't like the Beatles, then?"

"Oh, *si, si*," she said with a dismissive shrug, then added more cheerfully, "Lordo Byron, he died here in the water, drowned in his ship like a star."

"Like a what?"

"You know, like a pop star."

"Oh really, I thought it was a friend of his—*un amico*."

"No, no, Lordo Byron. *Guarda, guarda*—" and she tossed her dark head and pointed through the bus window at a little café. Its pink neon sign read: Hotel Byron.

"I see what you mean." I rose to clamber down the gangway to the door. For a moment I caught her eye moving from Claire's picture to my face and back again, and a quizzical smile flashed across her angelic features.

"*Arrivederci*," I said.

"See you, okay," she replied with a thoughtful slow nod.

The bus was stopping at the village of San Terenzo, a small string of sea-front hotels and cafés, with a domed church behind on the hill. I swung my pack on one shoulder and, chewing my gum hard, padded across the pavement and jumped the low wall down on to the beach. I felt curiously hot and shaky, and hurried across to the rocks to bathe. I swam and duck-dived for several minutes, opening my eyes in the clear green-blue water and watching the languorous seaweed swaying on the ocean bed. Climbing back out on to the rocks, I cut my hand. I saw that all the coastal rock was volcanic, twisted and honeycombed, like a fine froth of baroque lace. Its edges were as sharp as blades. It came to me that a drowned body, floating in those beautiful seas, would be soon cut to ribbons.

The bay of Lérici is about two miles across, a horseshoe shape, steeply wooded behind with pine and ilex and with a number of sandy coves between each descending spur of rock. Lérici itself, a small fishing port and holiday resort, occupies the left or southern tip of the horseshoe. San Terenzo, in those days still not much more than a seaside village, is situated at the right or northern tip. Geographically, the bay is one small loop in the larger sweep of the Tuscan coast, known as the Gulf of Spézia, and commanded by Portovénere on the sea-run between Genoa and Livorno.

All these places had by now a special meaning for me. Shelley had his boat, the *Don Juan*, constructed in the shipyard at Genoa; Portovénere was the point where he would turn back from the open sea and race the Italian feluccas home to Lérici; Livorno was the port where he last saw Lord Byron; and of course San Terenzo (not Lérici) was the place where in 1822 he set up his last house with Mary and Claire, four years after he had first come to Italy.

Far out to sea westwards, now turning smoky-blue and chrome in the late afternoon light, lay two low humped islands, very black against the skyline. These were Palmária and Tino, where Shelley often used to sail on days of high wind, saying that the humming from the bowsprit was actually the call of a siren from the cliffs. Palmária now has an automatic lighthouse, to guide belated fishermen safely home through these uncertain waters, quickly whipped up by the sudden squalls of tramontana or sirocco.

While Lérici has had a good stone quay providing sheltered moorings since the eighteenth century, San Terenzo was for a long time little more than a shallow beach partially protected by an artificial reef of piled rocks. Fishermen's boats had to be anchored temporarily offshore or dragged up on the sand, where Shelley used to keep his coracle built of reeds and canvas as a tender to his yacht.

Drying myself and patching my cut hand, I looked back up San

Terenzo beach. There, beyond the rowing-boats and fishing nets and instantly recognisable, was the white stuccoed frontage of his house, the Casa Magni, with its characteristic open ground-floor, with seven white arches forming a kind of loggia. It was this big, open ground-floor room like a boathouse that Trelawny found full of driven sand, tarred ropes, broken oars and old nets, many weeks after the drowning. I recognised it too from Mary's detailed description in her letters, one of which even contained a ground-plan of the front rooms, showing that she and Shelley had separate bedrooms; and also from an old Victorian photograph I had found of the beach-front, taken about 1870.

In the photograph Casa Magni still stood by itself, jutting over a primitive sea-wall; but it looked in bad repair, the walls dark with damp patches, and the metal awning over the first-floor balcony sagging and rusty. An atmosphere of melancholy hung over it, and the trees behind on the hill were dark and forbidding. But now, in the afternoon light, with its fresh stucco and crisp air of seaside simplicity, it looked innocent of all history. I knew I would have to work on it, absorb the atmosphere and take stock. But the thing was, the last house had been found.

As the sun began to set into the sea I sloped up and down the little cafés and beach shelters, unable to concentrate, bemused, worrying about my dwindling supply of lire and starting to feel the night air. San Terenzo has a ruined castle on its northern cliff, and I thought perhaps I could camp there and live rough for a few days, like my old times in the Cévennes. But it was nearly November now, cold and damp at nights, and besides I wanted a table to spread my books—the letters, the journals, the poems—to read and reflect on the problems of Shelley's exile.

I felt the need to slow everything down, to settle into a kind of alert stillness, to drop down below all the practical demands of daily affairs. I wanted to become quiet in a little room overlooking Shelley's sea; to concentrate like a fisherman sitting over a pool, waiting for the surface to stir and glint.

I suppose I felt I had him cornered: his back, as it were, against the wall of the western sky. Here was my last chance. Shelley had never stood still, either geographically or imaginatively. The hunting, restless quality of his spirit had been borne in on me, more and more, as I had tracked him across Italy. Nor had his houses usually been so easy to find, so symbolically positioned and distinct. In the first eighteen months after his arrival at Milan, in April 1818, he had rarely stopped more than a few weeks in any one place, always finding some excuse to pack his bags and move on.

From his first crossing of the Alps and his momentary visit to Lake Como his progress describes a rapid, plunging path southwards, in a series of wild meanderings across the map of Italy. From Pisa and Lucca in the west he swept across to Venice and Este on the Adriatic, then dashed south via Ferrara, Bologna and Rimini to Rome; then southwards again to winter in Naples. In the spring of 1819 he moved north to Rome, then spun upwards once more to Florence (but omitting Siena, alas) and west again to Livorno, then back to winter in Florence. Only in January 1820 did he definitely settle in Pisa, remaining there at various addresses (which presented their own puzzles), with summer expeditions to the Bagni of San Giuliano, until 1822.

Of course the household was very young in 1818: Shelley only twenty-six, Mary twenty-one, Claire twenty; and the three children —William, Clara and Allegra (Claire's child by Byron)—little more than infants. They were free and high-spirited, passionately keen to absorb the art and landscapes of Italy and, though not rich, had an assured income of one thousand pounds a year from the Shelley estates. This was quite enough on which to experiment with living, to rent lodgings as they chose, hire boats and horses, buy innumerable books, commission portraits of themselves, print Shelley's poems, and write long formal travel-letters and amusing accounts of their adventures for circulation among their friends tied to regular jobs and family commitments back in dull old England. For them, Italy was "the paradise of exiles"—revolutionary exiles perhaps, but something of a dream playground nevertheless.

Yet, especially in the first gypsy-like years of their existence abroad, the tensions within the household were extraordinarily high. Shelley was writing with a creative intensity he had never before achieved. Besides the mass of letters, essays and translations he produced, most of his finest major poems belonged to this Italian period: *Julian and Maddalo* begun at Venice; *Prometheus Unbound* at Este and Rome; *The Mask of Anarchy* at Livorno; the *Ode to the West Wind* and a mass of shorter lyrics at Florence; and *Epipsychidion* (his verse autobiography) at Pisa. The one remaining major, visionary work—his unearthly *Triumph of Life*, a poem much influenced by Dante—was not begun until the last months, when he had come to his final *point du départ*, the white house at San Terenzo by the sea.

Almost alone among the Romantic writers Shelley sought no refuge in drugs or alcohol, but stoically consulted doctors, took hard physical exercise, kept a vegetarian diet and rose most days at dawn; yet he frequently made himself ill with the strain of producing this immense fountain of poetry, and the household as a whole suffered from profound anxieties and family disruptions. For a start, they had left great unhappiness behind in England. Shelley's family regarded him as an outcast, and Mary's family—the Godwins—badgered them endlessly with their debts. Shelley's two children by his first marriage were wards of the Chancellor's Court and farmed out to a family; while the ghost of poor Harriet, their mother, drowned in the Serpentine in 1816, still haunted them all. So too did that other tragic suicide, Mary's half-sister, Fanny Imlay, the saddest part of the Wollstonecraft inheritance.

Nor were they safe from misery and death in Italy. Partly because of the very nature of their nomadic, unsettled existence they lost their two surviving children by Mary—baby Clara who died suddenly, after a strenuous period of coach-travel, at Venice in 1818; and the beloved "Willmouse", four years old, the darling of them all, who died of fever in Rome in spring 1819. Claire's child too, Allegra, was unwillingly left behind—much against Shelley's wishes—with Byron in Venice, to be callously dumped in an expensive Catholic convent by his Lordship, where she too died in 1822.

So the idealist household was childless for many months, and Mary herself suffered a nervous breakdown, as she recounted in her semi-autobiographical novel *Mathilda* (for there was nothing, at least, that could stop them all writing). Politically too the outlook was gloomy, and they clutched desperately at any signs of a post-Napoleonic liberalisation—radical reform in Britain, a Carbonari uprising in Italy, a revolution in Spain, a war of independence in Greece . . . none of which then seemed to be forthcoming.

Shelley's previously optimistic and enthusiastic temperament was scarred by terrible periods of doubts and gloom, especially at Naples, most beautiful of Italian cities, where many private poems —never seen by Mary until after his death—are witness to his deep misery and depression. Of course, he was maturing too, learning to live with his responsibilities and write a more adult, complex, subtle kind of poetry, of greatly increased imaginative power. Yet there was a sense of personal crisis, a crisis of faith and hope in the "great experiment", which touched on his most intimate relationships. Something of this is expressed in his "Stanzas Written in Dejection" (was he thinking of Coleridge?) composed in the winter of 1818 on a beach near Naples. The second stanza catches the luminous, sparkling beauty of Italy—the dream of their exile together, the great flashing sea of their hopes for the future. Yet Shelley feels isolated and alone:

141

> I see the Deep's untrampled floor
>> With green and purple seaweeds strown;
> I see the waves upon the shore,
>> Like light dissolved in star-showers, thrown:
>> I sit upon the sands alone,—
> The lightning of the noontide ocean
>> Is flashing round me, and a tone
> Arises from its measured motion,
>> How sweet! did any heart now share in my emotion.

The sudden, broken and stumbling rhythm of that last, long line shatters the radiant dream and prepares for the solitary, confessional cry of the next stanza, with its bleak, disillusioned list of negations and failures, almost as if everything were lost:

> Alas! I have nor hope nor health,
>> Nor peace within nor calm around,
> Nor that content surpassing wealth
>> The sage in meditation found,
>> And walked with inward glory crowned—
> Nor fame, nor power, nor love, nor leisure.
>> Others I see whom these surround—
> Smiling they live, and call life pleasure;—
> To me that cup has been dealt in another measure.

Again, that deadly long last line. Of course, everything was not lost; indeed, in creative terms almost everything worthwhile was yet to be done. Yet I was convinced that here was some radical rupture in Shelley's life, his very identity—the emphatic denial of peace "within", of "inward" glory, of personal affections, pleasure, love—which presented a profound biographical problem. More and more, as I followed them from house to house, city to village, river to seashore, I felt that the heart of this problem lay in the involved triangle of relations between Shelley and Mary and Claire. It came to puzzle and haunt me, with growing force, until the day I came down to San Terenzo.

What Shelley had hoped to do in Italy was not merely to create a new life—for himself, Mary, and Claire, the three children as they then were and any friends he could persuade to join him. Even as late as October 1821 he was writing to Leigh Hunt, who *did* eventually come: "Hogg will be inconsolable at your departure. I wish you could bring him with you—he will say that

I am like Lucifer who has seduced the third part of the starry flock."

What he wanted to create was a new *form* of life, a new *kind* of community, in which the rules of existence could somehow be rewritten. What his lost mother-in-law, Mary Wollstonecraft, had glimpsed for a moment in the Paris of the French Revolution Shelley tried to project into his "obscure community of speculators" (the phrase is from his unfinished novel, *The Assassins*), travelling in exile through Italy, waiting, hope against hope, for some new dawn, some new spring which could not be "far behind".

The sources of his inspiration—the political and moral radicalism, the visionary poetry, the new openness and risk in emotional relationships, the passionate belief in "love" as the law of life—all these things corresponded to what I had myself seen and witnessed, what my whole generation had seen and witnessed (but how quickly they were forgetting!) in Britain and Europe during the Sixties. These parallels, I felt, I could not use explicitly; I could not follow step by step quite as in the old, innocent Stevenson days. But because the parallels existed I had a unique chance to follow and reinterpret Shelley's life, almost from the inside. I felt I held the password.

Yet this very sense of being an almost privileged witness produced its own difficulties for me. The pursuit became so intense, so demanding of my own emotions that it continuously threatened to get out of hand. When I travelled alone I craved after intimacy with my subject, knowing all the time that I must maintain an objective and judicial stance. I came often to feel excluded, left behind, shut out from the magic circle of his family. I wanted to get in among them, to partake in their daily life, to understand what Shelley called the "deep truth" of their situation. I was often in a peculiar state, like a displaced person, which was obviously touched off by some imbalance, or lack of hardened identity, in my own character. It reminded me of one of my earliest childhood dreams, a recurrent one, in which those I loved were constantly hiding from me or somehow racing away, hurrying on ahead; or, strangest of all, changing their size and scale. One minute they would be like huge trees above my head, sublime and unreachable; and the next like tiny insects, diamond-precious, after whom I blundered with that infinite dream slowness, clumsy and desperate.

A ludicrous image, perhaps. But that is how I sometimes felt in Italy: a laughable figure, ridiculously unsuited to my task, and no longer protected by the adolescent enchantment of Le Brun.

Indeed I came to suspect that there is something frequently comic about the trailing figure of the biographer: a sort of tramp permanently knocking at the kitchen window and secretly hoping he might be invited in for supper. How many of Shelley's houses I stood outside, knocking and knocking!

2

Yet sometimes I was let in. I never knew quite what to expect, or even quite what I was looking for. The houses were often odd, inconsequential places in which to start a new life. Many were remote, and none of them was beautiful and luxurious like Byron's —whose stopping-places I seemed to find everywhere in North Italy, as if Milord advanced like an invading army on a wide front. Shelley infiltrated, moving rapidly and discreetly, and then lying low, in any place where he felt he could write.

In that first summer of 1818, after a brief stay at the Tre Donzelle Inn at Pisa (now an English tea-room, with lawyers' offices upstairs, shaded by green blinds) he retreated high into the wooded Apennines at Bagni di Lucca. Mary spoke in her letters of a little garden with a laurel grove at the end, where Shelley sat translating Plato's *Symposium* until twilight.

The house, known as the Casa Bertini, was rented from a local family called Chiappa. Allegra had by then been sent with their maid Elise to Byron at Venice, and Claire was restless, riding, and watching the dancing with Shelley at the little "casino" below in the village. But the household was cheerful and bustling, Mary happy with Clara and William, helped by Milly Shields, their English maid, an Italian cook and later a manservant, Paolo Foggi, who was to play an important part in their lives.

One of my first expeditions was made in search of this house. I set out from Pisa late one October morning, keeping a running record in my notebook as I went along, full of questions, talking to myself, to Shelley, always feeling my way, keeping alert to the unexpected thing, the revelation perhaps.

I took the local *direttissimo*, which is the slow train, winding up into the hills beyond Lucca. All along the line was shrouded in vines, big luminous leaves, bean bushes on sticks, coloured marrows nesting in the earth and globe peaches I could almost pick from the carriage window. Shelley's fragment was a perfect image of this Italy:

Stevenson in 1879, shortly after he followed Fanny Osbourne to America. He has cut his hair and put on a knitted tie in place of the Bohemian cravat. The photograph was originally owned by his friend, the critic Edmund Gosse.

Fanny Osbourne in 1876, at the time she first came to France and met Stevenson. Her jacket is edged in velvet and her tie declares Left-Bank independence. The steady gaze struck everyone who knew her.

William Wordsworth after the heady days of the French Revolution. Hazlitt later described his 'Roman nose, cheeks furrowed by strong purpose and feeling, and a convulsive inclination to laughter about the mouth, a good deal at variance with the solemn, stately expression of the rest of his face'. *Picture by Robert Hancock, 1798: National Portrait Gallery.*

Mary Wollstonecraft after she had returned from France and Scandinavia. The portrait was painted by John Opie about 1797, and hung in William Godwin's study above his desk, where Shelley saw it in 1814. *Picture: National Portrait Gallery.*

Fervour of the Revolution: Looting the abandoned house of an aristocrat in Paris, 1792. The Revolutionary mob consists equally of men and women. A contemporary lithograph.

Fervour of the Revolution: CRS troopers stand guard over the remains of a cobblestone barricade across one of the main Left-Bank boulevards in Paris, 1968.

Shelley in Rome, painted by Aemilia Curran in spring 1819. The large eyes, with their intense gaze, were described as seraphic by his friend Hunt. *Picture: National Portrait Gallery.*

Claire Clairmont, also painted by Aemilia Curran in her studio near the Spanish Steps, Rome 1819. Claire's dark good looks, fine singing voice and slight embonpoint were greatly admired by Italians. *Portrait: Nottingham Museums, Newstead Abbey.*

The back garden of the
Casa Bertini, Bagni di
Lucca, where Shelley
translated Plato's
Symposium in summer
1818. Little William
Shelley's ghost peers
round the plane tree on
the right.

Casa Magni and the
wooded cliffs of San
Terenzo, where the
Shelleys stayed in 1822,
photographed some fifty
years later. The first-
floor terrace, where they
ate, played chess, wrote
and listened to Jane's
guitar, was in those
days not covered over.

Gérard de Nerval, photographed in Paris in 1855, according to Nadar a few days before he committed suicide. He was probably wearing two shirts to keep out the cold; Gautier said he owned no overcoat. No biographer has yet remarked on the fact that Nerval smoked: but the poet's nervous nicotine-stained hand tells its own story. *Photo: Bibliothèque Nationale, Paris.*

Théophile Gautier, also photographed by Nadar around 1854–5, in the rue Saint-Lazare studio. He is wearing the Turkish jacket and silk scarf he preferred for writing his column in *La Presse*. A sensualist, as his face shows; the Goncourts said after his friend Gérard's death that he was 'haunted by unknown presences'. *Photo: Bibliothèque Nationale, Paris.*

> Flourishing vine, whose kindling clusters glow
> Beneath autumnal sun, none taste of thee;
> For thou dost shroud a ruin, and below
> The rotting bones of dead antiquity.

The journey from Pisa took one hour ten minutes, about thirty miles. By horse that would be maybe four or five hours' ride. Why did Claire keep falling off her horse? I asked myself. Did she stay with Shelley in Lucca when they rode there together?

Arriving at the tiny station at the Bagni and finding it deserted, I walked across the lines and then up the hill. All the way they were burning piles of leaves. I passed through the long colonnades of chestnuts and plane trees, the leaves dropping around me, the smoke rising white and blue in the light, the sky full of leaves, beautiful and purgatorial. Shelley wrote at length in his letters about these trees, the water, the sky, the stars at night, entranced by them.

Below me was the River Lima, meandering between shingle banks down the valley to Lucca where it joins the Serchio. There was magic in those names—Lima, Lucca, Serchio—soft words in the mouth, that seemed to affect Shelley's poetry, opening the vowels and quickening his rhythms. The children learned Italian easiest, William quickly became almost bilingual, but Claire already spoke it well and felt at home.

The road to the Bagni turned through a complete circle, wrapping itself in its cloak of trees, shades of Milton's Vallombrosa, producing the enclosed landscape that Shelley, surprisingly, often favoured for his houses, nestling in a hillside or under sea-cliffs. There was a small logging industry, with logs stacked neatly in clearings, but little other signs of activity. The modern Bagni has developed down the hillside and across the river—the "Bagni alla Villa", they called it. But the old road twisted up and up into the woods, the tarred surface eventually giving way to a broken stone track on yellow sandy earth. There were no indications of a Casa Bertini, but old moss-covered plaques marked other more famous names—a Villa Byron (when was he here?) and one lived in by Montaigne. Then the track ran out.

I drifted back down through the trees, with that familiar lost and invisible feeling. There was an English cemetery, modern Spa buildings closed up, a sense of a forgotten, genteel world of summer exiles and invalids, all departed, a place for a story by Chekhov or Katherine Mansfield. It was borne in on me that Shelley had been really hiding himself away here—how he hated the English abroad, the tea-parties and soirées, the gossip, the evening promenade. Instead he hired horses and rode to Il Prato Fioreto; disappeared into the woods with his books; or played in the rivers naked and scrambled up waterfalls like a child. The old question returned to me of Mary's modesty, compared to Claire's willingness to slip out of her clothes and bathe, as during the 1814 tour in France.

Shelley's letters to Peacock described all this—"spray over all my body while I clamber up the river crags with difficulty"—making similes for his poetry. He had a love affair with the waters of Italy: not conquering them like Byron with his swimming feats and races but giving himself up to them, submitting and revelling with a passive pleasure. This was later captured by Trelawny's story, apocryphal perhaps but interesting, of how the poet jumped into a deep rock pool and seemed to lie on the bottom like a fish until he was hauled out.

My sense of invisibility reached its next stage, a complete lack of self-consciousness and social embarrassment. I began to chat to anyone I saw: an old lady knitting blue wool in a window, a housewife hanging out washing, a woodsman roping up timber, a man in a dark suit strolling to his car. It was a Lancia and I admired it. "Temperamental, like a beautiful woman," he replied in English to my faltering Italian, and asked me what I was looking for. It was obvious that I was looking for something. Somewhere to stay? No, somewhere where someone else stayed—an English poet.

Once again it was like a password, and my luck had changed. For this was Signor M---, the director of the local Assurance Agency, a delightful man who knew all the property at the Bagni, knew the Mayor, knew the station master, knew everyone. The idea of Shelley's lost house intrigued him, a professional challenge, and instantly he joined in my search. We drove up and down for an hour, calling at cottages and villas, even interviewing the Mayor who was playing billiards in the back room of the social club. Everyone knew the Villa Byron but no one had heard of the Casa Shelley, until I suddenly mentioned the Chiappa family; and it was as if nothing had changed in five generations.

Of course, there was a Villa dei Chiappa, right back where I began, at the point in the hills where the tarred road became a track. We drove back up, and there in the old wall was the original stone sign, worn smooth with age, which Signor M--- scraped delicately with the tip of a silver penknife. *Ecco!* It was two stone cottages run together, set back above the road, three storeys with weathered walls like a farmhouse, old Tuscan tiled roof and yellow flaking shutters. Signor M--- tapped at the door, made introductions and explanations, laughed at the unlikelihood of it all, and went off assuring me I now had the run of the place, "to speak to my poet in peace".

I shall never forget this man's kindness, one further link in my long mysterious chain of providential guides, whose sense of the past as a living presence made him understand my pursuit instinctively. At the last moment he gave me the fragment of another life story, which deepened that sympathy to something more.

"Oh yes," he said, smoothing the wing of his gleaming car. "We are all lost sometimes in our lives. An Englishman lost in Italy, or an Italian lost in England. I was a prisoner there, you know, a prisoner of war for three years. It makes you think of Liberty. Your English poets understand Liberty. Liberty!—Ah, temperamental, like a woman!"

He patted the car, shook my hand and shot off down the track in a fine spray of damp earth, an operatic exit perfectly timed.

It was the top storey of the Villa dei Chiappa which fascinated me at first. Unlike the rest it had not been converted: the beams were bare, the lathes of the roof exposed, a fire of logs and twigs burning in a nineteenth-century iron grate. The view from the front overlooked the little corkscrew road, and then across the valley of the Lima to the wooded hillside opposite, beautiful but slightly claustrophobic. I recalled with what relief Mary later greeted the open panorama of the Lombardy plain from Este. But then, from the back window, there was the little garden, shrouded in foliage. I hurried down, out through a small door with an old brass handle lovingly polished, and up four steps to a narrow sanded walk.

The garden was long and narrow, hedged round by shrubberies and wild vines. It was about twenty foot wide by forty foot long, with a small aisle of surprisingly large plane trees running on either side of the walk, like the pillars of a church. Shelley later invented the term "upaithric" to describe such an open-air temple, like the roofless colonnades of the Roman ruins in the south, which he said were like ideal forests in stone. The trunks of the plane trees were peeling, giving them a stippled look, grey-green bark falling away from pale wood, like flakes of used-up sunlight. There at the end of the garden was still a grove of laurel, and far below to the right the glittering curve of the Lima, exactly as Mary had described.

I walked into the grove and turned back, seeing in one flash what Shelley saw as he looked up from his table, with his Greek lexicon and his Marcello Ficino and his scattered paragraphs of Plato.

The light was fading and there was a smell of damp leaves that reminded me of England. The wind stirred and dropped, and everything was still.

I sat on a piece of wood in the laurel grove making notes, then pulled out my camera. It was a thirty-year-old Ensign, with a bellows lens, taking big two-and-a-half-inch negatives of great sensitivity, though all the settings had to be calculated and done by hand. I set the aperture and field of focus to cover ten foot to infinity, the timing at one-fiftieth of a second—the longest I thought I could hand-hold—and breathed deeply like a swimmer about to dive to the bottom of the sea. Then gently I squeezed off a couple of shots, taking one-fiftieth of a second somewhere out of time. Ten foot to infinity, I think, is exactly the range of focus required by a biographer—from the close-up portrait to the full historical perspective.

There was a little scurry of leaves, an odd impression of movement, then voices sounded in the house, the garden door clicked open, a towel was drawn in from the iron balustrade, and I was being called in for a grappa.

At the big mahogany table in the kitchen we had our thimbles of clear fire, children appeared round doorways and pattered across the tiles in bare feet, and Signora wrote her name in my notebook. She did it gingerly, like someone signing an open cheque. Maria Pellegrini, Casa dei Chiappa gia Bertini, Bagni alla Villa, Bagni di Lucca. Then she smiled a little wearily, brushed back a lock of hair, shushed the children.

"Soon they will go to school," she said. "You have children?"

"No—Shelley had children. Two of them lived here."

"Ah, so maybe you have children after your book is finished."

"Maybe after my book, yes."

"Writers should have children, I think, or they get lonely."

"Yes. Shelley wasn't lonely here. He was very happy."

"Good. We are happy too. You will be happy when you have children, I think."

I made the long walk back, unwinding down through the trees in the gathering dark to the station. All the time leaves were falling through the sky, and bonfires showed little mouths of fire. Ever after the name Lucca has meant "leaves" to me: the Bath of Leaves. Waiting for the last *direttissimo*, I watched the green signal light gleam along the rail, and reread Shelley's letter on Jupiter, the evening star that guided him home on his rides through the hills. I felt I had come very close.

This particular day, which set the pattern for much of my

subsequent wanderings through Italy, also had a curious foot-note—or rather, footstep. It was a little one, but showed how much can happen without one realising it at the time.

Weeks later I had my sheet of contact-prints for the Lucca area and found only one very dark shot of the garden at Casa Bertini had come out. It was a vague vertical of trees framing a grey façade with a little balcony. It seemed hardly worth having the photo-graph printed up to full size, but on an impulse I marked it "print for maximum light", and filed the resulting half-plate photograph in its chronological sequence, June–August 1818, cross-referenced "Symposium".

Much later still, when writing this section of my biography, I was going through the photograph file for possible illustrations when I came across the picture again. It seemed rather clearer than I had first thought, and I held it under my desk lamp for closer inspection. I frowned and took a second look. Between the first and second plane tree, in the shadows on the right, stood a small child. It was a boy, aged between three and four, almost dwarfed by the trees, up to his ankles in leaves, and with a pair of dark eyes fixed on the camera. A faint tingling sensation passed over the top of my scalp. I felt I was looking at a photograph of little William, Shelley's dead son.

Shelley was more fond of this child than any other. He was Mary's first surviving child; he had been with them on their previous trip abroad to Switzerland in 1816; he was adored by Claire, who talked to him in Italian. He was of a sunny, bubbling disposition, and in many ways held the household together—a focus of warmth and love and their hopes for the future. When he tragically died, in Rome in April 1819, they were more than heartbroken: some mainspring within the circle was permanently damaged. Mary broke off writing her journal for many months; Claire began to worry obsessively about Allegra. Shelley, turning for solace to his poetry, tried and signally failed to write a poem about his son. For once the poet was over-whelmed by the father, and the elegy broke off after a few lines:

> Where art thou, my gentle child?
> Let me think thy spirit feeds,
> With its life intense and mild,
> The love of living leaves and weeds
> Among these tombs and ruins wild;—
> Let me think that through low seeds
> Of sweet flowers and sunny grass
> Into their hues and scents may pass
> A portion . . .

This deep grief only found its full expression after another two years, when Shelley was writing his lament for another death, that of John Keats, in *Adonais*. The faltering hope for some pantheistic transformation into the "living leaves and weeds", some seed-like resurrection into a redeemed "portion" of Nature, at last became articulate in one of Shelley's most triumphant and memorable passages:

> He is made one with Nature . . .
> He is a portion of the loveliness
> Which once he made more lovely: he doth bear
> His part, while the one Spirit's plastic stress
> Sweeps through the dull dense world, compelling there,
> All new successions to the forms they wear . . .

All that seemed to be implicit in the leafy garden at Casa Bertini, and the little figure staring at me. Besides, I too was very fond of "Willmouse". Who could forget how he had pointed at the beautiful stippled trout lying on the slabs of the Roman fish market, and made Shelley laugh by his solemn exclamation: *"O Dio — che bella cosa?"* Many such things flashed through my mind as I sat at my desk unmoving, astonished by the presence I had conjured up.

Then the moment passed and my critical faculties returned. I bent again to look at the half-plate photograph, smelling the damp leaves, and concentrated more carefully. No illusion, certainly — it was a child indeed, a little boy peeping mischievously round the tree-trunk. But one hand was in the pocket of a pair of modern flannel shorts and the jersey was a fashionable polka-dot. It was none other than little Master Pellegrini, come to spy out the funny foreign fellow scribbling in his exercise book. The Inglese didn't see anything at all — he was quite lost in another world, like Papa doing the lotto.

So Willmouse escaped me again. But I included the photograph in my book, wondering if someone else, someday, might experience for a moment the same tingling surprise. And besides, I thought, this was almost a symbol of what my biography should try to achieve. It should summon up figures like a magic photograph plate, and hold them through time, at ten foot to infinity, with the soft shock of recognition, perfectly alive.

But that was not quite all. For what I had photographed, most strangely, was also my own recurrent dream in childhood. Here was the small boy lost in a timeless world, among huge trees — trees that were perhaps other people, the people he loved, transformed into a world of nature, enduring and monumental, "new successions to the forms they wear". That dream I cannot now explain at all; or quite guess what it might mean as a symbol of some larger imagination at work.

3

My early investigation of the Casa Bertini set the pattern of my researches in one specific way. Many of the questions in my Bagni di Lucca notebook already concerned Shelley's relations with Claire Clairmont. This relationship became a vital element in the main biographical problem of Shelley's inner nature, his mature identity, that I tried to solve, or at least to clarify (the pun ran in my head), in Italy. What was the true character of their friendship? How did it affect Shelley's attempt at the "new life", and his fluctuations between hope and despair? And above all what impact did it have on his imaginative writing?

The received biographical image of Shelley's adult character had three powerful components, or filters. The first was the "angelic" personality of popular myth, the "Ariel" syndrome, with its strong implication that Shelley was insubstantial, ineffectual, physically incompetent. This I intended to explode (I felt quite violently about it) by re-creating a daily detailed texture of Shelley's life, showing a man who loved travel and hard intellectual work; who rode, sailed, shot a pistol as well as Lord Byron; who argued elegantly but occasionally got into brawls; who laughed, teased and made jokes; who addressed public meetings and lost his temper with officials; who put up with much ill-health and much scandal-mongering; who fathered six (or so) children and published some twelve books of poetry in less than twelve years. In short, to show a man whose physical impact on life, and on those around him, was intense and unforgettable.

The second component concerned his radical politics. The tendency had always been to treat these as essentially juvenile, and incompatible with his mature lyric gift as a writer. It was said that Shelley progressed from the schoolboy anarchism of Godwin to the sophisticated idealism of his Italian Platonics. There was no connection, for example, between his Irish revolutionism and *Prometheus Unbound*. This apolitical, conservative, aesthetic interpretation of Shelley had to be more subtly altered. Writing from the perspective of the Sixties I wished to show that Shelley's poetic and political inspirations were closely identified; that there was a continuity of revolutionary and reformist thought throughout his work; and that his lyric gift was only one element in his main creative effort towards the writing of large, carefully structured poems. Moreover, I believed it was impossible to understand his private life—his journeying, his unstable households—without appreciating his political enthusiasms.

The third component concerned the inner nature of those households, and Shelley's emotional and sexual make-up. It was here that I felt it vital to give Claire her full and proper place in Shelley's life, from 1814 to 1822. I did not think this had ever been done before, and I knew perfectly well that it would be provocative. The prevailing attitude to this subject had been set eighty years before by Matthew Arnold, in an essay based on a review of Shelley's first biography by the Professor of English at Trinity College, Dublin, Edward Dowden. Arnold perfectly expressed the Victorian position—knowing, yet fearful and distasteful of what it knew—or thought it knew:

> In one important point Shelley was like neither a Pythagorean nor an angel: he was extremely inflammable. Professor Dowden leaves no doubt on the matter. After reading his book, one feels sickened for ever on the subject of irregular relations; God forbid that I should go into the scandals about Shelley's "Neapolitan charge", about Shelley and Emilia Viviani, about Shelley and Miss Clairmont, and the rest of it! I will only say that it is visible enough that when the passion of love was roused in Shelley (and it was aroused easily) one could not be sure of him, his friends could not trust him. We have seen him with the Boinville family. With Emilia Viviani he is the same. If he is left much alone with Miss Clairmont, he evidently makes Mary uneasy; nay, he makes Professor Dowden himself uneasy.

He did not make *me* uneasy. Anyone who had grown up in the Sixties could understand Shelley's attitude to marriage and divorce; his principle that love was "free"; his ideal of the equal partnership and mocking attitude to conventional monogamy; his belief in the liberating force of love. How else could one make any sense of poems like *Epipsychidion*, written at Pisa in 1821? Besides, Arnold seems to have thought that Shelley was some Byronic seducer—"inflammable"—going off like gunpowder whenever a pretty woman came into his orbit. That was hardly the case. Shelley was a much rarer and more interesting species—the man who acted on principle, who acted out of sympathy and truth of feeling, who deliberately defied convention—and, to his utter dismay, caused chaos as a result. And it was *this* that made me uneasy, and fascinated me.

Many of my friends, married, living together or living in various forms of communities and groups seemed to be going through the experiences and crises that Shelley's various households went through. This was enormously important to me. When I wrote about Shelley I seemed to be writing about my own friends, practically at first-hand. Most unsettling of all—when I wrote about Shelley's women friends and lovers—I seemed to see faces, hear voices that I already knew. I do not say I knew them in the same way as Shelley—that would be absurd—but I had met people very like them, and seen them in situations very similar, and knew that they existed.

Moreover, I slowly realised that part of the fascination of the Shelley story was that it would be the same for every reader of my generation. For us, and maybe for others, the story was a continuing one. It was, in Shelley's own phrase—so often used mockingly—"a pure anticipated cognition". It was, as he wrote of the Maniac in *Julian and Maddalo*, a story which, "told at length, might be like many other stories of the same kind: the unconnected exclamations of his agony will perhaps be found a sufficient comment for the text of every heart."

The role of Claire within this life was crucial. What had happened in Shelley's first marriage to Harriet Westbrook was sufficiently well known and understood. The causes of their unhappiness—their differences of background, their intellectual incompatibility, their extreme youth—were clear and indeed almost commonplace, though no less sad for that. But the second marriage to Mary Godwin—beginning with the elopement to France and Switzerland, together with Claire—was something altogether different. It was a deep relationship, and not a simple one. It could be interpreted in one of two ways. Either it was a conventional marriage that survived, under great stress—often a creative stress —various outside entanglements and internal explosions, and brought Shelley and Mary side by side as far as the Casa Magni. Or else it was from the start a radically unconventional marriage, a dynamic and unstable relationship which required a second woman (and possibly a second man) to keep it in working equilibrium. On this interpretation the second woman was Claire Clairmont.

In a life so varied and free, as they lived in Italy, it would be easy to underestimate the tension within the marriage. Following them from one house to the next, I could never forget it. Two private journal entries—one by Mary, one by Claire—came to represent this for me, and to serve as constant and bitter reminders. On 4 August 1819—Shelley's twenty-seventh birthday—at their turreted seaside house near Livorno, Mary wrote in her journal for the first time since William's death: "Leghorn—I begin my Journal on Shelley's birthday. We have now lived five years together; and if all the events of the five years were blotted out, I might be happy; but to have won, and then cruelly to have lost, the associations of four years, is not an accident to which the human mind can bend without much suffering."

I never found the Villa Valsovano where Mary wrote this—it was allowed to fall into ruins at the turn of the century. But I found an old photograph of it, a large four-square Tuscan farm, with thick stone walls, plain square windows and a shallow tiled roof. It was set on sloping ground, within sight of the sea just south of Livorno, with its own garden and a little olive plantation. Mary recalled sitting on a garden seat in one of the stone arbours of the *podere* wall, listening to the peasants singing popular tunes from Rossini. She may well have written this journal entry there.

Above her, on the roof of the farmhouse, was the tower that Shelley had adopted as his study, and where he retreated to bask in the sun with his papers and books, trying to forget the misery below. In the photograph the tower shows up as a kind of greenhouse, mounted in the centre of the roof, with large hemispherical windows on each side, and what looks like the palisade of a little balcony. Here Shelley wrote his play about incest and patricide, *The Cenci*; and *The Mask of Anarchy*. At midday the tower grew so hot with the sun that Shelley alone could stand it, sitting half-naked at his desk. As I wandered about the little lanes of Monte Nero—I found Byron's villa, of course: very grand, with statues on either side of the entrance steps—I realised that their "Scythrop's tower" had become a local architectural fashion. All along the beach road were holiday villas, each with their Tuscan tower—Gothic turrets in pink or orange stucco, modernist blockhouses in white concrete, fairy-tale campanili with dark Tuscan tiles and arched windows and barley-sugar pillars.

Claire's journal entry was made three years later, in 1822, shortly after Shelley's death. She had finally decided to leave Italy for good—the first person of Shelley's circle to act so decisively—and had set out by coach to stay with her brother Charles in Vienna. She may have had a brief affair with Trelawny—but her mind went back to other things. This is what she wrote on 20 September 1822 after leaving Florence for the last time:

> We set out for Bologna. During the first part of the road I was too occupied with my own thoughts to attend to the scenery. I remembered how hopelessly I had lingered on Italian soil for five years, waiting ever for a favourable change, instead of which I was now leaving it having [lost every object—*deleted*] buried there every thing that I loved . . . Not withstanding the rain which came by fits very heavy, I walked up the steep hills, hoping by fatigue of body to dull the painful activity of mind . . .

So Claire's last entry in her Italian journal—the fourteen remaining pages are blank—ends in streaming rain, clambering up the hills above Tagliaferro. She says she has buried "everything" that she loved: so not her child Allegra only, but also Shelley, and perhaps others too. Did she mean little Willmouse, of whom she was so fond? Did she mean Shelley's mysterious "Neapolitan charge"? Who else did she mean? "Having buried everything that I loved " —not lost, but specifically "buried". I puzzled over this internment of loved ones. And the "favourable change" she waited for during five long years: presumably that was a change in Byron's attitude towards her and Allegra. But was this all? Was there also a change in Shelley's attitude that she waited for?

To begin with, what I wanted to know about Claire was very simple. Had she ever slept with Shelley? There were at least three periods of their life together when this might have happened. During the ménage at Kentish Town in the spring and winter of 1814–15, after they had returned from the elopement, was the first. They were all very young—Claire only sixteen—Mary pregnant with her first child, and Hogg apparently in love with Mary. The extraordinary scenes of those months—rows, walk-outs, midnight terror sessions, hide-and-seek with the bailiffs—suggested intrigues and emotional cross-currents. But, as I learnt to expect at later moments of private drama, the relevant pages of journals and diaries were missing—either torn out, or lost, or subsequently destroyed. The whole six months can be summed up in a phrase from one of Claire's own letters to her stepsister Fanny Imlay, written from Lynmouth on 28 May 1815, after she had been temporarily driven out by Mary: "so much discontent, such violent scenes, such a turmoil of passion and hatred."

It can be added that when, a year later, Claire became Byron's mistress in London, she made a point of saying that she did not believe in marriage and that Shelley would vouch for her character. Byron always accepted that Allegra was his child by Claire, but he also implied that he thought Shelley might previously have been Claire's lover—and this was to prove, at the least, a source of jealousy and suspicion between the two poets. Nor did Claire, in her many subsequent and heart-breaking appeals to Byron, ever say that she had been a virgin when they met. None the less, Claire always declared that Byron had been the great love of her life—and she claimed it with a lasting bitterness that is utterly convincing.

Many years later, in 1827, she wrote to Jane Williams of her relationship with Byron:

> I am unhappily the victim of a *happy passion*. I had one; like all things perfect in its kind, it was fleeting, and mine only lasted ten minutes, but those ten minutes have discomposed the rest of my life. The passion, God knows from what cause, from no fault of mine, however, disappeared; leaving no trace whatever behind it except my heart wasted and ruined as if it has been scorched by a thousand lightnings. You will, therefore, I hope, excuse my not following the advice you give me in your last letter, of falling in love . . .

It is sobering to find Claire still writing in this way of events that had taken place during one spring and summer, eleven years previously. But it also suggested to me that, whatever else, her relationship with Shelley was not of the same order of intensity. Nor was it likely to have involved a child—or, at least, not a child like Allegra, separated from her mother, and an endless source of Claire's bitterness and recriminations. The relationship would have been of a different kind; and inevitably so, for while Claire had never lived with Byron for more than one night at a time she had lived more or less continuously under Shelley's roof—despite everything that Mary had felt—from 1814 to 1820. At the very least they were old friends.

The second period when they might have been lovers was in that first summer in Italy, between August and October 1818. But it could not have been at the Bagni di Lucca in Mary's presence, but rather two hundred miles away, on the other side of Italy, in the Euganean hills south-west of Venice.

Letters from Allegra's nurse in Venice, Elise, had persuaded Claire that she must visit her child without Byron's knowledge. Shelley decided to accompany her, leaving Mary and his own two children at Casa Bertini. The details of their journeyings and their scheme to deceive Byron, with the help of the British Consul at

Venice, Richard Belgrave Hoppner, are characteristically involved, for Claire always had a genius for complicating life. But the upshot was that Shelley and Claire were alone together from the day they left Florence by *vettura* on 18 August to the day an exhausted Mary and two rather sick children arrived to rejoin them at the Villa Capuccini, at Este, in the Euganean hills, on 5 September. This was a total of nineteen days, or just under three weeks.

Shelley and Claire were again alone together at inns in Padua for several odd days during late September and early October, when Claire was "attending the medico" for some mysterious illness. And finally they were again alone at the Villa Capuccini, except for Elise and Allegra, for four days over the last weekend in October, while Mary remained in Venice.

The only adult witness to these unusually extended periods together was Elise, the nurse, at Este. And Elise was reliably reported to have said, some two years later, that Shelley and Claire had indeed been lovers, and that Claire had in fact conceived a child by Shelley. Her evidence has of course been bitterly disputed by everyone—most of all by Mary—and came to be known as "the Hoppner scandal".

Once again, Claire's journal covering the time at Este is missing. Both Shelley and Mary lovingly describe the villa, with its pergola and garden on the brow of a hill, and the summer-house where Shelley began both *Julian and Maddalo* and *Prometheus Unbound*. To the north, just across a sunken lane, was "an extensive Gothic castle, now the habitation of owls and bats, where the Medici family resided before they came to Florence". To the south was a wide view of the plains of Lombardy. In the evenings Shelley would do owl-calls for Allegra and Willmouse, and the owls would answer back with quivering echoes from the dark battlements of the castle—like young Wordsworth's owls calling back across the lakes in Cumberland.

The Hoppner scandal did not break until 1821, and then in a mass of conflicting evidence and testimony, a great deal of it concerned with what may have been a quite different problem: who were the father and mother of Shelley's "Neapolitan charge", a child registered in his and Mary's name on 17 February 1819 at Naples? But what puzzled me at Venice, as I stifled in little rooms filled with the pungent odour of ancient backwaters, was the lack of evidence concerning their behaviour, which actually dated from the autumn of 1818. No letters or notes from Claire to Shelley are known. There are a number of agonised references in Shelley's poems of the time which *could* be interpreted as alluding to Claire; but poetic evidence is, generally speaking, the least reliable, simply because it assumes the poet is speaking autobiographically—a perilous assumption at the best of times.

There is indeed one letter of Shelley's to Claire, written from Venice on 25 September. But this appeared to be exclusively concerned with quite another, and very tragic event, the sudden death of baby Clara. I read this letter over and over in the published text. "My dear Claire," it begins, and proceeds to narrate the story of Clara's convulsions on the journey with Mary to Venice; how they called first one, then a second doctor to the inn; how "in about an hour—how shall I tell you—she died—silently, without pain". And how "this unexpected stroke reduced Mary to a kind of despair". Well, that fact alone might lead Shelley to draw a veil over anything else. Yet it remained puzzling. Surely Shelley would have made some remark, *some* slight gesture, towards Claire? Unless of course there had been nothing special between them at this time after all. The letter ended simply, sadly and directly: "All this is miserable enough —is it not? But must be borne . . . And above all, my dear girl, take care of yourself. Your affectionate friend, PBS."

Nothing more to be said, it would seem.

Venice disappointed me. The most religiously preserved of the North Italian cities, despite all the depredations of the sea, it seemed encrusted under so many other associations, so many waves of visitors and pilgrims, that my Romantics were quite lost. The Palazzo Mocenigo was like any other on the Grand Canal, and it was easier to imagine Thomas Mann's Aschenbach dying here than Byron swimming races and climbing balconies. The Lido had been Shelley's lovely, desolate

> . . . bank of land which breaks the flow
> Of Adria towards Venice: a bare strand
> Of hillocks, heaped from ever-shifting sand,
> Matted with thistles and amphibious weeds,
> Such as from earth's embrace the salt ooze breeds . . .

But this abandoned beach had become one of the great hotel fronts and rich playgrounds of the northern Adriatic. I returned like everyone else to San Marco and watched the pigeons swoop, and black battered gondolas ride uneasily at their posts. One post was empty; it stood bare out of the waters, worn by invisible ropes, as if something were missing.

Yes, something was missing all right. Something so small that I did not realise it until I was in Rome, sitting one day in the long grass of the Forum. The text of Shelley's letter to Claire was not quite complete, as published. The three dots in the penultimate sentence had an editorial note attached: "one line is here erased." This is common in Shelley's letters, and is usually of little significance; when checked against the manuscript the erasure or deletion is minor. But here the manuscript was in America, and could not immediately be checked. It was only some time later that I recovered the full text, held by the Pforzheimer Library of New York. The end of Shelley's letter from Venice, to Claire at the Villa Capuccini, now read very differently. This is what it said: "All this is miserable enough—is it not? But must be borne. *Meanwhile forget me & relive not the other thing*—And above all, my dear girl, take care of yourself. Your affectionate friend, PBS."

So there, after all, was exactly that gentle but secret message between them that I had expected. The additional sentence crossed through in contemporary ink—either by Shelley, therefore, or most likely by Claire herself. The very deletion carries its own implication. It does not prove of course that they were lovers at Este; but it does show that Shelley shared something secret and special with Claire, and that now—with little Clara's death and Mary's despair —the situation had changed, and he wished to damp it down. "Forget me & relive [or *revive*] not the other thing": but if Claire were pregnant (as Elise was to say) it might not have been so easy.

There was a third period when Shelley and Claire might have been lovers: the time between October 1820 and March 1822 when she left Shelley's household (partly as a result of the Hoppner scandal) and went to stay as a lodger and governess with the Italian family of Dr Bojti in Florence. In the week this parting occurred Claire wrote in her journal: "Think of thyself as a stranger & traveller on the earth, to whom none of the many affairs of this world belong, and who has no permanent township on the globe."

She was desolate and lonely, and it is clear that life had little meaning without Shelley—except for the endless, nagging possibility that she might still do something to get Allegra back from Byron.

During these next eighteen months Shelley and Claire met frequently—often in secret at Livorno, or at Pugnano outside Pisa. They also corresponded, with Claire using the poste restante at Pisa, and a false name—the wonderfully banal "Mr Joe James"—on Shelley's instructions, so that Mary should not know of it. Once again, most of these letters have disappeared, but a revealing set of five from Shelley to Claire remain for the final months of their separation between December 1821 and March 1822. It is evident from these that Shelley was missing Claire greatly, and the tone of affection and regret is set by the opening paragraph of a letter of 11 December:

> My dearest friend, I should be very glad to receive a confidential letter from you—one totally the reverse of those I write you; detailing all your present occupation & intimacies, & giving me some insight into your future plans. Do not think that my affection or anxiety for you ever cease, or that I ever love you less although that love has been & still must be a source of disquietude to me ... Tell me dearest [*deleted*] what you mean to do, and if it should give you pleasure come & live with us.

Claire of course did finally come to live with them again, four months later in April 1822, at Casa Magni. Yet it is clear that, but for Allegra's death, Mary would never have assented to it: she was finished for ever with any radical ménage. To those outside Shelley's immediate circle it was obvious how strange and difficult the triangle of relations between the three had become. Claire's protectress at Pisa, Mrs Mason—the erstwhile Lady Mountcashell, once a pupil of Mary Wollstonecraft in Ireland—could see the situation in a calm and commonsense light. She could see that Claire would never marry or make an independent life of her own, and that Mary would never be able to enjoy a normal marriage, until Shelley and Claire were permanently separated. She wrote as tactfully as she could to Shelley in May 1822:

> I wish Claire had some determined project, but her plans seem unsettled as ever, and she does not see half the reasons for separating herself from your society that really exist ... I regret Mary's loss of good health and spirits, but hope it is only the consequence of her present situation [*ie her pregnancy*], and therefore merely temporary, but I dread Claire's being in the same house for a month or two ...

"I dread Claire's being in the same house"—strong words. And words which brought me back once more to Casa Magni. For it was here that I began to realise that the question of Shelley and Claire as lovers, in a simple sexual sense, was a very superficial one. The relationship required much deeper understanding. It was the human quality of their long, passionate and restless friendship which was important. For Claire brought out in Shelley something that Mary never did: a dark side, tortured and dissatisfied, full of wild schemes and desperate hopes, which in fact gave much of his writing its most characteristic—and least lyrical—edge. It was too, I think, the side of his dreams and nightmares, and his ultimate realisation of the need to transcend his situation in Italy.

What did Shelley himself say about this relationship? He too was inclined to treat the sexual side—and all the speculation it aroused—with a certain nonchalance, even with flippancy. On the occasion of the Hoppner scandal he admits that "the living with Claire as my mistress" would have been a "great error & imprudence" but not a "crime". In no sense would it have been a moral evil, such as "abandoning a child"—explicitly Claire's supposed baby—an act which he always most vehemently and convincingly denied. Yet even when writing to Mary at such a tense moment he most carefully avoids actually *denying* that he and Claire had ever been lovers. Indeed, he is almost teasing on the subject, with a flash of the old rebellious, coat-trailing Shelley of much earlier days. He tells the appalled Mary: "Elise says that Claire was my mistress —that is all very well & so far there is nothing new: all the world has heard so much and people may believe or not believe as they think good."

That was all he was prepared to say; and all the comfort Mary was to get on the subject in writing.

On the general question of his friendship with Claire, Shelley adopted a different tone. It was already obvious to me from his letters that he bitterly regretted the fact that after 1820 Claire had to live apart from them in Florence. But he reveals this most clearly in his autobiographical poem of January and February 1821, *Epipsychidion*. In this poem, adopting the Petrarchan courtly-love convention, he assigns a cosmological symbol to each of the women in his life: Mary is the Moon, Emilia Viviani the Sun and Claire the Comet. The poem thus has unusually reliable biographical significance. Using this symbolism (like a modern roman à clef) he begs Claire to return from Florence, and looks back with extraordinary anguish at their difficult, passionate, involvement:

> Thou too, O Comet beautiful and fierce,
> Who drew the heart of this frail Universe
> Towards thine own; till, wrecked in that convulsion,
> Alternating attraction and repulsion,
> Thine went astray and that was rent in twain;
> Oh, float into our azure heaven again!

This, in its way, is remarkably explicit. The nature of their relationship, says Shelley, was fiery and violent, dynamic and unstable, "alternating attraction and repulsion". Claire's heart was finally driven "astray" by the "convulsion" of emotions; while Shelley's was "rent" in two—he seems to mean permanently divided between Claire and Mary. He even goes on to make a mournful little joke about Mary's attitude: if Claire will come back to them, Mary will relent: "the Moon will veil her horn/In thy last smiles."

A relationship of such power and intensity, lasting over eight years, was unlikely to be based solely on sexual infatuation, or indeed frustration. Claire appealed and responded to what was most imaginative in Shelley as a writer—both his poetry and his radicalism. In a way this is surprising, for it was surely Mary—the enormously gifted daughter of Godwin and Mary Wollstonecraft, and the well-read author of *Frankenstein*—whom one would expect to fulfil this role. I knew for example from her journal how she and Shelley read together every day; how Mary copied and criticised much of what Shelley wrote; how she took part most fully in the professional side of his life. Yet the fact remains that Claire had a spontaneity, a vividness and almost violence of response to life that Mary lacked—and for which Shelley always hungered.

I first became fully aware of this when I left Venice for Rome.

4

I arrived in the capital late one night, after hitching down the Autostrade del Sole. From a boxroom above the Via Cavour I gradually worked my way into the labyrinth of tiny streets immediately north of the Foro Romano, until by the third day I had a small annex room off the Via Leonina, with a view of pink and white washing strung above a stone fountain—or rather a stone obelisk with an iron pipe—gently splashing on to the cobbles.

This miniature piazza, itself not much larger than a room, came to symbolise modern Rome for me—it had a baker's shop, a motor-cycle repair shop and a sort of bottling plant smelling darkly of old red wine. It was never quiet at any hour of the day or night, except for the two hours of siesta, when even the radios were muted. Outside each doorway stood a wooden chair with a wicker bottom, occupied either by a cat or a grannie, depending on the position of the sun. Above rose a cliff of geraniums, alternating with underwear and birdcages, until a hot blue square of Roman sky was reached.

My room had a folding bed and a window-ledge, on which I

spread my books. I read and made notes during the night, using the white ecclesiastical candles I could purchase in the churches. At dawn, when the bottling plant started up, I closed the shutters and went to bed. At siesta I got up and went out on my tours—again and again to Shelley's three favourite places, the Pantheon, the Forum and the huge ruined Baths of Caracalla. Occasionally I would work on the manuscripts in the Keats-Shelley Museum above the Spanish Steps, or drift through the Capitoline Museum, or sit in the room containing the Hermaphrodite statue in the Palazzo Borghese.

Shelley left many fragmentary notes on the statues of Rome, and his appreciation shows—besides his instinctive understanding of classical legends—his unabashed pleasure in erotic imagery. Of one unidentified "Athlete" he wrote: "Curse these fig leaves; why is a round tin thing more decent than a cylindrical marble one?" And of a "Venus Genetrix": "Remarkable for the voluptuous effects of her finely proportioned form being seen through the folds of a drapery . . ." While of a disappointing statue of "Leda" he exclaimed frankly: "Leda with a very ugly face. I should be a long time before I should make love with her."

Shelley did not come to Rome like an ordinary English tourist, content to gaze. He came to find active inspiration, a new sense of history and the works of art and mythology that he could incorporate into his own poetry. He rejected much that he saw—the hateful imagery of Imperial Rome, the contemporary Rome of the Pope and the slaves working in chain-gangs in St Peter's Square. Yet his favourite sites became sacred places for him, not monuments but living sources of power, symbols of Liberty. Ignoring as far as I could the modern tourist round, dislocating my hours, I tried to immerse myself in these places, living a double life as monkish tramp and nineteenth-century ghost.

It was just here that I began to appreciate the quality of Claire's companionship. Shelley was in Rome from 5 March to 10 June 1819, and for once Claire's journal exists almost in full for this whole period: from 7 March till 3 June—the day Willmouse first became seriously ill. While Mary's journal remains its usual, brief laconic self—a list of sites visited and books read—Claire's is characteristically full and vivacious. But more than that: she succeeds in showing Rome as Shelley saw it, through his eyes. In many of her entries I could catch Shelley's own words and reflections on what they were seeing: his speaking voice, puzzling, meditating and enthusing. I could begin to understand how close they really were.

On Sunday 14 March, for example, Mary enters the following in her journal: "Read Montaigne, the Bible, and Livy. Walk to the Coliseum. Shelley reads Winckelmann."

It is of course a help to know that Shelley was reading the great German art historian Johann Winckelmann's epoch-making study *The History of Ancient Art among the Greeks* (1762). It indicates how Shelley was already interpreting Rome as a philhellene, and how European his thinking had become (the book was not translated into English for another forty years). Yet what were his personal reactions to the great ruins of the Coliseum? Was he impressed by them? Did he go inside? Did he stay long? Mary tells us nothing of this.

Here is Claire's entry for the same day:

> Go to the Capitol and the Coliseum—We range over every part —along the narrow grassy walks on the tops of the arches— above us on the nodding ruins grew the wall-flowers in abundance. The Coliseum resembles a mountain, its arches and recesses appear as so many caves, and here and there are spread as in the most favoured of Nature's spots, grassy platforms with a scattered fruit or thorn tree in blossom.

Immediately I could see them bounding along those precipitous paths above the arches (now frequently fenced off for safety), spying the wild flowers and choosing the little hidden lawns terraced into the ruins—"grassy platforms"—for sitting under a blossoming tree. Already Claire has seized on the idea that enchanted Shelley about the ruins both of the Coliseum and the Baths of Caracalla: that they had reverted to kinds of natural landscape —magic mountains with their caves and alpine lawns. It was exactly these dream-landscapes that he was to build into the great visionary settings and backdrops of *Prometheus Unbound*, and to describe at length in his long letter to Peacock of 23 March.

Claire completes her entry: "I think there can be nothing more delightful than a daily walk over the Capitol to visit the ruins of the Forum. In ancient times the Forum was to the city what the soul is to the body—the place in which is concentred all the most powerful and the best.—In the evening I go there again with Shelley—and see it under the grey eye of twilight."

This walk became their evening ritual while they were living in that quarter of Rome: to visit the "soul" of the ancient city—as defined in Shelley's own words, after Plato, as a "concentring of the powerful and the good".

Shelley also wrote a little-known fragment about the Coliseum: an unfinished story describing an old man visiting the ruins during the "Feast of the Resurrection". The old man is blind, but accompanied by a young woman—Helen—"apparently his daughter". He questions her as to the appearance of the Coliseum and, listening to her replies, he weaves his own imaginative interpretation on what he hears from her. In a sense this "rebirth of the imagination"—an Easter theme—is partly the meaning of the piece; but also it seemed to me to reflect something of the continual imaginative interchange between Shelley and Claire.

The young woman describes the towering ruins, the "dark arcades", the mossy lawns covered with clover and wild flowers, the "shattered arches and the isolated pinnacles". Then the blind poet remarks that the ruins sound more like "chasms rent by an earthquake among the mountains than like the vestige of what was human workmanship". He goes on, with a wild, almost surreal flight of the imagination: "Are they not caverns such as the untamed elephant might choose, amid the Indian wilderness, wherein to hide her cubs; such as, were the sea to overflow the earth, the mightiest monsters of the deep would change into their spacious chambers?"

This is already close to the descriptive language of *Prometheus*, but recognisably spiced by Shelley's sense of fun, his love of the mysterious and strange, his passion for teasing Claire. It was as if the Coliseum lay deep beneath the sea, and they swam about it like pearl-divers, half-expecting some sea-monster, some slumbering Kraken, to surge out of its dark caverns and devour them both.

Claire, unlike Mary, also shared Shelley's impatience with the expatriate socialising that English visitors were expected to take part in—the dreaded Conversazione in the smart salons of the Via del Corso. She left one amusing glimpse of such a Sunday soirée: "In the evening go to the Conversazione of the Signora Marianna Dionigi where there is a Cardinal and many unfortunate Englishmen who, after having crossed their legs & said nothing the whole evening, rose up all at once, made their bows, & filed off."

It was Claire, too, who made contact with the woman who was to become the trio's closest friend in Rome, the painter Aemilia Curran, an old friend of William Godwin and one of the original circle of feminists who knew Mary Wollstonecraft in London in the 1790s. They soon moved from their lodgings in the Corso to take rooms next to Miss Curran in the Via Sistina, above the Spanish Steps, where the three portraits of Shelley and Claire and Willmouse were done in May. The third was lost for many years;

the first—partially repainted after Shelley's death—now hangs in the National Portrait Gallery.

My own social life was very odd in Rome. Reading Shelley's letters and poems on the sites where he wrote them, especially in remote corners of the Forum, I perched illegally in the crumbling brickwork of the Caracalla while whole afternoons seemed to drift by in absolute, autumnal solitude. I was once shut in by the guards, having missed their whistles, and had to climb out through a vegetable garden next door, becoming inextricably involved with bean-netting and finally escaping over the lattice-work of a pear tree tied to a wall, terrified that I should damage its beautiful old branches and earn the undying enmity of the genius loci. I climbed with shoes tied round my neck.

My favourite point on the Palatine Hill, high above the Temple of Jupiter, was also temporarily out of bounds to the public, owing to subsidence, although it commanded by far the finest vista of the entire Forum. I used to arrive there during the siesta when no one was about and work undisturbed for an hour or two, until a particular guard—who got to know my routine—came and shouted at me from the far side of the wire.

One afternoon I showed him the picture of Shelley by Joseph Severn, working with his books in the ruins (actually in the Bagni di Caracalla, but I glossed over that), and this subtly changed the atmosphere of our daily encounters. Thereafter this long-suffering man used to arrive from his luncheons, buttoning up his dark-blue tunic, and calling genially—"Okay, crazy Shelley, you leave now, crazy man."

But my only real friends were at the rakish little worker's *hostelleria* in the Via di Tre Conti behind Trajan's Market. More than three tales were told there. In the daytime it was a bustling café-restaurant with six long wooden tables, a steel serving-counter and a huge old fridge—looking more like a gangster's safe stuck over with pictures of the Pope and Sophia Loren and Michelangelo's Adam and Eve cast out of Paradise. At night, after nine, it became a cabaret, in the old sense, a place where people drank and told long involved jokes and sang sentimental songs.

It was here that I fell in with two gentleman drifters, expatriates and dreamers of the old school, who welcomed me into their circle at the end of the fourth table where they were perpetually to be found in front of large tumblers of *rosso*. They were a fantastic pair, melancholy and humorous by turns, who vied in a courtly way for the favours of the waitress, Monica, a thin lady in her forties who wore a red ribbon in her long black hair. Each night they told me their life stories, which I would write down in the left-hand side of my notebook on my return to the annex room.

Why I liked them was that the details changed slightly every night, depending on their mood and the poetic demands of the occasion. In effect they had had at least half a dozen lives each, and they encouraged me to show an equal largesse. "Tell us," they would begin, "when you were at Oxford, when you were at Cambridge, when you were at the Sorbonne, when you were at Princeton . . ."

Best of all, they would always ask me the latest news of Shelley, and Claire, and Mary. How was Shelley's poem progressing? How were Claire's singing lessons getting on? How were Mary's moods? What galleries had they visited today? And, with great tenderness, how was little William's health? They listened to my replies with care, nodding gravely, shaking their heads, smiling, sometimes sighing deeply, agreeing that more *rosso* was called for, perhaps. "You must find out . . ." they would reflect; "you must ask them . . ."; and finally, "that reminds me . . ." and so their own lives would begin again, with some new adventure.

The tall one, Boris, had distinguished grey hair, a signet ring, and always wore a long black tweed coat. He was, he said, a White Russian who had been born in Cairo, divorced in Rome and longed to go to Scandinavia. He could quote the poetry of Cavafy in French. His two passions were Soviet Imperialism, which he hated, and cold blonde Scandinavian women, whom he loved. Sometimes even these leading details would alter, and on one memorable night he described vividly how he had been brought up in Helsinki and fallen in love with a gypsy girl in Cairo.

His friend, Alfredo, was a short swarthy man who wore a black leather jacket and a series of brightly coloured scarves. He came, he said, from Chile and had once worked on the newspaper *L'Amicità*. He had big mournful eyes and could sing in a fine tenor voice. His love-life had been so tragic that he had renounced women for ever; and perhaps for this reason it was to him that Monica's smiles were most often directed. His political hatred was reserved, despite everything Boris could contend, for American Imperialism, and there were many lurid accounts of a journalistic assignment in Saigon.

Both agreed however that "imperialism was the number one evil of our time", and when I described Shelley's radical views they nodded gloomily: "You see, nothing has changed, it is Liberty that the people want."

"Liberty or death," said Alfredo.

"Life, Liberty and the pursuing of happiness," said Boris.

The *rosso* went round.

Why do I record these two unlikely figures? Partly because their romantic expatriatism did teach me, by a strange analogy, something of the dreamy timeless world of European exiles. For they were, essentially, men in exile—full of mad hopes and slumbering regrets—for whom the borders between remote possibility and the immediate practicalities of life had become permanently blurred. Yet their shared notion of Liberty was not unreal, and not laughable. They were waiting upon events, upon some sudden turn in luck, some unexpected current that would draw them back into life and action. For the time being they were washed up, comic in their dignity, but resilient and self-mocking: the tide might turn again, might float them off. I remembered the ring that Shelley had had made for himself in Italy, with the inscription: "*il buon tempo arriva*." The good time will come.

But more important to me than this was their sense of fantasy, of the malleable properties of their own lives. You could dismiss them as bar-flies, tellers of tall stories. But that is not what I saw. They were people not wholly different from a man like Trelawny, for whom the truth about themselves and others had to be given a mythic shape. Much of what they said was to do with what *might* have happened to them, what they wanted to happen rather than what actually happened. They lived in a kind of subjunctive mode, especially the past subjunctive; but this world of possibilities was no less part of them, part of their truth as personalities, than the more normal grammar of reality and the everyday recorded fact. We are what we dream, in the same way that we are what we eat. I began to realise that a biographer had to become fluent in this subjunctive language; to manipulate and interpret it with the same confidence as all the other tenses of the past. He should be neither drowned by it nor frightened of it. It was simply one more dialect of the past—dialect of the memory—that he would have to master.

Besides, I liked Boris and Alfredo. Their warmth, their eagerness to share their fantastic existence, appealed to me. I felt at home with them; a *marginal*, as the French say, no less than they. They made clearer to me something in the contradictory nature of my own vocation. For here I was, living a largely fantasy existence precisely in order to establish the most exact, daily and domestic truth about other people's lives.

The Shelleys' life in Rome was, in a sense, much more real than my own. My life was a figment of my own imagination, whereas theirs was to me an absolute, historic reality—no detail of which could be invented or falsified, not even the weather. When Boris and Alfredo asked about Shelley I was scrupulously exact, except for the fact that I spoke in the present tense. When asked about myself, I was considerably more vague and picaresque. After all, the Shelleys' lives were simply so much more interesting than my own.

The game of speaking about them as contemporary visitors to Rome soon became far more than a bit of shared make-believe. It became more like Coleridge's definition of poetry: a willing suspension of disbelief. But, unlike poetry, it had rigour and absolute rules—everything had to be verifiable. I remember they were always asking me to discover why Shelley was attacked in the post office on the Via del Corso, and by whom. But I could never bring them a satisfactory answer, or even proof that it had occurred.

"It probably happened," was all I would say, "but maybe not quite as Shelley remembered it."

"I expect it was by Imperialist spies," said Boris in a hollow voice.

"CIA," said Alfredo.

The last night I ever went to the *hostelleria* it was somebody's birthday—I never found out whose, the festivities were too far advanced by the time I slipped in. Monica gave me a free plate of lasagne, and the rest remains hazy. I wanted to tell them about Shelley's wonderful description of the Arch of Titus in the Forum:

> The keystone of these arches is supported each by two winged figures of Victory, whose fair hair floats on the wind of their own speed, & whose arms are outstretched bearing trophies, as if impatient to meet. They look as if it were borne from the subject extremities of the earth on the breath which is the exhalation of that battle & desolation which it is their mission to commemorate.

I think I felt that both Russia and South America were, in their own way, "subject extremities of the earth". But my notebook says only that Boris sang "a Russian drinking-stamping song" and laughed and capered "like a tall grey winter bear"; while Alfredo sang "a lovely soft *canzone d'amore*" with his eyes shut and a dreamy smile on his face, of which "I could only make out one word— *febrile*". Then there was a highly complicated drinking game, involving forfeits and toasts, with an elected Master of Ceremonies who dictated the terms on which the *rosso* could be drunk. I couldn't understand most of it, but the laughter was wonderful, warm and somehow sad, full of sentiment and nostalgia—rising to the ceiling like smoke, an exhalation of deepest feelings, quite un-English. It moved and embarrassed me. The toasts were serious and bawdy by turns—family, loved ones, politics, home towns far away. Then they toasted Shelley—as a fellow-exile—and his name rang to the roof. I sat there looking at my plate dangerously close to tears. I came back on wings down the Via dei Fori Imperiali, determined to write my book for people like them too, who would never read it, people who had lost most things except hope. There were stars above the Arch of Titus, a black shape under the sky of the Eternal City.

5

Shelley had originally intended to return to Naples from Rome in the summer of 1819. He had completed the first three Acts of *Prometheus Unbound* in his "upaithric" study in the Baths of Caracalla and by May was working on his verse-play about Beatrice Cenci—the sinister old Cenci palace still exists down by the Tiber near the island. One of the reasons for this planned return southwards must have been his "Neapolitan charge" Elena, and I was surprised to discover that he commemorates her registered birth date, 27 December, in *The Cenci*:

> I beg those friends who love me, that they mark
> The day a feast upon their calendars.
> It was the twenty-seventh of December:
> Ay, read the letters if you doubt my oath.

The reference is doubly surprising in that, in the play, Cenci is talking about the day two of his children *died*; and once again this raised for me the whole problem of Elena's identity, and Shelley's depressive crisis at Naples. What complex meaning had Shelley hidden here?

The circumstantial evidence strongly suggested that Claire Clairmont had conceived a child by Shelley early in 1818, and that the baby Elena Adelaide Shelley, registered as born in Naples and left there with foster-parents until she died two years later, was indeed Claire's. But as I came gradually to know Claire's character, and the way she bitterly regretted leaving her child Allegra with Byron, it became less and less likely to me that she would ever leave behind her—to foster-parents, guardians, friends, or least of all to a Foundling Hospital (as Elise Foggi would claim)— a second child, and that by Shelley.

Moreover, if Claire had some special interest in the child one would have expected *her* to be the one urging Shelley to go south again; and Mary to be understandably reluctant. But in fact the roles were almost reversed: Claire showed no particular desire to go back, while Mary frequently spoke of Naples as the city where she had been most happy, even in preference to Pisa. As late as April 1822 she was writing to Maria Gisborne: "Pisa certainly agrees with [Shelley] exceedingly well, which is its only merit in my eyes. I wish fate had bound us to Naples instead."

In the event, William's death was to drive them north to Tuscany, on 10 June.

A further puzzle arose when I examined copies of Elena's official Italian registration, originally discovered by N. I. White at Naples. If she had really been Claire's illegitimate child one would have expected Shelley to proceed in the most discreet manner possible. In a city rich with expatriate gossip he would have avoided anything which linked the child to their residence at 250 Riviera di Chiaia. But the birth registration showed that not only had the ceremony been witnessed by a local midwife, Gaetana Musto, but that two local shopkeepers from the Riviera di Chiaia district were also co-opted as witnesses. Shelley himself signed the birth register, formally stating that Elena Adelaide Shelley was the child of Mary Shelley and himself, born to them nearly two months earlier at No 250.

This presented a further mystery: why had he waited until 17 February, the day before their final departure from Naples, to formalise the registration? It all suggested a decision taken at the last possible moment, almost on impulse, and with no particular attempt at discretion. Moreover it would not have provided convincing cover for Claire, even if the child had been hers. For who would ever believe that Shelley and Mary would leave their *own* child behind in Naples, with Italian foster-parents? The document was self-evidently false, and this must have been known by all the local signatories. There would have been many ways of hushing up an illegitimate birth in such a city as Naples—the child need never have been registered there at all—and I could not believe that this was one of them. Shelley must have had a different purpose in making this legal declaration.

Nevertheless it seemed inescapable that Claire *had* been compromised in Naples in some way; and that Shelley (but not Mary) had been close to despair about it. The blackmail that Paolo Foggi and Elise began—"Paolo's infernal business"—in June 1820, immediately after Elena's death in Naples, eventually required the services of an Italian lawyer, Del Rosso, to silence it. So there must have been some basis in fact, though not necessarily what the blackmailers alleged. Elise seemed genuinely sure that Shelley and Claire had been lovers at Este; and her wild tale of the illegitimate child born at No 250 was obviously based on local gossip, or something of which she had personal knowledge. Then there was that crucial date, 27 December 1818. How could one avoid it?

The date appears quite separately in three significant documents. It is the day recorded for Elena's birth on the official register. It is the date recorded in Mary's own journal for Claire being "ill". And it is the date carefully chosen by Shelley in *The Cenci*, as a kind of bleak memorial of some tragic occurrence in the family.

I worried at this problem ceaselessly. The details are far more convoluted than I have sketched here, and in the end I wrote a separate appendix on the subject for my biography. There is for example Elise's recantation, written in Florence in 1822, stating that she had seen "*rien de pervers*" in Claire's conduct at Este after all; and also Claire's letter to Mary saying that Elise would sign whatever she dictated, but—significantly—that she did not know how to phrase it.

Nevertheless I came to feel that there were three likely truths underlying the Hoppner scandal, and somehow they had to be reconciled. The first was that Shelley and Claire had very probably been lovers at Este, that some of what Elise said was indeed true, and that there were sufficient grounds for Paolo Foggi's blackmail, for Shelley's acute depression at Naples and for Mary's growing desire for Claire to leave their household. The second was that though the baby Elena, the "Neapolitan charge", undoubtedly existed as a source of grief and embarrassment to Shelley, something that he always tried to keep secret, she was *not* in fact Claire's illegitimate child. The third was that, none the less, the date of 27 December was especially significant in the whole affair. Somehow it linked the baby Elena with Claire's compromised position.

The light that these conjectures threw on Shelley's marriage was considered radical and even somewhat outrageous at the time that I wrote. But they are now widely accepted by Shelley scholars and readers, because the unconventional nature of Shelley's relationships is regarded with much more sympathy and understanding. But they do not of course provide a biographical solution to what actually happened; nor is there really sufficient evidence to do so still. Nevertheless I felt insistently, and perhaps misguidedly, that a solution had to be provided.

My own solution in the published book was stark. It had two parts: that Elena was Shelley's illegitimate child by the maid Elise; and that Claire had also been pregnant by Shelley, but had had a miscarriage at four months on 27 December. In retrospect, I now think that the first part of this hypothesis is both unnecessary and extremely unlikely. But I am more than ever convinced that the second part—Claire's miscarriage—alone represents the true solution to the mystery.

The baby Elena was, I now believe, a Neapolitan foundling child, which Shelley impulsively adopted from the Naples Foundling Hospital as an act of atonement for Claire's suffering. He chose a child born on the date of Claire's miscarriage (her "illness")— hence the crucial coincidence of 27 December—and intended to bring it up with foster-parents at his own expense. Hence Elise's notorious accusation was partly based on a misunderstanding, or misinterpretation of what she genuinely thought had occurred.

Even as I write this I am seized with my old doubts. So much evidence really does point to Elena being Claire's illegitimate child. It is only my interpretation of Claire's and Shelley's characters that stands against it. And how can one really interpret Claire's behaviour, with her diary entries missing for those eight crucial months between the end of June 1818 and the beginning of March 1819? And why was the diary missing—or destroyed—anyway?

Yet a biographer does become slowly convinced about his subjects' characters. After studying them and living with them for several years he finds they become one of the most important of all human truths; and I think perhaps the most reliable. This sense of character eventually grows very strong, and in an extraordinary way a relationship of *trust* seems to be established between you. There are several things that I concluded about the quality of this trust, while I was in Italy.

First there is the whole question of people acting "true to character", or "true to themselves". In daily human affairs notoriously, we all do sometimes act apparently out of character—especially in situations of great stress or temptation or depression. In such situations one could say that a person's sense of their own identity is diminished, and that they act almost in spite of themselves. Yet the biographer views and witnesses these daily human affairs in a special and privileged perspective. He gains a special kind of intimacy, but quite different from the subjective intimacy that I had first so passionately sought. He sees no act in isolation; nor does he see it from a single viewpoint. Even the familiarity of a close friend or spouse of many years suffers from this limitation. The biographer sees every act as part of a constantly unfolding pattern: he sees the before and the afterwards, both cause and consequence. Above all he sees repetition and the emergence of significant behaviour over an entire lifetime. As a result I have become convinced of the integrity of human character. Even a man's failings, sudden lapses, contradictory reactions, sudden caprices, seem in the long run to fall within a pattern of character. One could say, paradoxically, that people even act out of character in a certain way: there is always, so to speak, meaning in their madness, provided one has full knowledge of the circumstances. (Though that is the great proviso, together with Henry James's, "never say you know the last word about any human heart".)

The real error in my first hypothesis, that Elena was the child of Shelley and Elise, lies in the fact that, had she been so, it would have been utterly out of character for Shelley to leave the child in Naples. In character for Byron, but never for Shelley. Shelley's attitude to children, legitimate or illegitimate, had been amply demonstrated by the long chancery case bitterly fought in England for custody of the children by his first marriage; and by his support of Claire when she gave birth to Allegra. Shelley was simply not the sort of man to abandon children whatever the social pressures. And this objection, as I have already said, applies with even greater force to any child of his and Claire's. In trying to solve a domestic mystery by mechanical, almost forensic explanation, I violated what I had learned much more deeply of the laws of character. I had in effect broken the terms of the biographer's trust. It was a cardinal mistake.

By the same token, I had maintained that trust, almost in the teeth of the evidence, as far as Shelley and Claire were concerned. The whole pattern of their relationship pointed to a sexual affair, a compromising situation and a probable pregnancy. Yet nothing in the character of their intimacy either before or, even more important, afterwards at Florence and Pisa allowed me to concede that they had abandoned a love-child to the Naples Foundling Hospital, or callously farmed it out to foster-parents. The tragic miscarriage became the logical solution to the mystery.

The second thing about this trust is, of course, that one may be wrong about it. As in all human affairs, trust may be misplaced or betrayed; or one's judgment of character may be simply incorrect. This possibility of error is constant in all biography, and I suspect that it is one of the elements which gives the genre its peculiar psychological tension. I do not here speak of simple errors in documentation; or even less of the deliberate slanting of an account. I mean that the reader can see, from the outside, an honest relationship developing between biographer and subject, and the deeper this becomes the more critical are those moments —or areas—in which misunderstanding or misinterpretation become evident.

At the point where the reader believes he can see more truly or fairly into the state of the case than the biographer himself then the very nature of the book he is reading seems to change. Essentially, the dramatic nature of the biography—its powers of re-creation—are fatally undermined. The literary illusion of life, the illusion that makes it so close to the novel, is temporarily or permanently weakened. In short, where the biographical narrative is least convincing its fictional powers are most reduced. Where trust is broken between biographer and subject it is also broken between reader and biographer.

The great appeal of biography seems to lie, in part, in its claim to a coherent and integral view of human affairs. It is based on the profoundly hopeful assumption that people really are responsible for their actions, and that there is a moral continuity between the inner and the outer man. The public and the private life do, in the end, make sense of each other; and the one is meaningless without the other. Its view of life is Greek: character expresses itself in action: and can be understood, if not necessarily justified.

Inevitably I took the mystery of Elena north with me again, to Florence and then Livorno, where the Shelleys settled in late summer 1819. It was here, almost exactly a year later, that the story—as opposed to the scandal—had its sequel. At the end of June 1820 Shelley heard of the baby's illness; and on 7 July her death. Both Claire's and Mary's journals exist in full for this period, without significant deletions; as do several letters from Shelley to his close friends the Gisbornes, then in London. So in many ways it is the most revealing time of all in the whole sad affair: what did they each say?

Mary, as so often, says nothing at all on the matter; though there is a letter showing that she knew of Paolo Foggi's blackmail attempts. Claire's diary shows no evidence of grief or upset, though an ironic reference of 13 July to "those who threaten to take to the law" indicates that she too knew of Shelley's efforts to silence

Paolo. On 4 July there is also a stinging aside about her quarrels with Mary, in two lines of doggerel:

Heigh-ho, the Clare & the Ma
Find something to fight about every day

—but this hardly indicates any shattering revelation or dispute. In fact there is a lot about Naples in Claire's diary throughout this summer, but it all concerns her enthusiastic reception of the revolution there against the King, an enthusiasm which she shared with Shelley, and which helped to inspire his "Ode to Liberty" of that year. There is nothing that could be remotely connected with grief or remorse over Elena's death.

By contrast, Shelley has a lot to say. He had taken the Gisbornes into his confidence over Paolo, and it was they who had originally helped him employ the lawyer Del Rosso. Clearly they also knew about Elena, and it is to them that Shelley unburdens himself. On 30 June he writes: "My poor Neapolitan, I hear, has a severe fever of dentition. I suppose she will die, and leave another memory to those which already torture me. I am awaiting the next post with anxiety, but without much hope. What remains to me? Domestic peace and fame? You will laugh when you hear me talk of the latter . . ."

To this he adds a PS dated 1 July: "I have later news of my Neapolitan. I have taken every possible precaution for her, and hope they will succeed. She is to come as soon as she recovers."

Of course it is this last sentence that strikes one: if Elena really had been his illegitimate child, so carefully secreted away in Naples, why should he now risk everything by proposing to bring her to his household at Livorno? And if she had been Claire's would not Claire be in a fever of anxiety to know the outcome of this radical change in plan? Then, on further reflection, there are the omissions: why does Shelley write so impersonally of the baby—never using her name, Elena, never making the slightest hint about her mother, never suggesting an impending domestic crisis? On the contrary, he seems to suggest that the baby's death will simplify things, leaving him "domestic peace". His grief is real enough—a memory to "torture" him—but it is impersonal, and above all it shows no guilt. Could he have written that way about Claire's child? I find it difficult to believe.

Then, about a week later, around 7 July, Shelley wrote again to the Gisbornes in a mood of great bitterness and disillusion. It is this letter that shows something more than grief, a sense of being hounded and oppressed, so that even his good actions seem to be turned to evil. If Shelley did adopt Elena as an act of atonement for causing Claire such misery, then I now feel I can interpret and understand a voice that ends in despair and fury:

> My Neapolitan charge is dead. It seems as if the destruction that is consuming me were as an atmosphere which wrapt & infected everything connected with me. The rascal Paolo has been taking advantage of my situation at Naples in December 1818 to attempt to extort money by threatening to charge me with the most horrible crimes. He is connected with some English here, who hate me with a fervour that almost does credit to their phlegmatic brains, & listen & vent the most prodigious falsehoods. An ounce of good civet apothecary to sweeten this dunghill of the world.

The exclamation from *King Lear* comes from the old king's famous speech of disgust, "Let copulation thrive . . ." Paolo, at least, was forced to leave Livorno within twenty-four hours. I meanwhile continued on my way to Pisa.

6

I found the calm of the old riverside city, with its dreamy hints of Moorish architecture and the ancient sea-trade of the southern Mediterranean, curiously deceptive. From 1820 onwards Shelley was to rent various apartments here along the crumbling banks of the Arno, and Pisa became his most settled home in Italy ("our roots were never struck so deeply as at Pisa"), with an outwardly contented Mary and their third and only surviving child, Percy, born the previous November. Gradually the last expatriate circle of his friends formed around him: the bearded, piratical Edward John Trelawny; the charming Old Etonian Edward Williams, an ex-Indian army officer, with his voluptuous wife Jane Williams (actually the separated wife of a brother officer); and, in late 1821, Byron and Teresa Guiccioli. Life took on an almost domestic surface, and Shelley for the first time unpacked fully his cases of books, while Mary grew plants in pots on the window-shelf.

I wandered about Pisa for many days, feeling my way into the place, talking to the university medical students (term had begun and the tourists gone home), reading of Galileo and the Pisanos, hanging over the parapets of the bridges and gazing up at the mace-headed tower where Dante says Count Ugolino was imprisoned and starved until he ate his own children. But all the time I was thinking of the absent Claire.

Two or three hundred yards down the Lung'arno, Byron's establishment, the Palazzo Lanfranchi, which Shelley found and hired for him in autumn 1821, still dominated the street. Its mullioned windows and sculpted door-lintel looked directly on to the sleepy, curving river. It was in fact a town house, dating from the seventeenth century, rather than a "palace" in the English sense, but it maintains its superiority by being the only building which has its own stone landing-steps still cut into the river wall.

To reach Shelley's modest apartment a skiff would have taken you from these steps diagonally downriver almost to the old city wall on the far bank; or else a brisk four-minute horse trot would have led you round by the bridge. But I arrived a little too late, as American bombers had destroyed the last two old buildings in the row, including Shelley's, in 1944.

It occurred to me that though the house was gone I could still photograph the *view* from the house that Shelley would have seen every morning, as he stepped out with his books to go walking in the woods—"the Cascine, near Pisa"—or to take the skiff with Williams. This reversal of perspective, looking *outwards* from within Shelley's life rather than the more usual attempt to look inwards from the outside—the view *from* the window, rather than the view of the window in the façade—became for me one of the important techniques of biography. In a sense it was merely a device, a trick of perspective using the same materials. But it also expressed a principle, a definite method of recapturing time, by turning the viewpoint inside out, if only for a moment.

The photograph that resulted from this discovery largely made up for the disappointment of finding Shelley's house gone. For me it expressed so much of the feel of Shelley's Pisa—not the tourists' Pisa of Leaning Tower and Baptistery, but the residential Pisa, standing quietly along the Arno, elegantly crumbling, its buildings reflected in water, as described in Shelley's tone-poem, "Evening: Ponte al Mare, Pisa". A painted skiff with its long bird-like prow rested on the nearside bank, and, beyond the white façade of the Palazzo Lanfranchi, were the jutting irregular lines of the tiled roofs against the Tuscan sky, the stone walls tufted with grass, the shimmering ripples breaking and re-forming the old city like a mirage:

> Within the surface of the fleeting river
> The wrinkled image of the city lay,
> Immovably unquiet, and forever
> It trembles, but it never fades away;
> Go to the East . . .
> You, being changed, will find it then as now.

"Immovably unquiet"—a typical Shelleyan paradox about the passage of time, so subtly put that it was easy to overlook it.

By capturing it in my lucky photograph I was drawn again to reflect on the paradoxes of time as they affect the biographer. In a photograph, it is conventionally said, an "instant of time is frozen", like a bucket of water taken from a flowing river or a tableau held in a theatrical production. But in my photograph of Pisa from Shelley's lost house I felt that I had established a *continuity* of time, a linking of one "instant" to the next across many years, with a dissolving (rather than a freezing) of much that was temporary and ephemeral. "You, being changed, will find it then as now." Without people, without vehicles, with only the boat and the roofs and the river, Pisa could be seen very much as Shelley would have seen it. Biography too had to achieve something like that.

From the moment of Claire's departure from Pisa, Shelley's shaking of his domestic chains becomes, as it were, audible. To his cousin, Tom Medwin, who was travelling through the Alps with Edward Williams, he wrote in July 1820:

How much I envy you, or rather how much I sympathise in the delights of your wandering. I have a passion for such expeditions, although partly the capriciousness of my health, and partly the want of the incitement of a companion, keep me at home. I see the mountains, the sky, and the trees from my windows, and recollect as an old man does the mistress of his youth, the raptures of a more familiar intercourse . . .

It seemed to me that this was written partly with Claire in mind; and that Mary had long since ceased to be Shelley's "companion" in the delights of such wandering.

Shelley continued to associate Claire with his wilder schemes, as a letter to her three months later, at the end of October 1820, makes explicit. The somewhat mysterious dream of a great sailing expedition to the East which it describes became one of Shelley's deepest escape-fantasies in the last months of his life. It appears again and again disguised in such poems as "Evening: Pisa" and *Epipsychidion*, and it is secretly present in the entire plan to settle on the seashore at Casa Magni, which Shelley understood—more or less unconsciously—as a jumping-off point, a point of departure, rather than—as Mary thought—a temporary and highly impractical holiday home.

Shelley wrote to Claire in Florence:

> I have read or written nothing lately, having been much occupied by my sufferings, and by Medwin, who relates wonderful and interesting things of the interior of India. We have also been talking of a plan to be accomplished with a friend of his, a man of large fortune, who will be at Leghorn next spring, and who designs to visit Greece, Syria, and Egypt in his own ship. This man has conceived a great admiration for my verses, and wishes above all things that I could be induced to join his expedition. How far all this is practicable, considering the state of my finances, I know not yet. I know that if it were it would give me the greatest pleasure, and the pleasure might be either doubled or divided by your presence or absence. All this will be explained and determined in time; meanwhile lay to your heart what I say, and do not mention it in your letter to Mary.

Shelley in Egypt, Shelley in Greece: it is an intriguing possibility, a whole new perspective on his dreams. Was it a realistic scheme?—I never managed to discover who that "man of large fortune" was, or even if he ever existed. Certainly Mary never got to know of this plan—and she had become the touchstone of reality in Shelley's household. The letter seems to imply that Shelley wanted Claire to come with him, but not Mary—the phrasing of his invitation is curiously echoed in the "free love" passage of *Epipsychidion* in the following year:

> True love in this differs from gold and clay,
> That to divide is not to take away.

But the destruction of his marriage was not, I am now convinced, what Shelley intended—consciously at least; nor do I think that Mary, so difficult yet so long-suffering and so absolutely loyal to Shelley would ever have allowed herself to be left behind. But it does show how Mary, by this date, was being excluded from one whole part of Shelley's mind; and how Claire was still a warm and secret sharer.

Claire, in this sense, gradually became a key witness in my biography, even a kind of collaborator. I felt her presence urging me on whenever I found myself attacking or contradicting the conventional view of Shelley, especially in matters political or amorous. "Claire and I," I found myself thinking, "we know the truth about this." Indeed, I now think Claire was the source of much mischief at certain points, and frequently led me to be unfair to Mary. The light did not dawn until long afterwards, when a friend remarked with a flash of mockery, "Of course, trust you to fall in love with Claire Clairmont!"

I was not the only one, it seems. Several of Shelley's friends saw her as the dark, unstable, poetic element in his life, as against the blonde, domestic, pacifying one. Thomas Love Peacock had already guessed and celebrated the importance of this dynamic when, years before, he gave Mr Scythrop, with his "passion for reforming the world", a divided love-life in *Nightmare Abbey* (1818). Peacock tactfully mixed up Claire and Mary's qualities (with a dash of Harriet Shelley), and presented Scythrop as perpetually and comically incapable of choosing between the raven-haired intellectual, Stella, and the fair-haired, musical, adoring Marionetta.

Trelawny too never quite recovered from his infatuation with Claire, and his fascination with the emotional drama she generated around Shelley's attempts to live out his radical ideas. In January 1870, nearly fifty years after the events that had first drawn them together in Italy, he wrote an unpublished letter to Claire, which still shows him teasing the old lady, and playing nostalgically with the wild possibilities that their lives had touched on:

The present and the future are nothing—so I look back, and the Shelleyan episode in my life is the most interesting. Bye the bye, why did he not project a sect on the Mormon plan? I would gladly have joined him and founded a settlement. As Man is everywhere, and at all periods has been, ingrained with superstition, we must have had ours—the heathen mythology would have done, with adaption to our present state. The poet should have had his fifty wives—five would have done for me . . . You say he was womanly in some things. So he was, and we men would all be much better if we had a touch of their feeling, sentiment, earnestness, and constancy. But in all the best qualities of man he excelled. The best qualities of the sexes he had—not exactly all—he was inconstant in Love as men of vehement temperament are apt to be—his spirit hunting after new fancies. Nothing real can equal the ideal. Poets and men of ardent imagination should not marry; marriage is only suitable to stupid people.

Why was Claire's role in Shelley's life so important to me? Why did I question it more closely than almost anything else, except Shelley's political radicalism? Why did I give up so much time and thought to Claire in Italy that I was almost certainly unfair—or at least unsympathetic—to Mary: his wife, his biographer and his literary executor? These are questions that I find it hard, and even quite disturbing, to answer fully. But they reveal something of the biographer's hidden or secret impulses.

In terms of research, the explanation may seem obvious. Shelley's relations with Claire were simply that part of his private life that had been least freely explored by previous writers. Claire's diary was the last major document from Shelley's inner circle to be published—not until 1968—and many of her letters still had to be consulted in manuscript. I felt that she had never been given her proper place in Shelley's story.

It was the same with Shelley's radical politics. It was the political, visionary poems like *The Revolt of Islam* (1818) or the political, visionary prose like *A Philosophical View of Reform* (1820, but not published for a hundred years after) which had previously received the least attention. Indeed, the subject of Claire and the subject of radicalism were in a sense complementary. One represented the most extreme edge of Shelley's private life while the other showed the most extreme element in his public concerns. Both had, I felt, been bowdlerised by my predecessors. The safe Shelley, the known Shelley, the acceptable Shelley was the figure in the middle-ground—Mary's unworldly husband, the lyric poet, the romantic exile, the gentle idealist: "our ideal Shelley", as Matthew Arnold called him. But this was a Victorian figure. I wanted to show what I met for myself: a modern Shelley still speaking to us, a Shelley who had penetrated the darkness at the edges of existence; a bright flame, certainly, but a flame flickering in shadows.

Claire, more than anyone else in the whole story perhaps, saw and understood this restless, reckless side of Shelley—being temperamentally, if not intellectually, very much inclined that way herself. She never allowed me to forget this vital, fiery, darting element in Shelley's character.

Their passionate friendship—for that is what finally I think it was—had a symbolic importance to me, as an emblem of the Romantic revolt, a refusal to conform to the conventional patterns and expectations of society. I did not want it to die out, either smothered by the familiarities of domesticity or blasted by the failure to live up to the responsibilities of an illegitimate child. I am still convinced that neither of these things happened, and that as part of Shelley's "experiment in living" the relationship contained much that was best and most revolutionary in Shelley's attitude to love.

None the less, it cannot be said to have brought much happiness to those concerned. Nor can it be said to have been a conventional "success". As I stood back and tried to consider Shelley's overall situation at the time he finally left Pisa for the Gulf of Spézia I was aware of almost nothing but the contradictions in his life, the suffering and the sense of sublime refusal to face any reality he had created, outside that of his own poetry. In one sense he was a formidably brave, kind and creative man; in another he was self-deceiving to the point of cruelty to those most dear to him.

Certainly the underlying domestic problem between Claire and Mary was never finally resolved. The last letter Mary was to write to Shelley is from the Casa Magni and dated 3 July 1822. It has survived only in a fragment, because it went down with him, probably folded in one of his pocket-books, in the wreck of 8 July. The damaged paper, torn and disfigured with sea-water, carries only a few phrases, none of them complete. But it refers specifically to Claire. Mary mentions her wish for a house "all our own", the lack of "order and cleanliness" at Casa Magni, and begs Shelley to seek Mrs Mason's help at Pisa—and "talk to her also about Claire". It had been Mary's refrain for seven long years.

7

The move to the Casa Magni in April 1822 was thus for me the final act in a biographical drama of immense complexity. As I drifted through San Terenzo that late autumn afternoon my gaze turned constantly to the sea. I remembered how Shelley had sailed out into the bay in his slim twenty-four-foot schooner, fitted out by the handy Edward Williams with bookshelves and lounging cushions, and felt that his life had never achieved such a level of magic transcendence.

"My boat is swift and beautiful," he wrote, "and appears quite a vessel. Williams is captain, and we drive along this delightful bay in the evening wind, under the summer moon, until earth appears another world. Jane brings her guitar, and if the past and the future could be obliterated, the present would content me so well, that I could say with Faust to the passing moment, 'Remain, thou art so beautiful.'"

The reasons for the removal to San Terenzo, after his two comparatively peaceful and settled years at Pisa, confronted me with this final sense of mystery, and the enigma of Shelley's deepest emotions. Outwardly there were practical explanations that were easy enough to understand. The boating scheme (largely Trelawny's invention); the increasingly awkward relations with Byron in Pisa; and the immediate need to soothe and distract Claire, because of the news of her child Allegra's death—all these provided pretexts for such a move.

Yet the moment I arrived at San Terenzo I was overwhelmed by the improbability of it all, the wildness of the place, the deliberate extremity of the whole position. There was something desperate and irrational here. More than ever before, Shelley seemed to be moving into a world of fantasy. The Casa Magni, with its seven white open arches standing only a few feet from the sea, seemed more a vision than a house of stone and stucco and pebble dash. And Shelley had foreseen just such a house a year before, in *Epipsychidion*:

> This isle and house are mine, and I have vowed
> Thee to be lady of the solitude. —
> And I have fitted up some chambers there
> Looking towards the golden Eastern air,
> And level with the living winds, which flow
> Like waves above the living waves below . . .

Of course, Casa Magni faced west, not east; but the rejected prefaces to *Epipsychidion*—which speak of "fitting up the ruins of an old building" on one of the "wildest of the Sporades"—and a remarkable letter to Mary of August 1821, where he also speaks of retiring to "a solitary island in the sea", where he would build a boat and "shut upon my retreat the floodgates of the world" all convinced me that the idea had been long in his mind, and that San Terenzo was the nearest thing to his magic island, his last retreat.

Yet in ordinary, mundane terms, Shelley's move here still made little sense. He had no ostensible reason to think his life was over. He was not yet thirty, his career had barely begun, and he stood to inherit a large estate on the death of his father back in England (Sir Timothy Shelley was already seventy-one). His own son, Percy, was a robust little boy of two and a half; and Mary was again pregnant.

His scheme to launch a new magazine, *The Liberal*, with Byron and Leigh Hunt showed that his literary ambitions were far from extinguished. Events in Greece—about which he had dashed off his choric drama, *Hellas*—now fed his political hopes once more, so central to his inspiration as a poet. Even in England the tide was slowly turning in favour of a more liberal outlook: the first time, really, for two decades. Within the next five years the agitation for Parliamentary Reform would turn into a gathering storm. In all outward circumstances, Shelley had everything to live for. Yet by coming to San Terenzo he seemed to be courting obscurity, self-abandonment and imminent disaster for himself and his family.

Dumping my pack in the corner of a little taverna, decorated with faded blue seascapes, I got talking to a fisherman who said he had a brother, who had a wife, who had an ancient aunt who could help me . . . I had long got into the habit of drifting with unlikely currents of this kind. Passed from hand to hand through the village, with much laughter and some singing in a back kitchen, I was finally taken up to the top of a crumbling block of flats behind the little church. Here I was introduced to Signora T---, an old lady dressed in black, who sat very upright in a cane chair with a cluster of diamonds on her left hand.

Her apartment was almost dark, except for a beautiful marine lamp, and she seemed nearly blind. I was told to sit down next to her and tell her about my life. She listened intently, occasionally smiling and shaking her head. In turn she told me she had been a cook in Kensington during the War, and had been very lonely and read the English poets. Then she had met Mario, and come home, and life had been good to her. Mario was dead now, but she had inherited an old house on the seafront, and she had let out the rooms as a *pensione* for old people and widows like herself, so they could take a holiday from the big cities, from Genoa, from Florence.

"Old people like looking at the sea. It brings back their memories, their lives. It is like looking at a fire. It is a sort of dream."

Here she made a smoothing gesture with her hand, and I was sure that she was blind. She smiled again.

"But old people cannot afford very much money. And nor can young people. That is all right. Life has been good to me. You must have a room in my *pensione*, if you wish, and dream about your *poeta inglese*."

I was ushered out, and left her sitting, dark and upright against the steady glow of the glass lamp.

Her *pensione* was next door but one to the Casa Magni. The room was on the first floor, looking directly over the sea, with a big stone balcony carved with fleur-de-lys. It was the best room I ever had in Italy, and also the strangest.

The windows were hung with old brocade curtains, the floor was tiled with patterned marble, smooth and warm to my naked feet. In one corner was a huge old mahogany armoire, with pier-glass mirrors; in the other an enormous double-bed with spiral-carved bedposts and the tattered remnants of a canopy. In the middle of the floor was a white tin table, and a beautiful high-backed cane chair with curving arms. Strangest of all, against the far wall, were not one but two cradles, also made of cane, on wooden rockers with small, embroidered tent-like lace veils over each head. Their design was certainly nineteenth century. I felt I was moving in with a whole family.

For this enchanted room I was asked to pay the equivalent of one pound ten shillings a week, in advance. I moved the table out on to the balcony and unpacked my books. Overhead was a canvas awning with a loop of washing-line clipped with wooden pegs. Out in the bay the lighthouse on Palmaria had begun to wink. I craned over the balustrade and looked across to the balcony of Casa Magni. Then I sat down and began to write my daily notes, the long continuous imaginary conversation I had with my subject.

I was full of questions. The first thing I did not understand about San Terenzo was its remoteness. It wasn't just a summer holiday; Mary hated it from the start. It was nothing like the Bagni di Lucca, with its little baths and stables and casino. There was no civilisation near it. Food supplies came from Salzano, four miles inland across the river. Even the mail came by boat, once or twice a week through the Harbour Master of Lérici, Signor Maglian. The buildings that make it this small modern resort are all recent, that is to say late nineteenth century, except the church. Early biographers wrote indiscriminately of Casa Magni being actually at Lérici, or "Santa Renzo", so obscure was it. Mary says Casa Magni was originally built as a boathouse, and the proprietor of the estate on which it was situated was insane: "He had begun to erect a large house at the summit of the hill behind, but his malady prevented its being finished, and it was falling into ruin."

That must have amused Shelley, and given the place its demonic touch. Whenever he describes it in his letters of May and June he mentions *Faust*, and implies he too has made some sort of pact with the devil. The sea, the boat, the storms, the moonlight immediately enter his poetry with unearthly force; and Dante's underworld—the Inferno—shapes *The Triumph of Life*. None of the last short lyrics are addressed to Mary; all are to Jane Williams—except perhaps the lines, "We meet not as we parted, We feel more than all may see," which may have been to Claire. Shelley was tortured by Allegra's death. At Casa Magni he had to think of all that trail of dead children marking his course through Italy during the last five years—Clara at Venice, Willmouse at Rome, Elena at Naples, and now Allegra at Bagnacavallo, a stepping-stone path of little tombs.

Was he running away from all that at Casa Magni—or trying to isolate himself and face it in his poetry? Was he turning, at bay, in his magic fortress? There are references to *The Tempest*, Shakespeare's last play, and the idea of reincarnation in the "Ariel to Miranda" poem, written like a guitar tune for Jane:

> Your guardian spirit, Ariel, who,
> From life to life, must still pursue
> Your happiness;—for thus alone
> Can Ariel ever find his own.
> From Prospero's enchanted cell,
> As the mighty verses tell,
> To the throne of Naples, he
> Lit you o'er the trackless sea,
> Flitting on, your prow before,
> Like a living meteor.

Shelley's image of himself is now that of a meteor, burning itself up; a preoccupation which persists through May and June. The self-destructive idea had begun in *Adonais*, where he seems to foresee his fate with startling clarity:

> . . . my spirit's bark is driven
> Far from the shore, far from the trembling throng
> Whose sails were never to the tempest given . . .

As I put down these scattered last notes, there on my balcony, and thought about them during the final days of swimming and walking about the bay it was borne in on me how far Mary Shelley had been struggling with the same questions. Because she was ill with her pregnancy and frequently confined to bed, or to a sofa dragged out on to the terrace of Casa Magni, she must have felt like a spectator—helpless amidst events she could not properly control or understand. There may have been some degree of wisdom after the event in the *Notes on the Poems of 1822* which she wrote seventeen years after, in 1839. She only kept the sketchiest daily journal between May and June 1822, and there are only three known letters written from Casa Magni: one to Maria Gisborne of 2 June; another—a brief line to Hunt—on 30 June; the last—the scrap to Shelley—in July.

Yet her recollections of 1839 carry great conviction:

> During the whole of our stay at Lérici, an intense presentiment of coming evil brooded over my mind, and covered this beautiful place and genial summer with the shadow of coming misery . . . The beauty of the place seemed unearthly in its excess: the distance we were at from all signs of civilisation, the sea at our feet, its murmur or its roaring forever in our ears,—all these things led the mind to brood over strange thought, and, lifting it from everyday life, caused it to be familiar with the unreal.

The note to Hunt, sent with Shelley on their last expedition down to Livorno in the *Don Juan* on 1 July, when Mary was left behind on her terrace, confirms this sense of doom and helplessness most vividly. I read it again as the last light drained away behind the castle and faded beyond Portovénere:

> My dear Friend—I know that S. has some idea of persuading you to come here. I am too ill to write the reasonings only let me entreat you let no persuasions induce you to come, selfish feelings you may be sure do not dictate me—but it would be complete madness to come. I wish I could write more—I wish I were with you to assist you—I wish I could break my chains and leave this dungeon.

Mary had not seen Hunt for four years, since they left England. Yet she speaks directly and urgently to him—of "madness", of her "dungeon". It is clear that she was desperately unhappy at Casa Magni, and felt cut off from the normal world.

The house was primitive, uncomfortable, overcrowded: five adults—including Claire—and three children (two belonging to Jane Williams), sharing three main rooms and the servants' quarters. Yet Shelley had surrendered their apartment in Pisa, put all their furniture in store at Lérici and given himself up to boating and writing. He seemed no longer interested in building a proper private life together with Mary, but had gone back instead to his old dreams of a communal existence, lived from day to day and hand to mouth. He might even invite the Hunts—with their four children—to join them.

After four long years of trying to establish a real home, with real roots, in Italy, Shelley's improvident flight to Casa Magni must have nearly broken Mary's heart. With Pisa gone, what did their future hold? Would Shelley even remain with her, Mary must have wondered in those summer nights, gazing up at the rough white-washed ceiling of her room, hearing the sound of the waves beating and sighing on the beach: "The gales and squalls that hailed our first arrival surrounded the bay with foam; the howling wind swept round our exposed house, and the sea roared unremittingly, so that we even fancied ourselves on board ship."

Did Shelley intend to leave Mary and Percy with the Hunts and their children at Livorno? Did he plan some extended sailing expedition?—there was already talk with Williams of sailing across to Corsica. Maybe he would go further—to the Balearic islands, the coast of North Africa, Greece, the Levant? Or was his restlessness, his increasing elusiveness, evidence of some irrevocable shift of emotion—towards the attractive, guitar-playing Jane Williams? Or towards Claire once more, so tragically bereft of her child but also free now of Byron, dark and restless—"*la fille aux milles projets*"—and still only twenty-four? Or, worst of all possibilities perhaps, because least preventable and most absolute, was Shelley unconsciously tempting fate, challenging his destiny on the water, and deliberately flirting with death, with suicide?

I knew that within weeks of Shelley's drowning Mary would be bitterly reproaching herself for her doubts about Shelley, for her coldness at Casa Magni, for the way that *she* had held herself back from *him* In her poem "The Choice", not published until fifty years after it was written (probably at Monte Negro in 1823), she says that her heart accused her of not having requited Shelley's love:

> It speaks of cold neglect, averted eyes,
> That blindly crushed thy soul's fond sacrifice:
> My heart was all thine own,—but yet a shell
> Closed in its core, which seemed impenetrable,
> Till sharp-toothed misery tore the husk in twain,
> Which gaping lies, nor may unite again.
> Forgive me! . . .

A "shell closed in its core, which seemed impenetrable": a bitter self-accusation, full of uncomfortable sexual undertones, and bleakly miserable. Yet how much more so, had Mary known the contents of Shelley's last letter to the Gisbornes, written just three weeks before he died. Italy he finds "more and more delightful". Yet he misses old friends, and feels cut off from Mary:

> I only feel the want of those who can feel and understand me. Whether from proximity and the continuity of domestic intercourse, Mary does not. The necessity of concealing from her thoughts that would pain her, necessitates this perhaps. It is the curse of Tantalus, that a person possessing such excellent powers and so pure a mind as hers, should not excite the sympathy indispensable to their application to domestic life.

He adds that he finds Jane and Edward Williams "very pleasing" by contrast, "but words are not the instrument of our discourse".

Many of Shelley's friends in Italy—Leigh Hunt, Jane Williams, Trelawny to some degree—were later to accuse Mary of coldness towards Shelley, especially in those last months. No doubt there was much truth in this. Yet something else struck me as I read over that letter. It was written on 18 June. This was a mere *two days* after a near fatal miscarriage which Mary suffered at Casa Magni, in circumstances of pain and terror and humiliation. How could Shelley have been so utterly unfeeling to write such things at such a time?

Here was the final, sad example of how differently their lives together could be perceived by two people, even two as close as Shelley and Mary. Shelley seems to have regarded the miscarriage —consciously, at least—as a domestic mishap of no great importance. Indeed, in describing it he almost seems to put himself and his own reactions to the fore. Mary's situation, he writes:

> for some hours was alarming, and as she was totally destitute of medical assistance, I took the most decisive resolutions, by dint of making her sit in ice, I succeeded in checking the haemorrhage and the fainting fits, so that when the physician arrived all danger was over, and he had nothing to do but to applaud me for my boldness. She is now doing well, and the sea-baths will soon restore her.

But Mary was not soon restored. On the contrary, for her the whole episode was traumatic: she was in great pain for many days, and convinced that she was going to die. The lost child was one more link in the "leaden chain" of fatalities, and to her it proved just how

hopeless, how crazily unrealistic, was the household at Casa Magni.
As she later exclaimed: "No words can tell you how I hated our house
and the country around it . . . the beauty of the woods made me weep
and shudder."

Her own description of the miscarriage (also written to the
Gisbornes) is much more factual than Shelley's, and far more
devastating:

> On the 8th of June (I think it was) I was threatened with a
> miscarriage, and after a week of ill-health on Sunday 16th this
> took place at eight in the morning. I was so ill that for seven
> hours I lay nearly lifeless — kept from fainting by brandy, vinegar,
> eau de Cologne etc — at length ice was brought to our solitude — it
> came before the doctor so Claire and Jane were afraid of using it,
> but Shelley overruled them and by an unsparing application of it
> I was restored. They all thought and so did I at one time that I
> was about to die . . . My convalescence was slow . . .

In fact Mary did not leave her bedroom, or the terrace beyond her
door, for the next three weeks — indeed not until after Shelley had
departed on his last trip to Livorno. It was only the sinister
rumours of the sinking of the *Don Juan* that finally got her on her
feet again, for a terrible all-night carriage ride to Pisa and then on
to Livorno to find Trelawny. As much as seventeen years later she
recalled that day of her miscarriage in her journal as the first time
she had "had the opportunity to look at Death in the face".

Yet Shelley, of all men, could not be described as unfeeling. This
was the contradiction. Having followed his life through Italy,
nothing so convinced me as the extreme sensitivity of his feelings
for those around him. Above all, it was the emotional intensity of
his relations with Mary and Claire which had formed the centre
of his life. Moreover his poetry, and writing generally, drew directly
on this passionate intensity of feeling. Without it he could never
have been the extraordinarily productive poet that he was. It was
inconceivable to me that he should not have reacted most violently
to Mary's sufferings and blamed himself only too acutely for her
misery at Casa Magni. It was only a question of how he would
manage to express it.

It was clear that he could not do so to his friends, or in a normal
way to Mary herself. Another man would have packed up the
household and moved back to Pisa or Livorno, to some sort of
civilisation. But that was not the Shelley I had watched driving
himself to this edge of existence. Shelley would act, would express

himself through his imagination. Casa Magni in this sense became a dream place, a theatre of his mind: and this was one of the reasons that I myself entered it with such mixed feelings, even misgivings.

The story of Shelley's visions and nightmares during those last weeks is well known. They are the last part of the received myth of his life that any biographer has to confront in an attempt to explain without trying to reduce or deny. In my room at the *pensione*, full of those strangely empty cradles and the sound of the sea coming through the windows beyond my own balcony, I tried to consider them calmly, though not at first very objectively. I wrote my daily notes, I kept my own dream diary, I wandered about the little beach long after dark and sat late into the night on my cane chair drinking Chianti from a straw-cased flask. Several mornings, before dawn, I walked to Lérici along the cliff road and stood on the harbour quay looking back across the bay through borrowed binoculars, watching the sunlight spill down through the olive trees and light upon the empty terrace of Casa Magni. Often, as I raised those lenses, I wondered what figures I might glimpse.

Shelley's imagination erupted six days after Mary's miscarriage. In Edward Williams's characteristically laconic diary entry for 23 June: "Shelley sees spirits and alarms the whole house." Mary's sketchy journal makes no mention of this, nor do Shelley's own letters say a word. But for the fact that Shelley died just over a fortnight later and Mary went over those last days in great detail in her long letter of 15 August to Maria Gisborne—perhaps the most remarkable and moving letter she ever wrote—there would be no way of knowing just what those "spirits" were. However, Mary explains in great detail, and almost for the first time I felt I was looking into the secret, hidden life of Casa Magni; as if the glittering shapes had risen, momentarily, from the deep towards the surface.

This is what Mary wrote: "As I said Shelley was at first in perfect health but having over fatigued himself one day, and then the fright that my illness gave him caused a return of nervous sensations and visions as bad as in his worst times."

This itself immediately alerted me, for Mary had never previously written about Shelley's "visions"—yet she now implied that they had occurred often: perhaps throughout their time in Italy.

Her account continues:

I think it was the Saturday after my illness [in fact Sunday 23] while yet unable to walk I was confined to my bed—in the middle of the night I was awoken by hearing him scream and come rushing into my room; I was sure that he was asleep and tried to waken him by calling on him, but he continued to scream which inspired me with such a panic that I jumped out of bed and ran across the hall to Mrs Williams' room where I fell through weakness, though I was so frightened that I got up again immediately—she let me in and Williams went to S. who had been wakened by my getting out of bed—he said that he had not been asleep and that it was a vision that he saw that had frightened him.

Mary may have been terrified indeed; but typically she remained perfectly rational, for she observed logically: "as he declared that he had not screamed"—and Shelley had screamed enough to wake the whole house—"it was certainly a dream and no waking vision." The following morning she calmly questioned him about what he had seen, and gradually two "visions" emerged: the first concerning the Williamses (who were sleeping together in the room next to Shelley's), and the second concerning herself. Both visions reveal clearly enough Shelley's deep underlying anxiety, and his sense of guilt at the way he was treating Mary.

She records what he "saw" unflinchingly:

What frightened him was this—He dreamt that lying as he did in bed, Edward and Jane came into him, they were in the most horrible condition, their bodies lacerated—their bones starting through their skin, their faces pale yet stained with blood, they could hardly walk, but Edward was the weakest and Jane was supporting him—Edward said, Get up Shelley, the sea is flooding the house and it is all coming down. S. got up, he thought, and went to his window that looked on the terrace and the sea and thought he saw the sea rushing in.

The laceration of those bodies puzzled me for a moment, until I remembered the volcanic rock around the bay. Both Edward and Jane were, in Shelley's eyes, drowned people—and the house itself had become the boat, foundering beneath stormy seas. To a literal interpretation this might seem like a direct presentiment of their shipwreck. But I came to think of it much more as symbolic: Shelley's unconscious realisation that his dream of the "island house" at Casa Magni was doomed, that they would all be swept away by outside forces, that ordinary life would break in upon them, and that he must rouse himself and face reality before it was too late.

The second part of the vision moved to Mary's room: the room in which she had so nearly bled to death. To get there, Shelley would have to have opened his bedroom door, crossed the dining-room in front of the big terrace windows, and burst through the door opposite, altogether a distance of some thirty feet. So this was no ordinary nightmare; at the least it was sleep-walking—common in childhood (Shelley had sleep-walked regularly at Syon House, his prep school, where he was desperately unhappy) but rare in a normal adult. Mary's account continues, now breathless, the manuscript showing that she wrote with increasing speed, hardly bothering to punctuate:

Suddenly his vision changed & he saw the figure of himself strangling me, that had made him rush into my room, yet fearful of frightening me he dared not approach the bed, when my jumping up awoke him, or as he phrased it caused his vision to vanish. All this was frightful enough, & talking it over the next morning he told me that he had had many visions lately—he had seen the figure of himself which met him as he walked on the terrace & said to him—"How long do you mean to be content" —Not very terrific words & certainly not prophetic of what occurred. But Shelley had often seen these figures when ill . . .

It is interesting that Mary, still amazingly logical and objective, specifically denies that Shelley was somehow prophesying his own death. It would have been so easy, in her distraught state, to make an "anecdote" of it, to show her beloved poet foreseeing his last days on earth. (Trelawny hints at this continuously in the *Records*.) Again she says that Shelley often saw such visions "when ill". But what she leaves unsaid is how the murderous "strangling" image must have come to Shelley. For surely it is evident that Shelley's mind was running obsessively over those awful hours after her miscarriage. He would have remembered those unstaunchable flows of blood on the sheets; the tin hip-bath full of water and lumps of ice; lifting Mary into it, fainting, her head back in his arms; holding her down in the freezing water; the appalled faces of Jane and Claire—especially Claire—wondering if the shock would kill her . . . So he woke the house with his screams.

But Mary says nothing of all this. What could a biographer say? "He *would* have remembered . . ."; the fatal past subjunctive, which marks the passage from fact and evidence, to fiction and self-projection. I walked beside the little modern marina at Lérici and watched the Italians in their crisp white trousers and blue espadrilles, rolling sail canvas, emptying plastic buckets, calling to each other, preparing for the end of the season. Stacked on the quay were wooden boxes of silvery sprats. I returned the borrowed binoculars.

"You could see well? You found what you were looking for?"

"Not really. But they are beautiful glasses."

"Sometimes the weather is too hazy. It is a sort of sea-mist. But it is wonderful for sailing here in the bay. Outside it is rougher. Outside it can be dangerous."

"I have heard."

I thought for a long time about Shelley seeing the figure of himself. "How long do you mean to be content?" Did Mary know that these words came from Goethe's *Faust*? Claire must have known, for she was slowly translating the poem into English. Shelley had arranged this translation for Byron—who could not read it in the original—telling his Lordship that he had commissioned the work from a friend in Paris, and extracting a fee of sixty crowns. It was typical of the way Shelley quietly continued to look after Claire, and brought her—often secretly—into all his schemes up to the very end. But the "double", the fatal *doppelgänger*, also figured in his own poetry, and here I could begin to make a tentative connection between these disturbed dreams and involuntary visions and the deliberate, often learned, process of his creative work.

In Act One of *Prometheus Unbound* there is a haunting passage in which Shelley describes the "two worlds of life and death". Combining classical ideas of Hades, Platonic notions of the intermediary sphere of daemons and the Dantean vision of the Christian Inferno, he suggests the existence of a world of "doubles", of "shadows" which repeat or mirror everything on earth, "all forms that think and live". These are not so much ghosts of the dead as ghosts of the living. We all have our doubles in this second world (the idea is most familiar nowadays in science fiction rather than poetry). Only at the moment of death or destruction are the real and the double united, "and they part no more". Thus to meet your double, or to see it attacking someone, signified imminent peril: death perhaps, or the invasion of the real, normal world by the world of shadows. It was precisely this problem that Shelley seems to have been facing at Casa Magni. In modern psychological terms, he was refusing to acknowledge the realities of his situation, so fraught with suffering, and his unconscious mind was rebelling. Of course, that was crudely put: but it gave me a frame in which to consider the "deep truth" at the end of his life.

In the poem it is beautifully put. The person who sees his double is a magician, the part legendary and part historical Zoroaster. A Persian wise man, supposed to have lived about 1000 BC (but also identified with one of the Magi who visited the infant Christ), he founded the Parsee religion with its dualistic theology of Good and Evil (hence Nietzsche's and Richard Strauss's *Zarathustra*). Zoroastrianism had always fascinated Shelley and appears throughout his poetry from *Mont Blanc* (1816) onwards.

In *Prometheus Unbound* the figure of the Earth describes how Zoroaster met his own double and came to a knowledge of the shadow world:

> . . . Ere Babylon was dust,
> The Magus Zoroaster, my dead child,
> Met his own image walking in the garden.
> That apparition, sole of men, he saw.
> For know there are two worlds of life and death:
> One that which thou beholdest; but the other
> Is underneath the grave, where do inhabit
> The shadow of all forms that think and live
> Till death unite them and they part no more;
> Dreams and the light imaginings of men,
> And all that faith creates or love desires,
> Terrible, strange, sublime and beauteous shapes.

Several points now gave a new meaning to this passage. The Earth describes Zoroaster as her "dead child", a phrase which surely had personal meaning for Shelley. The description of the shadow world containing "terrible, strange, sublime and beauteous shapes" was exactly how everyone talked about San Terenzo. And I began to wonder if, at some level, during these last days Shelley was almost identifying with Zoroaster, seeing himself as a poet-magician, like Prospero in *The Tempest*, somehow attempting to exorcise all their pain and suffering—Mary's, Claire's, his own—by natural magic and his own poetry, at Casa Magni. Or was this a fantastic suggestion, more appropriate to fiction than to biography?

I never quite resolved that tension between a mythical and a strictly historical view of Shelley's last days; and I am still not sure if it can—or should—be done. The mystery of his inner nature remains until the end. Yet all this summed up for me the final act of his search for the new life, the final revolutionary attempt: it was not self-destruction in the mundane sense, but a magic self-transcendence at the level of the imagination. Shelley never gave up the Romantic struggle he had inherited, never finally gave up hope that the great forces of regeneration were on his side. As he wrote in bold black ink on the front inside cover of his last working note-book, bleached with sun and sea-salt: "The Spring rebels not against winter but it succeeds it—the dawn rebels not against night but disperses it."

For Mary, the survivor, Shelley's drowning on 8 July 1822 was also a transformation of their lives into the world of the imagination, but of a very different kind. Within two months she was writing of the extraordinary sea-change that had overtaken the memory of her husband. To Jane Williams—now her "best, dearest, only friend" —she wrote from Genoa on 22 September of the summer that they had shared together, lamenting her departure for London and looking back with bitter regret to the "paradise" she and Shelley had known at San Terenzo:

Ever since you quitted me I am overpowered by a melancholy and misery no human words can describe and no human mind can long support . . . You are gone, the last link of a golden chain leaving me bound by a leaden one alone. You the Eve of a fair Paradise—Now through Eden take your solitary way. I was never the Eve of any Paradise, but a human creature blessed by an elemental spirit's company & love—an angel who imprisoned in flesh could not adapt himself to his clay shrine & so has flown & left it—& I feel as poets have described those loved by superhuman creatures & then deserted by them—Impatient, despairing—& resting only on the moment when he will return to me.

It was impossible not to sympathise with Mary's overwhelming grief. That remorseless, gnawing grief, moreover, of the widow who feels that she has somehow failed to do justice to her spouse in life and must therefore make a cult of him in death. At the Keats-Shelley Museum in Rome I had noted the disturbing fact that even the handwriting of Mary's letters changed sharply after Shelley's death and became virtually identical with his own, as if it were the "automatic writing" of the spiritualists, guided by his disembodied spirit. But in biographical terms Mary's profound mourning and her transfigured memory of "the angel imprisoned in human flesh" was to prove a disaster. Within two generations it was to produce that apotheosis of the Victorian Shelley in Matthew Arnold's essay, describing the "beautiful ineffectual angel beating his luminous wings in vain". So the great aim of my biography finally came clear to me.

I left my balcony at San Terenzo early one crisp November morning, determined to bring that angel to earth, and to do justice to Shelley's lifelong dream of a better world here below. The bay was empty of boats, and a light pearly mist rose off the glittering water. The bus to La Spézia was almost empty.

FOUR

1976 : Dreams

1

Shelley's drowning was like a death in the family. I went back to London and wrote his *Life*, some eight hundred pages of it, virtually non-stop every day for fourteen months. I was possessed by it, and in the end it became something like an act of exorcism, and his death was a release. I can remember very little of that period, except that I slept on an ex-army camp-bed most of the day, and began writing at dusk, usually in deep depression. Once some friends took me to Torbay for the weekend at the beginning of February, and one midnight I took to the cold sea and swam out towards the end of the pier. I remember the sound of the waves running in from the dark and slapping the pier stanchions, a sound like death, and thinking if I could get round the end of the pier I could come back and finish the book. It was a long pull. My friends drove their car on to the edge of the promenade and switched on the headlights facing straight out to sea so as I finally rounded the black point I found a long glittering tunnel of yellow light, and swam back dazed and stupid, and stumbled up the beach. Six weeks later the book was done.

At the end of 1974 I went back to Paris, supposedly to write a novel. I had had enough of facts; I wanted some fiction, and some daylight. I bought my set of coloured notebooks at Gibert Jeune on the place Saint-Michel, found my hotel room and my morning café, enrolled at an Institute to teach English to French schoolchildren two evenings a week, and settled down to await inspiration. This time I would follow no one else's footsteps but my own. My bible was Hemingway's *A Moveable Feast*, with its wonderful clear wintry opening: "And then there was the bad weather." Only the weather was beautiful.

The Paris I now rediscovered was a calm, picturesque city; that is to say, a city of pictures. It celebrated the idea of the *flâneur*, the man who drifts round the streets, gazing at everything that meets his eye. From the mirror-life and postcards of the big cafés, and the huge displays of prints and posters along the quais and through the

Latin Quarter, I moved effortlessly into the great galleries of the Grand Palais, the Jeu de Paume, the Beaubourg and ever-changing exhibitions in the rue de Seine. After that it was the cinemas, thicker on the ground than in any other city in Europe, and not only in the tourist quarters. At the place Clichy, where the eighth arrondissement joins the eighteenth, you could stand at the top of the Metro steps and, turning through a circle, see the posters and *horaires* for no less than twelve different feature films at a single glance.

I became absorbed in this city of images. I learned my colloquial French in the *films noirs*; and in the evenings made up gangster plots, trials and detective stories for my schoolchildren to act out in colloquial English. The rumour ran among the ten-year-olds that Monsieur Holmes was directly descended from Le Grand Sherlock.

But, despite myself, the pictures led me inexorably back into the past again. An exhibition at the Kodak Gallery in the rue Jacob, and a grand retrospective at the Bibliothèque Nationale, just across the rue Vivienne from White's Hotel, taught me that Paris was the birthplace of the portrait photograph. At the very time that the Impressionist painters were starting on the long march to modern Abstraction, the early photographers were beginning to produce a wholly new kind of Realism. Men such as Adam-Salomon, Carjat, Nadar and Disderi—many of them originally minor painters and cartoonists—produced a visual revolution in the twenty or thirty years following the invention of the wet-collodion photographic plate in 1850.

Photography became a craze, and the Parisian critics began to debate fiercely whether this novelty was really a new art form. Some called it "sun sculpture", while others like Baudelaire described it as a morbid disease, a kind of narcissism, or else as a mere piece of technology, a "science of memory". I recognised the seeds of a debate that I had already met among biographers. Was their work an art form, like the novel or narrative history? Or was it merely an analytic technique, a social science of compilation and character analysis, skilfully combining personal data with social and political history? There were enthusiasts of photography who spoke of the "alchemical magic of the black box", its semi-occult powers to freeze time, to divine the inner secrets of personality, to resurrect life after death. The well-known anthropological tale of the Indian or African tribes who believed that the photograph stole away a bit of their souls appeared in the very earliest discussions of photography. And here too I recognised some of my own wilder speculations about twentieth-century biography, and its magical properties.

The first semi-professional photographers in Paris during the 1850s worked much more like biographers than painters. There were those who produced soft-focus landscapes like Adam-Salomon, or ludicrously staged allegorical and historical tableaux, or risqué nude "Academy" poses, or grand tourist set pieces like Maxime du Camp's studies of the Pyramids taken during the celebrated voyage to the Orient with Gustave Flaubert. But for the most part they were interested in "distinguished personalities": the politicians, actors, artists and musicians of the day. For the first time in history, they had produced an exact visual record of the entire generation of remarkable and creative men and women of the period. Indeed, they seemed to have altered something about the very nature of history and the past itself. I began to realise this when I discovered the astonishing archives of Felix Nadar, in the Bibliothèque Nationale.

Nadar himself really belongs to the history of publicity. His name is itself an invention, a publicity "logo". He was born in Lyon in 1820, two years before Shelley's death, and came to Paris under his real name, Felix Tournachon, to work as a hack journalist and cartoonist. He was a political Romantic, and in 1848 marched with an ill-fated French legion under the name Nadarsky to liberate Poland, where he spent some time in an internment camp. He came back penniless and slept rough in Paris until he was discovered by another journalist with an odd name, who knew the back streets well: Gérard de Nerval.

Nerval introduced him to a successful Republican newspaper editor of the day, Alphonse Karr, who left the following memorable reminiscence of the future photographer:

One day in 1848, Gérard de Nerval came into my office with a sort of giant under his arm: a figure with immensely long legs, exceedingly long arms, extensive torso, and on top of all this a head of shocking red hair surmounted by a pair of large, intelligent, darting eyes, full of wild lights . . . "This is Tournachon," announced Gérard, presenting him to me with a theatrical flourish. "He is full of ideas, but he's a bit simple. You must find him work on *Le Journal*; he has his mother to support and he adores her. He's full of mischief, but basically he has a heart of gold and is absolutely honest. The day before yesterday he was Polish; but he's just resigned his nationality . . .

Within five years of this eccentric introduction, Nadar had become the most famous cartoonist in the satirical magazines of Paris, and had created his *Pantheon Nadar*, an enormous lithograph containing three hundred of the best-known literary figures of the day, led by George Sand, Balzac and Victor Hugo. They paraded in a serpentine cortège of grotesque homunculi with enlarged heads and shrunken bodies—not unlike the modern literary cartoons of David Levine.

To complete this lithograph, and to keep it up to date for future editions, Nadar began keeping a special file of sketches and daguerreotypes of all his subjects. The invention of the wet-collodion plate, with its much faster exposure time, allowed him to work in his own apartment, using an upstairs room with skylights as his studio, and preparing and developing his own pictures with a small chemistry apparatus.

Many of his subjects first came to visit him informally, as lunch guests; and Nadar began to produce a particular kind of *portrait intime*, full-face, searchingly frank, without any of the conventional trappings or drapes or formal costumes. These soon became far more interesting to him than the highly mannered cartoons for which they were originally intended to serve merely as documentation.

The range of this earliest series of portraits, taken between 1854 and 1860, was a revelation to me. Here was the next literary and artistic generation after Shelley and Byron, suddenly brought back to life—their hairstyles, their wrinkles, their buttoned jackets, their scuffed shoes, their watch-chains or necklaces, their pince-nez, their frayed shirt-cuffs, the smile-lines round their eyes, the worry-lines over the brow, their mouths turned up with hope or turned down with disappointment—in a way that made them almost completely contemporary. Moreover, everyone seemed to be there: painters like Corot and Delacroix and Manet; musicians like Verdi and Offenbach and Rossini; writers like Dumas, Hugo, Flaubert, Saint-Beuve, Zola and Gautier. I was dazzled by it all, as I sat in the Cabinet d'Estampes of the Bibliothèque Nationale, or leafed through the files of Roger-Viollet, the famous *archives photographiques*, just outside the Institute at the bottom of the rue de Seine.

It struck me that from 1850 onwards a wholly new kind of biography might be possible—because of photography. For here was the beginning of the "modern age": these people would never be lost in "history". Here they were, alive, like us, flesh and blood, and touched by the marks of life.

Indeed, it was those marks, those imperfections, which made them so human: the thinning hair, the gnarled hands, the lined cheek, the unsightly wart or skin rash. The complexions of nineteenth-century city-dwellers were noticeably bad, a combination of crude sanitation, bad air and unbalanced diet—and this was particularly marked in the writers. These mundane things told a story that no diary or letter would mention. In fact the very process of aging itself—which is the existential equivalent of the biographer's chronological narrative—was one of the most touching facts of this vast gallery of portraits. Nadar chose as his first subjects friends of his own age (he was thirty-four when he began photography) or people who had already reached a certain eminence in life. The signs of effort, suffering, wear and tear were already upon them. The face of the poet and literary journalist Théophile Gautier was more deeply lined and tracked at forty-five than W. H. Auden's was at sixty-five. Henry Murger, the author of the carefree, sentimental *Scènes de la Vie de Bohème* upon which Puccini based his opera, was already bald and hollow-eyed at thirty, his face haunted by anxiety. Only a very few were caught in the first flush of successful youth: Gustave Doré at twenty-two, with a raffish check scarf knotted round his collar, or the teenage Sarah Bernhardt, with a thick mass of dark curls clustering over her naked shoulders.

But it was the ageing of Charles Baudelaire that most impressed me as a piece of biographic evidence. Nadar knew Baudelaire well from the early newspaper days and admired him greatly. They were almost exact contemporaries. Baudelaire was one of his first sitters, in 1854, three years before the *Fleurs du Mal* was published, after which Baudelaire became famous—or at least notorious. Nadar continued to photograph him regularly over the next eight years, and I found individual portraits taken in 1854, 1855, 1860 and 1862. The story they told of his physical and spiritual decline was unforgettable. In the first photograph, aged thirty-three, Baudelaire is still the young dandy-intellectual, buttoned into a thick topcoat with a high, loose, stylish collar. His face is pale and fresh, the features finely drawn, the long mouth with its beautifully shaped lips set in a determined line. The eyes look out at Paris like a young Lucien de Rubempré (the hero of Balzac's *Les Illusions Perdues*), challenging, hopeful, with a glitter of arrogance. The right hand is thrust into the front of the topcoat with a Napoleonic gesture. His hair, cut quite short in the then fashionable English manner, curls slightly over his ears and recedes in a rather elegant way at the temple. He wears a thick black silk cravat, tied in the loose floppy bow of the professional *littérateur*. He is proud of what he is, and what he will become. The future is full of hope.

Two years or so later the picture has already changed sharply.

Baudelaire lounges back in a decorated chair, with what looks like a cushion behind his head. His hair has been cropped very short, exactly as it can be seen in Gustave Courbet's picture *The Artist's Atelier* in the Louvre—where Baudelaire sits on a table at the extreme right, reading a folio book, while just behind his head can be seen the face of his mistress Jeanne Duval, partially painted out by Courbet for reasons of discretion. The left hand is raised to his cheek in a curiously effete gesture, while the facial skin has become heavier, and the corner of his mouth seems marked by a cluster of skin spots. The exposure of the photograph is much darker, which adds perhaps artificially to the atmosphere of brooding and unease—or disease. Nevertheless there is now something skull-like about the face, and the eyes seem dark and unfocused. One could almost say it was the photograph of an alcoholic or an opium addict.

By 1860 something much harder and older has entered the face. Yet it has gained in dignity too, and the self-conscious dandy has almost entirely disappeared. Baudelaire wears a coat with a velvet collar, like a prosperous banker, and the black silk cravat is more tightly and economically tied. The hair has been allowed to grow longer again, but it is now distinctly thin on top and grizzled at the sides, curling over the collar at the back in a dishevelled way that suggests neglect and the life of a lonely bachelor. The mouth has become thinner and harder, the cheeks have the downward lines of suffering and suggest inner struggle, perhaps deprivation. Above all the expression in the eyes has changed; they have become more watchful, distrusting, full of irony. It is the picture of someone who knows the world, and is embittered by it. It is someone who has experienced cruelty, yet retains a kind of nobility. This photograph corresponds to the period after the trial of the *Fleurs du Mal* for obscenity and immorality, when six poems were condemned, and Baudelaire's whole career in Paris was jeopardised. He was only thirty-nine, but he looks ten years older.

The final photograph in this moving sequence belongs to about 1862, shortly before Baudelaire embarked on his disastrous lecture-tour to Brussels in search of financial security. It is a portrait of extraordinary inner power, showing a man at bay, turning to face his fate head-on. His jacket is thrown open, his dark waistcoat unbuttoned almost to the waist, both hands thrust fiercely into his trouser pockets with the white frayed cuffs hanging negligently down—no longer dandyish, but disarrayed. The hair is unkempt, and the long mouth now turned down in a stubborn refusal to surrender. There is something pugilistic about the whole stance, like a man challenging a rival to knock him down if he dares. Once again, the eyes are remarkable, staring straight out at the onlooker with a glare of absolute defiance. Here indeed is the *poète maudit* of later legend, the writer cursed and rejected by society.

Nadar's camera records it all without rhetoric or exaggeration. The frame is as bare as a police photograph, no chair, no drape, no conventional book or pen; only a thin concentration of daylight on Baudelaire's broad, high forehead—over which, he will soon write, he heard "the beat of the wing of madness" passing. Ahead lie increasing illness, poverty, the loneliness of hotel rooms and the final onset of general paralysis, until even the powers of speech are denied him, and he is carried back to his old mother, and to Paris, to die at the hydrotherapy clinic of Dr Emile Duval—haunting name—in the rue du Dôme, near the Etoile. I stared at these photographs for hours, transfixed. The old sensations of being drawn into another life began to assail me almost with a sense of fatality.

I shook it off briskly. There was too much I wanted to do and see in Paris, my novel about a group of friends caught up in May '68 was taking shape, and besides I had met new friends whose interests were forward-looking and who were full of zest for the life around us. I got to know a group of young teachers at the Ecole Normale Supérieure who discussed modern art and politics with Gallic passion; a young woman journalist who wrote profiles of the new feminist generation now making its mark in the media and the professions; a circle of Irish businessmen, romantic republicans all, who had visions of the future of modern Europe—and the insularity of Britain, and "the Brits"—beyond anything I had previously considered. They too were inveterate travellers, but of a new kind, whirling about the big cities of France and Germany clinching deals and setting up new enterprises—cider, salmon, woollen garments, machine parts—with enormous energy and charm. They were the first people I had ever met who made commerce seem almost as exciting as literature.

Moreover, all of these people treated the fact of my being a writer as something perfectly honourable and rational; I no longer felt an aberration, as I so often did in England. On the contrary, they seemed to talk to me with a particular kind of confidence—about their work, about their families or their affairs, about their hopes for the future and, above all it seemed, about their childhood and adolescence. Indeed it was from them that I learned how much everyone needs to talk about their own past, the forces and experiences that shaped them; and how rarely this constant need is satisfied in the competitive, pressurised world, except in moments of emotional crisis.

I found a new role as a listener, often aided by the very fact of linguistic difference, which makes questions seem natural and subtly forces people to clarify exactly what they are saying, or what they really feel or mean. I slowly realised that what I was getting from these new friends was a kind of living, spontaneous biography: they were showing me the patterns in their own lives, and by the act of telling—and the confidential rhythm of question and answer—were re-enacting the very process that I had first known as a lonely act of the imagination. Perhaps this was partly the old magic of Paris; or perhaps it was that I myself was beginning, at long last it seemed, to grow up and have something like my own identity.

It taught me at least two things. First, that the past is not simply "out there", an objective history to be researched or forgotten, at will; but that it lives most vividly in all of us, deep inside, and needs constantly to be given expression and interpretation. And second, that the lives of great artists and poets and writers are not, after all, so extraordinary by comparison with everyone else. Once known in any detail and any scope, every life is something extraordinary, full of particular drama and tension and surprise, often containing unimagined degrees of suffering or heroism, and invariably touching extreme moments of triumph and despair, though frequently unexpressed. The difference lies in the extent to which one is eventually recorded, and the other is eventually forgotten.

Hence the constant paradox of biography as a literary form: that everyone would like to be fully understood and appreciated, but few people want their privacy invaded, even by an imagined posterity. Sometimes I would think that everybody should have their official biographer, just as they should have their own doctor, or accountant, or priest; but this of course was a delusion of grandeur, confusing the writer with the Recording Angel. I was also reminded of Stevenson's wry observation that anyone who married had "domesticated" the Recording Angel; so the writer should not be confused with a spouse, either.

Nothing I did in Paris, and nobody I met, could drive away the images of Nadar's photographs however. The generation that reached their maturity in the 1850s—the Baudelairian decade, one might say—haunted me with their interesting, careworn, complicated faces. I wondered if, without being drawn in too far, I might write a biographical group portrait, using Nadar and his camera as the *point d'appui*, an innocent eye observing the progress of his friends. This idea of finding a central but relatively neutral or unfamiliar figure to tell the story of a famous group or circle has often struck me since as a promising new way for biography to proceed. It is something like the "central consciousness" that Henry James suggested as a way of narrating and combining the many viewpoints in a long novel. A figure like Robert Southey could provide this for the first generation of the English Romantics; or Ford Madox Ford for the great Edwardian novelists; or Cyril Connolly for the Modernists of the 1930s and '40s. The difficulty is that the "neutral" figure usually becomes of absorbing interest in his or her own right.

Certainly this was the case with Nadar, who besides being a cartoonist and photographer turned out to have had an almost fabulous career in Second Empire Paris. He became successively involved with the Impressionist painters, the great newspaper and magazine editors of the day, the scientists and inventor-eccentrics who pioneered aeronautics, the early balloonists like the Godard brothers, and the men who organised the first airmail post during the Siege of Paris using an early form of microfilm.

One of his greatest friends was the science-fiction writer Jules Verne, who finally put him into a novel, *De la Terre à la Lune* (1865), as one of the three astronauts who were to "carry into outer-space all the resources of art, science, and industry". Verne brilliantly changed Nadar's name, by inspired anagram, into "Michel Ardan": a Phaeton with replaceable wings, as he put it, and a boyish enthusiast who had "not yet outgrown the Age of Superlatives". The chances of keeping such an effervescent personality in the margins of a group biography came to look increasingly unlikely.

Moreover, there was something in the buoyant optimism of Nadar's temperament, the endlessly cheery egoism, the very naivety which so appealed to Verne, which curiously denied the reflective, questioning mood I found in his photographs, and which seemed to me essential to the 1850s. This was not really an age of superlatives at all, but one poised between the collapse of a religious culture and the rise of a scientific or materialist one: an age of doubt and scepticism which shadowed the more obvious achievements of capitalism, industry, exploration and empire. It was this shadowy world, half dying, half waiting to be born, that fascinated me. I remembered what Nadar's friend Gérard de Nerval had said of the photographer: he's full of ideas, but a bit simple.

Nadar comfortably outlived all his famous contemporaries. In 1900, when he was eighty, a spry old man still very upright, with a mane of silver hair, a huge retrospective exhibition of his photos was held in Paris. To coincide with this, he published some early memoirs, much of them written twenty or thirty years previously, under the title: *Quand j'étais photographe*. This is a remarkable little volume—surprisingly it has never been translated—full of mischievous anecdotes about his many sitters, particularly the vanity of ancient generals and politicians, posing before the camera. He observes typically that when a husband and wife came to collect family photographs the husband invariably looked at those of himself first; while the wife always asked to see those of her husband. It was the definition, he said mockingly, of a good French bourgeois marriage. Poets, on the other hand, were frightened of their own photographs, and only liked to gaze on those of their mistresses or actress-flames. As for actresses themselves, they were the easiest and least self-conscious of sitters, for they already knew—from hours of careful study—exactly the weaknesses and strengths of their features. Actresses had the least illusions of all.

There was one sentence in this gossipy memoir of Nadar's that took me by surprise. In fact, it took my breath away. In talking about Baudelaire and Gautier, Nadar casually mentioned how different their noble, expressive faces looked by comparison with the poor, battered visage of their friend and fellow-poet Gérard de Nerval. Poor Gérard's face, said Nadar, was marked equally by the memory of lunatic asylums and the foreboding of his tragic death. "Within a few days of this photograph, the only one that was ever taken of our beloved friend, he had committed suicide in that accursed backstreet down by the Seine, the rue de la Vieille Lanterne." The man who had introduced Nadar to journalism, and the first steps of his brilliant Parisian career, had himself died in poverty and obscurity by his own hand.

This discovery went through me like an electric pulse, and in a moment had rearranged all the diverse elements of the 1850s into the story I had unconsciously been looking for. It was based on a paradox, or a series of contradictions: between success and failure, between material and spiritual values, between recognition and obscurity, between the social and the solitary, between bourgeois and bohemian, between reality and dreams. But above all, Nerval's death seemed to hint at the ultimate historical fate of the Romantic spirit in Europe, that chimera I had been half-consciously pursuing for so long.

The evening I read Nadar's description, I left the Bibliothèque Nationale early and hurried through the lamplit colonnades of the Palais-Royal, across the place Royal and the dark gulf of the place du Louvre. It was a January evening, a cold wind blowing, with no tourists along the Seine. I ran across the pont des Arts (not yet removed) into the maze of little backstreets behind the quai des Grands Augustins to a second-hand bookshop I knew. The Mandragore, lit by Chinese lanterns, plastered with astrological posters, reeking of incense, carried a good stock of nineteenth-century texts traded in by students from the Sorbonne for cult-books, ecology pamphlets, and *bandes dessinées*. Here I bought my first well-thumbed *livre de poche* of Nerval, with marks of coffee-cups on the cover. For the first time—in that pungent half-light, with the rain suddenly beating on the windows—I read the poem of his life, "El Desdichado" ("The Disinherited"), which begins:

> *Je suis le Ténébreux,—le Veuf—L'Inconsolé,*
> *Le Prince d'Aquitaine à la Tour abolie:*
> *Ma seule Etoile est morte—et mon luth constellé*
> *Porte le Soleil noir de la Mélancolie.*

The words were simple and direct, as of someone introducing himself with an apologetic smile. Yet the images were strange, a kind of medieval heraldry, proud and desperate, like John Keats's knight—"alone and palely loitering". Nerval seemed to be introducing himself like a Prince out of a forgotten fairy-tale or Arthurian legend: behind him stands a shattered ancestral Tower, above him a burnt-out Star, and at his side a medieval lute emblazoned with a Black Sun. What did all these symbols mean? They carried overtones of destruction and loss; but they also had a luminous beauty about them, something other-worldly and gracious. It was difficult to connect them with the shrewd journalist who had marched into Alphonse Karr's newspaper offices with Nadar "under his arm".

Moreover, though the words appeared simple they were in fact extraordinarily difficult to translate into English prose with any real accuracy:

I am the man of shadows—the man in the shadows—the man of darkness—the man lost in the dark—the shadowy man you cannot see. I am the Widower; I am the Unconsoled, the disconsolate, the grief-stricken man. I am the Prince of Aquitaine (that region of south-west France between Bordeaux and Toulouse, through which the rivers Garonne and Dordogne run). I am the Prince with the abolished, shattered, stricken, or blasted Tower; or the Prince standing by that Tower. My only

Star is dead, burnt-out, extinguished—the noun is feminine. And my star-studded lute, or my lute marked with the constellations, or the zodiac signs; my lute carries, or is emblazoned with, the Black Sun of Melancholy or Melancholia.

Puzzling over these four mysterious lines in the Mandragore, I remembered how T. S. Eliot had used one of them in the famous last passage of *The Waste Land*; and he had not dared to translate:

> Shall I at least set my lands in order?
> London Bridge is falling down falling down falling down . . .
> *Le Prince d'Aquitaine à la tour abolie*
> These fragments I have shored against my ruins

I held a fragment in my hand. The rain poured steadily now. Somewhere between the doorway of the Mandragore and the brightly lit publicity photos of the cinema Saint-André-des-Arts round the corner I had abandoned my novel.

2

Proust called Nerval one of the three or four most important French writers of the nineteenth century. Yet to me, and I suspected to most other English readers, he was virtually unknown—certainly of a different order of magnitude to contemporaries like Baudelaire, Balzac, Dumas or Gautier. Almost the only thing that everyone knew about him was the famous, and perhaps apocryphal, story of how he used to go for walks in the parks of Paris taking a live lobster with him on a leash. This crazy anecdote was meant to sum up his reputation as a charming but lunatic poet; though in fact it sounds more like the thing one of the dandy-poseurs of the *bohème doré* of the 1830s would have done, in order to make a name for himself and *épater les bourgeois*, or shock the middle-classes, as was the fashion. It took me some time to track down the real source of this story, and when I did it gained an altogether different significance.

It was told by Nerval's oldest friend, Théophile Gautier, who had known him since early schooldays at the Lycée Charlemagne where they were pupils together. They had shared a theatre column in the daily newspaper *La Presse* during the 1830s and '40s, signing it "G.G." for "Gautier et Gérard"; and Gautier had often put

Nerval up at his apartment in Paris, or visited him in clinics during the bad times of his madness. Gautier was in fact Nerval's closest professional colleague, as well as being something like a brother to him; it was Gautier who was called down to the public mortuary to identify Nerval's body on the morning of his suicide. "My collaborator," Gautier called him, "and the faithful companion of my brightest—and above all my darkest—days." Gautier understood Nerval as well as anyone.

Gautier told the lobster story, not as an example of Nerval's exhibitionism or fashionable flamboyance—it soon became clear that Nerval was the most retiring and secretive of men—but as an example of his friend's obsession with symbols, and the extraordinary power of his inner imaginative life. The whole point, said Gautier, was that Nerval thought it was a perfectly reasonable thing to do. "He could not conceive why the doctors should be concerned if he happened to choose to walk in the gardens of the Palais-Royal leading a live lobster along on the end of a blue silk ribbon." When questioned about it, Nerval would answer quite rationally, dismissing all the ridiculous animals that smart Parisians chose for pets, and producing his own beautifully poetic reasons for preferring his lobster, as a symbol of true friendship:

Why should a lobster be any more ridiculous than a dog? Or a cat, or a gazelle, or a lion, or any other animal that one chooses to take for a walk? I have a liking for lobsters. They are peaceful, serious creatures. They know the secrets of the sea, they don't bark, and they don't gobble up your *monadic* privacy like dogs do. And Goethe had an aversion to dogs, and *he* wasn't mad!

Strange as Gautier's account is, and funny too, it does seem to be confirmed by Nerval's letters. He was fascinated by curious animals, especially exotic birds, insects and fish, and frequently used them symbolically in his work. He had great respect for the mythology of such ancient civilisations as the Egyptian, which assigned symbolic roles to creatures like the scarab beetle and the cat. He was very fond of parrots, and they appear as symbols of wisdom and memory in his stories. Often, on his wanderings through Paris, he would leave messages for his friends in the form of animals; and in his last desperate years I found that several surprised writers had come home to find lobsters or parrots waiting with a startled concierge, "a present from Monsieur Gérard de Nerval". All this seemed to promise a fine vein of tragi-comedy in Nerval's story.

But there was a further, and possibly darker consideration. Gautier was a brilliant journalist, and unlike his friend made an immensely successful career as a literary columnist, first in *La Presse* and later in the official paper *Le Moniteur*. He campaigned on behalf of the poets and painters he admired, continually attacking the values of his staid, bourgeois readership, and eventually becoming the spokesman for the *L'art pour l'art* movement of "purist" principles and the anti-utilitarian values. "Everything that is beautiful is useless," he would write. He stood, in effect, in polar opposition to a figure like Nadar, who so eagerly embraced all the progressive materialism and technology of the age.

So for Gautier, a writer like Nerval provided wonderful ammunition in the critical war against the bourgeois, utilitarian, rational and progressive world. Nerval was, in effect, a source of marvellous *copy*, of journalistic anecdote. His strange actions, his picturesque travels, his weird fantasies made him almost the summation of the now familiar Romantic poet who defied every social convention. Nerval was someone whom Gautier could *use*: the ideal poet-victim for the age. He was also someone that Gautier, and other writers, might exploit to fulfil their own fantasies of the artistic life. From their position of success they could, consciously or unconsciously, exploit his failure. He was a gift, a martyr, a sacrifice to the cause: the lobster poet, lost in the deep.

From the outset, therefore, I was aware of the possible complications of Nerval's story, and the distortions and deliberate myth-making I might have to encounter from his friends. But what I never realised—and had I suspected it for a moment I would have turned back—was the labyrinth that Nerval himself made of his life; a maze of fantasy and memory, from which a biographer might never escape. He too might be lost in a deep of his own making, and unlike the lobster might not be equipped with claws and carapace to survive.

I remember mentioning the lobster story to my friend Françoise, now herself a journalist, as we sat in her studio flat in the rue de Sévigné, just across from the rue Saint-Antoine where Nerval and Gautier went to school. Outside there was music from a small Turkish restaurant, and the bark of small dogs being taken on their evening promenade towards the quai. The buildings in this *quartier* were nearly all pre-Revolutionary, some even seventeenth-century, and the studio ceiling had bare old beams, as in an English country pub. The alcoves were stuffed with books mounted on bricks and planks, and lit with home-made lamps shrouded in blue and green shot-silk shades. From the little kitchen next door came the smell of coffee, lying freshly ground in its white paper filter, while the saucepan simmered on the gas.

"*Tiens, le homard!*" she exclaimed. "*Pas très joli, un peu maléfique même.*"

Why an evil influence? I asked, expecting some culinary joke.

"*Tu ne connais pas le Tarot, alors,*" Françoise replied with a finger raised and one of her provoking grins.

The Tarot is a set of medieval playing cards, which are used to predict the future, or, more subtly, to analyse the state of your love-life or career. Much in fashion just then in Paris, the Tarot had rather the same status as the astrology columns in English newspapers and magazines, that gave you your "star reading".

"*C'est un peu comme le météo—c'est à dire, pas une science exacte.*" She went over to one of the marine-lit alcoves and pulled out a small leather-bound book. "*C'est numéro dix-huit dans L'Arcane Major, je crois.*"

Number 18 was a card called The Moon. She handed over the book, and told me to read slowly, while she went to make the coffee. This is what I copied into my notebook:

Number 18, La Lune, the Card of the Moon and the Unconscious, the Irrational, the Feminine Mysteries, the Imagination. At the foot of this card lies a deep, mysterious pool, out of which a Crayfish or Lobster is attempting to crawl on to the dry land. A path leads up from the pool and twists like a ribbon towards the horizon. The path is guarded by two animals—in some Tarot packs these are both Dogs, in others they are a Dog and a Wolf. Further in the distance can be seen a pair of forbidding Towers, astride the path, which form a gateway to the mysterious regions beyond. Above, a full Moon hangs in the night sky. Drops of moisture like diamonds float in the air, as if being slowly drawn up from the Pool by the power of the Moon. The Lobster raises its claws from the water, and the Dog and Wolf lift their heads and bay at the Moon.

"*C'est lugubre, n'est-ce pas, ton jardin d'homard?*" called Françoise from the kitchen. I flicked on through the book, glancing at various commentaries on the symbolism and folklore of the cards. Number 18 had several longish entries, many of them concentrating on the Moon, its links with water and tides and fertility, and the ancient cults of Moon goddesses, Diana the Huntress, and the Egyptian divinity Isis associated with annual floodings of the Nile Valley. For the moment, none of this meant very much to me. Then I came across a footnote, printed under the heading, "Quest literature and the *rite de passage*, the 18th stage". In this commentary, the poet's lobster reappeared as a key image in the interpretation, and I was gripped by its weird connection with what I had already learned from Gautier and Nadar about Nerval's last years in Paris before his suicide. It also seemed oddly like a warning. The footnote was in slightly archaic prose, as if taken from an earlier text:

The 18th card illustrates the dark realm of Hecate, the Night Hag, the Muse in her menacing Aspect. At the base of the picture is a Lobster or Crab (seventh sign of the Zodiac), an emblem of the primitive and devouring forces of the Spirit or Unconscious which have to be overcome. In the middle-distance are the Wolf and the Dog, guides to the Land of the Dead, who are also unstable and not to be trusted. Behind them are the stone pillars of Hades, the portals of the dark Womb, gateway both of Life and Death, the Underworld, the region of Sleep and Dream. Reigning over all is the great Moon, Queen of the Night, who draws the souls of the living towards her with the irresistible powers of enchantment or death.

The Hero is at the critical stage in his journey, where his existence hangs suspended in the balance. If he allows himself to be entranced by the glamour of the Moon, his quest is at an end. His life will be drained from him, until he is only a hollow shell. If, on the other hand, the Hero forces himself onwards, not straying from the narrow path, nor deceived by the spells and illusions all around him, he will eventually win through the dark land and the dismal cavern, and emerge into the light of new day.

This section of the commentary ended with a brisk valediction: "the negative meaning of the 18th card gives a warning against the dangers of the uncontrolled imagination, when fantasy is indulged in as a means of escape from the world of sanity and reality."

I sat there for a long time, seeing the figure of Nerval and his lobster coming slowly towards me down the neat, geometrical *gravillon* pathways of the Palais-Royal. "*Moi, je n'aime point les homards*," said Françoise standing beside me. "*Ils ont quelque chose de monstrueux. Ils ont habités trop longtemps au-dessous de la mer*." But I was not to be warned.

That spring I left my hotel and my teaching classes, and moved into a little attic room, papered with asphodels, in the ninth arrondissement not far from the boulevard du faubourg Montmartre and the marché Cadet. It was a night-patrol from Cadet who had arrested Nerval in the street, on the first recorded outbreak of his insanity. So I felt I was on the spot. Gautier's house in the rue de Navarin, now carrying a plaque as the first headquarters of the Société des Gens des Lettres, was also four minutes away, off the rue des Martyrs. This was one of the axis streets of bohemia, rising gently from Notre Dame de Lorette (who gave her name to the "lorettes", or easy girls of the 1840s) to Pigalle, which became the artistic café-quarter of the 1890s, but is now lost to the neon. I embarked on an intensive period of research at the Bibliothèque Nationale, walking to and fro every day by the rue Cadet or the rue des Martyrs. My aim was simply to establish the outlines of Nerval's career, and to begin with everything went well. In the evenings I bought fruit and vegetables at the marché Cadet, cold meat from the *charcuterie* at the corner of the rue Lamartine and drank cold beer in the rue Condorcet. In the library I imagined Nerval's world; on the streets I studied it. Slowly the actors assembled.

Nerval had been born on 22 May 1808 at No 96 rue Saint-Martin, just north of the place du Châtelet, and about five hundred metres from where he committed suicide in 1855. His father, Etienne Labrunie, was a military doctor whose family came from Aquitaine. His mother, Marguerite Laurent, was the daughter of a well-to-do Paris shopkeeper whose family came from the Valois, the region of lakes and forests around Chantilly in the Ile de France. Gérard was their only child. Etienne and Marguerite were much in love, and when in April 1809 Dr Labrunie was posted to the military hospital at Hanover (it was the beginning of Napoleon's thrust to the East) Marguerite decided to accompany him on service with the Grande Armée. Gérard, not quite two years old, was left with the family of Marguerite's uncle, Antoine Boucher, in the Valois at the tiny village of Mortefontaine.

Here he grew up until the age of six, looked after by various cousins and aunts, running wild in the countryside, and having long letters from his mother in Germany read to him, describing her travels and adventures. Nerval recalled at the end of his life:

The letters that my mother wrote from the shores of the Baltic, and the banks of the Danube and the Spree were read over to me so many times! The feeling for the marvellous and my taste for distant travels, were doubtless the result of these earliest impressions, together with this long period I spent in the remote countryside in the depth of the woods. Often given into the care

217

of servant-girls and peasant folk, my mind was nourished on bizarre beliefs, local legends and traditional songs. In all this there was the stuff of which poets are made; but I am only a dreamer in prose.

During the course of Napoleon's Russian campaign, Dr Labrunie was promoted to direct the big military hospital at Gross-Glogau in what is now Poland. But his wife Marguerite caught a fever while crossing a bridge piled with bodies, and died tragically in 1812, at the age of twenty-five. She was buried in the Catholic cemetery of Glogau. Her son had never been old enough to remember her face. In some ways neither Dr Labrunie nor Gérard ever recovered from this blow. Caught up in the disastrous retreat, Dr Labrunie lost all his personal effects—including the pictures of his wife, and her jewellery—during the terrible crossing of the Beresina, when thousands of French troops drowned in the icy waters. In 1814 he returned to France, and rode to Mortefontaine to collect his little son. He was by now a hardened campaign officer, aged forty-three, and limped from the effect of two leg wounds.

Nerval recalled that traumatic reunion:

I was seven years old, and playing carelessly at my uncle's door, when three officers appeared in front of the house. The blackened gold of their uniforms barely gleamed beneath their military greatcoats. The first one hugged me to him with such emotion, that I cried out: "Father . . . you are hurting me!" All three were returning from the siege of Strasbourg. The oldest, saved from the waters of the frozen Beresina, took me with him to learn what were called my duties.

These two autobiographical passages, describing the earliest memories of his mother, his father and the magic childhood in the Valois, show the simplicity of Nerval's prose at its best. Everything is presented with quiet, factual observations, yet every detail carries a subtle weight of implied meaning. Four bitter years of warfare and final, crushing defeat of a whole Imperial dream is indicated by that "*or noirci de leurs uniformes*". While the rising and falling rhythm of the short descriptive phrases, and the tolling of the distant place-names—Baltic, Danube, Spree, Strasbourg, Beresina—convey an irresistible elegiac mood. The mixture of love and pain caused by his father's return—the embrace that causes hurt—became a permanent element in Nerval's feelings as an only child. So too does the unspoken question: why had Marguerite died—and who was to blame?

After 1815 Dr Labrunie set up a gynaecological practice in Paris. He never remarried, but Nerval implies that a number of women paid court to the doctor; the child was regularly bought presents, and often spoilt by maidservants and the Laurent relations. Discipline was benevolent but strict: Labrunie's batman was put in charge of the young boy, and often took Gérard for long walks before dawn over the hills of Montmartre and the surrounding Parisian countryside, still at that date a place of farms, vineyards and flocks of sheep. Ever after, Nerval was addicted to little excursions, or *promenades*, around Paris, and had an almost religious reverence for observing the sunrise. A sleepless night followed by the heady, slightly unreal sensation of a new dawn, became a constant theme in his "prose dreams".

In the evenings, at sunset, his father would sometimes play the guitar, singing Italian love-songs and laments, and crying over his lost wife. Nerval always recalled one song that began, "*Mamma mia, medicate . . .*", that is, "Oh my mother, heal this wound of mine, for pity's sake . . ." For the little boy, the lost mother became a sacred figure. For the widowed father, Gérard with his blond hair, grey eyes and angelic good looks served as a constant reminder of lost love. Together father and son made a sort of romantic cult of their bereavement.

Gérard was sent to the Lycée Charlemagne, where he became a model pupil, especially gifted in languages. According to his own account, he studied Italian, Greek, Latin, German, Arabic and Persian. He loved the poetic mythology of Ovid's *Metamorphoses*, and the Teutonic legends. Characteristically, he developed the most beautiful rounded handwriting—quite unlike the loose, racy script of many of his literary contemporaries—"elaborated and elegant like the most famous manuscripts of Iran". All the letters and holograph poems that I saw retain this physical clarity, this sense of "best behaviour", even in the later and extreme phases of his apparent madness. Dr Labrunie regarded him as a brilliant and gifted child and was immensely proud of him. He planned for him an ambitious professional career: either as a diplomat, with his love of languages and foreign places; or, with his apparently quiet and analytical approach to life, following in his father's footsteps as a doctor.

In the summer holidays Nerval was still sent back to Uncle Antoine Boucher's house at Mortefontaine, where he was teased and admired as "le petit Parisien", so modest and so clever. He recalls how he became romantically attached to a number of pretty country girls there, Héloïse, Sylvie, Fanchette (he gives them many names). His uncle, besides owning a parrot and a collection of antiquities, also had a remarkable library of archaeological and other specialist books, where he was allowed to browse, pursuing his taste for mythology and legends. The old man would discuss religion, in the eighteenth-century style of Voltaire and Rousseau, pouring scorn on the superficialities of conventional Christianity. Nerval later described the unsettling effect of this in his Preface to *Les Illuminés* (1850), a collection of biographical essays on seventeenth-century illuminati; and in *Aurélia*, the autobiography of his madness. His uncle was an amateur archaeologist, and collector of coins and fragments which he used to dig up in an allotment he owned just outside Mortefontaine, known as the "clos de Nerval".

The exact site of this clos or paddock is no longer certain, but one warm May afternoon, I caught a country bus for the first time into the land of the Valois, and found myself in another world of forests, lakes and blossoming hedgerows. I walked along the little winding road from Mortefontaine to the village of Loisy, following the stream of the Thène, and an old man putting up bean sticks leaned on his spade and pointed with his thumb to the wood running to the west; "*Il y en a des clos partout ici, voyez-vous. Mais c'est ça, le bois de Nerval. On y chasse les lapins, le matin.*"

Describing his uncle's hobby and its effect on his religious education, Nerval wrote reflectively:

The country where I was brought up was full of strange legends and bizarre superstitions. One of my uncles, who had the greatest influence on my early education, had taken up the hobby of studying Roman and Celtic antiquities. He sometimes found in his paddock, or round about, the images and medallions of gods and Roman emperors, which his learned admiration led me to venerate, while his books taught me their history. A particular Mars in golden bronze, a Pallas Athene or armed Venus, a Neptune and an Amphitryon carved above the village pump . . . were the household gods and guardians of this remote place. I admit they then inspired more reverence in me than the poor Christian images in the church, and the two shapeless statues of saints standing in the doorway . . . Confused in the midst of these many different symbols, I asked my uncle one day who God really was. "God," he told me, "is the sun."

It was the answer, said Nerval, of an honest countryman who had always lived as a Christian, but who had passed through the upheaval of the French Revolution. He himself always felt the heir to this confusion of beliefs, mixing the scepticism of the Enlightenment with the imaginative faith of Romanticism: the renewed fascination with classical mythology, magic beliefs, pantheism and the rich poetry of local superstitions.

I found the two "shapeless saints" still standing at the doorway of the little Romanesque church in Mortefontaine. One appears to be a statue of the Virgin, her face worn away into a curiously haunting smile made by a trick of the stone; she is nursing the remnants of a child. The other is probably St Denis, his head wearing his bishop's mitre, which he holds in the grotesque symbolism of Christian martyrdom detached in front of him, like a sacrificial fruit.

Gautier tells another famous story which bears on this weird polytheism of Nerval's. At a literary dinner-party in Victor Hugo's apartments in the place des Vosges, Nerval was leaning on the mantelpiece "whirling together the Heavens and Hells of several quite different religions with studious impartiality". One of the other guests remarked somewhat cuttingly that it was perfectly obvious that Nerval didn't believe in any religion at all.

"Gérard surveyed his interlocutor with an expression of immense scorn, and transfixed him with those glittering grey eyes of his, dancing with their strange scintillations. 'No religion at all? *I* have no religion?—but I have seventeen religions—seventeen at least.'"

It was a good story, and allowed Gautier to remark sententiously that the "fine Pantheon of Gérard's intellect eventually became a Pandemonium."

When Gautier first met Nerval at the Lycée Charlemagne he was already a byword among his fellow-pupils for his immense reading, golden good looks, modest demeanour and dizzy poetical ambitions. He was one of those sixth-form heroes, so beloved of later Victorian fiction, of whom parents and masters are overbearingly proud, and of whom great things are too confidently expected. Gautier was two years younger than Nerval, and though his own ambition was to be a painter—he soon became an unofficial student at the Rioult *atelier*, supported by doting parents—he hero-worshipped his fellow-pupil and saw him as a leader of the new Romantic generation who were to follow in Victor Hugo's footsteps. Indeed, at the age of eighteen, a year before he left the Lycée, Nerval published two small pamphlets of poetry, one patriotic—the *Elégies Nationales* —the other satirical, *L'Académie ou les membres introuvables* (1826).

But Nerval's greatest triumph drew on his German reading and his adolescent dreams of the tragic and romantic land beyond the Rhine. Shutting himself up in his room above the surgery in the rue Saint-Martin, he worked steadily through the winter of 1827 to produce a superb verse translation of Goethe's *Faust* (Part I). This was taken on by the commercial and literary publisher Renduel, and issued in 1828, bringing Nerval great critical acclaim, personal invitations to the soirées of ,Victor Hugo and Sainte-Beuve and later a request from Berlioz to use the translation for the libretto of his *Faust* opera. The edition was shown to the aging Goethe himself, who said that he "had never been so well understood". Nerval later completed *Faust* (Part II), and the book ran to a second edition; to this day it is still the text published by Garnier-Flammarion.

Nerval at twenty thus had a reputation as a scholar-poet and a prodigy; he was courted by newspaper editors; received the coveted permission to use and borrow books from the Bibliothèque Royale (now Nationale); sought after by tough professional writers like Alexandre Dumas in search of bright young theatrical collaborators; and even praised and supported by leading critics like Jules Janin.

Dr Labrunie was delighted with his offspring, seeing *Faust* as his son's passport to a professional career in newspapers, diplomacy or perhaps, still, as a fashionable young doctor. But for Nerval it was the golden key to a purely literary future—in poetry, literary translation and above all in the most glamorous of romantic forms, the popular theatre. Only two events shadowed his life at this moment: the death in 1826 of tante Eugénie, aged twenty-five, his mother's youngest sister and perhaps his closest woman friend; and two years later, in 1828, the death of grandmère Boucher, a beloved figure from the Mortefontaine summers of his childhood and adolescence.

Nerval bitterly missed these two maternal presences, and he wrote one of his best early poems about the latter, "La Grandmère", describing how he was unable to weep at her funeral—"I wandered through the house, astonished rather than griefstruck"—but later wept in secret when all else seemed to have forgotten her, so that as the months and years went by, "like a name carved in the bark of a tree, her memory sank in deeper!" Again, it is a typical Nervalian image, deceptive in its simplicity. But one implication seems to be that, while the names of the dead are carved on gravestones and gradually wear away, the names of loved ones are also carved in living materials and slowly bite deeper into our lives. *Mamma mia, medicate . . .*

3

It is from this time that I became aware of an increasing struggle within Nerval's own personality, which first expressed itself as a clash with his father over the question of his career. To begin with this did not seem particularly unusual. After the success of *Faust* Nerval began to lead a double life, divided as it were between bourgeois and bohemian personae, the model pupil and the eccentric young poet. This was a frequent dilemma for young nineteenth-century writers, who would normally depend on some form of financial allowance to get them launched, and hence on continuing parental support and approval. If Nerval had had a mother to intercede for him (as Gautier's mother so frequently did for her son) things might have been very different. As it was, Dr Labrunie clung close to the son of whom he was so proud, and constantly tried to manage his future. Nerval remained with his father at the rue Saint-Martin until 1834, when he was twenty-six. He was apprenticed in turn to a publisher, to a firm of lawyers and as a medical externe. During the cholera epidemic in Paris of 1832 he accompanied his father on more than fifty visits to sick or dying patients; the idea of serving society as a doctor or spiritual healer never left him, and recurs vividly in the last five years of his life.

At the same time, Nerval was pursuing a wild life as a leading member of the so-called Jeunes-France, with Gautier, Petrus Borel (Le Lycanthrope), the dandy-illustrator Camille Rogier, and the sculptor Jehan Duseigneur who cut a dashing medallion of Nerval's handsome profile in 1831. They were all members of the Young Romantics or *petit-cénacle*, who were in effect the literary groupies of Victor Hugo. Nerval attended the famous battle of *Hernani*, when the Romantics literally fought it out with the Classics during the twenty-five nights of Hugo's Spanish melodrama at the Théâtre-Français, though Gautier noted that Nerval always slipped out before the end so that he would not be late for supper with his father. Nerval was twice arrested during this time, once in 1831 for "breach of the peace at night", and again in 1832 for suspected involvement in political disturbances. He left an amusing account of his incarcerations at Sainte-Pélagie, in *Mes Prisons*. Above all Nerval developed an absolute passion for the theatre, submitting a number of scripts to the Odéon, including *Lara* and the *Prince des Sots* ("The Prince of Fools"), and cultivating platonic worship for various young actresses, as was the fashion, whom he hoped might star in his erotic epic-drama, little trace of which remains, entitled *La Reine de Saba* ("The Queen of Sheba").

Yet during this six-year period Nerval produced little work of value, except for a number of exquisite verse translations and some short lyric poems of which "Fantaisie" is the most justly famous. It is hardly surprising that Dr Labrunie became increasingly anxious and severe; nor would it have amused the ex-officer of the Grande Armée that his brilliant son now had a police record. He might have expected some wild oats, but this was a worrying crop; as Nerval would later say, they were "*les dents du vieux dragon*"—dragon's teeth sown in the mind, to bear strange and bitter fruit.

But what *was* going on in Nerval's mind during these early years? It was nothing like the youth of the English Romantics—no urges to reform the world, no great experiments in living, no passionate affairs or disastrous marriages, no concentrated bursts of literary self-expression. I puzzled over this. Everything seemed so much an external question of style, of fashion, of cliques, of cultivated bohemian dress and behaviour. It was all so artificial, so thoroughly—well, French.

The most solid professional fact appeared to be the vast sums of money to be made in the theatre, when writers like Hugo had overnight successes with *Hernani* (1830); or Dumas with *La Tour de Nesle* (1832) or Alfred de Vigny with *Chatterton*. "The pistols of young suicides," said Gautier, "could be heard cracking across all the attic rooms of Paris." There was also the rise of the daily newspaper, which began to employ well-known critics and literary columnists like Janin on high salaries, and to pay enormous fees for serial fiction—*feuilletons* —from novelists like Balzac. Both these outlets—the theatre and the press—were soon to shape Nerval's outward life. But the inner life: what of that? There were less than twenty surviving letters from Nerval up to 1834, almost all of them concerning publishing, and none of them really personal: none to his father, none to Gautier, none to any woman. There were no diaries. I felt uneasily that I still understood very little of his character, or the mysterious charm he exercised over his friends. He was still "*le ténébreux*".

Only two parts of his writing seemed to throw any light. First are a scattering of autobiographical lyrics from that time, "La

Grandmère", "La Cousine", "Le Coucher de Soleil", and above all "Fantaisie". The second is the opening of a much later prose work, *Sylvie*, which tries to analyse the feelings of those times explicitly, but in retrospect.

Proust said that the poem "Fantaisie", written in 1832, already held the seed of everything that would develop in Nerval's finest work of the 1850s. It is a sixteen-line lyric describing the effect on Nerval of a particular old tune, *"un air très vieux, languissant et funèbre"*, which we may guess to be one of the folk-songs of the Valois heard in his childhood. For this single tune the poet would give *"tout Rossini, tout Mozart, et tout Weber"*. Every time he heard it, a trance seemed to come over his mind, and his spirit went back in time by two hundred years; or, rather, it grew two hundred years younger. He was carried back to the time of Louis XIII in the seventeenth century, and saw a mysterious château, with its pink brick and white cornerstones, standing on a green hillside in the sunset. The château was surrounded by beautiful parks and rivers (not unlike the mysterious "pleasure dome" of *Kubla Khan*). It was obviously an emblem of some kind; of Paradise, perhaps, or the idea of an ancestral home containing the continuity of family love across centuries; or even the "house of the imagination" set in its fruitful grounds. Above all it was a permanent place, beautiful and safe, a Romantic heartland.

The implication is that the poet has travelled on a long journey and undergone many trials to reach it. "How few of us," wrote Nerval twenty years after, "reach that famous château of brick and stone dreamed of in youth." In the final stanza we find the château is inhabited: a woman with blonde hair and period clothes is waiting at a high window. Who is she? The Princess of the old legends, the Beloved, the Muse? The poet does not say. Only, in a skilfully managed shift of tense or time-frame, he suddenly reveals that he has seen her somewhere previously; he remembers that he remembers her: she is a dream within a dream.

> *Puis une dame, à sa haute fenêtre,*
> *Blonde aux yeux noirs, en ses habits anciens*
> *Que, dans une autre existence peut-être*
> *J'ai déjà vu . . . et dont je me souviens!*

Here already, at the age of twenty-four, Nerval is announcing the twin themes of remembrance and of the mysterious woman glimpsed in another place, or another life, which are so central to his work and which produced two acknowledged nineteenth-century masterpieces, his sonnet sequence *Les Chimères* and his prose dream of the Valois, *Sylvie*. Even in such a simple poem the displacements of time are already complex, and there is a hint of the Pythagorean doctrine of the transmigration of souls which was later to obsess Nerval. The poet's "old languishing air" takes him back to something like a race-memory, and within that two-hundred-year-old vision there is enclosed a further memory, a further sense of déjà vu, so that the poem suggests both an infinite series and infinite longing.

There are hidden autobiographical elements too, as I gradually discovered on my trips through the Ile de France. Nerval's Valois is a land of châteaux: there is a seventeenth-century château at Mortefontaine, in whose park he used to play as a child; and through the woods to the north-west is the magnificent château of Chantilly, with its blue slate roofs and turrets standing on its reflection in the lake. This was the ancestral home of the last Duc du Condé, who hanged himself in 1830 at nearby Saint-Leu, perhaps because of the unfaithfulness of his mistress the Duchesse de Feuchère. Nerval was fascinated by the story, and would later claim that he had seen the Duchesse riding through the woods in fancy-dress, as an Amazon huntress. This was quite possible, as she was a woman much given to theatricals and *fêtes champêtres*; her real name was Sophie Dawes, the daughter of an English fisherman—a perfect type of his *princesse lointaine*. Nerval called her Adrienne.

Indeed, the whole poem is not unlike a piece of theatre: the music strikes up, the curtains of memory part, the blonde actress stands at her high window in the flaring light of the *rampe* or gas footlights, while Nerval sits entranced in the audience. It was something he did every night that he could manage it, during these years. One further resemblance struck me: the bold emblematic quality of the poem reminded me of those descriptions of the Tarot cards—here was a symbolic landscape, which suggested a stage in Nerval's journey, the first phase of his magic quest which I was more deeply committed to following than I realised.

If this was Nerval's inner world, it was hardly something that Dr Labrunie understood. There was not only the gap between the down-to-earth doctor dealing with gynaecological problems and the intellectual young poet dreaming of blonde princesses in the sunset. There was also a generation gap, which many young writers experienced in post-war and post-Revolutionary France, disenchanted with the Napoleonic dreams of *la gloire* which had so held their fathers. De Vigny expressed something of this in his *Servitud℮ et grandeur militaires* (1835), and Alfred de Musset even more in the opening of his *Confession d'un enfant du siècle* (1836), in which he attempts to diagnose the peculiar *mal*, the restlessness and disillusion, that afflicted his contemporaries. Twenty years after, Nerval looked back and gave his own explanation in the opening of *Sylvie* (1854). And here I found, for the first time clearly described, that clash between the materialist confidence and the spiritual questioning which Nadar's photography had challenged me to explore.

"At that time we were living in a strange epoch," Nerval wrote,

> like those that frequently succeed to revolutions or the collapse of mighty dynasties . . . It was an age that combined frenetic activity with hesitations and indolence; brilliant dreams of utopia, religious or philosophic aspirations and ill-defined enthusiasms mixed up with vague hopes of some kind of renaissance; boredom with the conflicts of the past, with uncertain hopes for the future. It was something like the age of Peregrinus and Apuleius. Materialist man longed for a bunch of roses from the hands of the beautiful Isis that would spiritually regenerate him. She was the goddess, eternally young and pure, who appeared to us by night, and shamed us for our wasted days. But mundane ambition was irrelevant to us then, and the greedy scramble for places and honours alienated us from all spheres of practical activity. There only remained for refuge that ivory tower of the poets, where we climbed ever higher to isolate ourselves from the crowd below.

The roses of Isis and the ivory tower! How sentimental and post-Romantic it seems—all "blue and rosy hues"—until one realises the underlying bitterness with which Nerval wrote it. The "ivory tower" was a phrase first used by Sainte-Beuve of Vigny, but curiously enough it is this passage in *Sylvie* that gave it currency, and in Robert's great *Dictionnaire Français* its coinage is credited to Nerval. But in France the writers' sense of alienation from prosperous society was genuine, much more so than in England; and soon this was to be seized upon and developed by ideologues of a very different kind, like Charles Fourier with his *phalanstères* and Karl Marx with his *Communist Manifesto*.

The irony was that, in 1834, prosperity did suddenly come to Nerval. In January his maternal grandfather died, leaving him a considerable inheritance of some thirty thousand francs: money which he always regarded as his mother's posthumous gift to him. It is difficult to establish how much this was in contemporary terms, as the basic prices of food and lodging were comparatively low in those days, while the yields on stocks and Government "funds" were far more speculative and variable. Nerval later argued with Dr Labrunie that it would never have been enough to provide him with an independent income, even if it had been wholly invested; nevertheless, had he done so it would undoubtedly have freed him from regular dependence on newspaper work, and in the bullish state of the market in the 1840s would eventually have made him a very rich man. It was a sum equivalent to perhaps forty thousand pounds.

In the event, Nerval spent the greater part of it over the next three or four years: on clothes, on travel and on founding a quality illustrated magazine *Le Monde Dramatique*, given over to his passion for the theatre and consisting of dramatic reviews, essays and theatre-scripts, and racy profiles of well-known actresses accompanied by expensive, full-page steel-engravings, the equivalent of modern pin-ups. He also gave up his room at the rue Saint-Martin, and lived in a series of bohemian apartments, many of them shared with Gautier, of which the most famous was in the impasse du Doyenné.

The Doyenné was a picturesque cul-de-sac of crumbling seventeenth-century buildings off the place du Carrousel, running along the site of the National Convention in Revolutionary days, what is now the modern façade of the Louvre Palace. Nerval and his friends hired a vast attic studio where they lived together in a series of curtained-off alcoves and boxrooms, dossing down on piles of Turkish cushions or in silk-hung hammocks. They gave a number of memorable parties there between 1834 and 1836, culminating in the legendary "*bal des truands*", packed with young painters, writers, diplomats, actresses and *filles de joie* ("*les cydalises*"). They hired a cabaret orchestra to play illegally in the grounds of the royal stables next door, which they reached through a hole in the fence at the end of the impasse. There are numerous memoirs of this "*bohème galante*", left in later days by Gautier, Arsène Houssaye (who became director of the Théâtre-Français), Camille Rogier and others. Nerval wrote his in 1852, an amusing and wistful collection of poetry and prose entitled *Petits Châteaux de Bohème*.

For all its colourful eccentricities—Gautier in Spanish costume, Chasseriau painting nudes on the door panels, La Cydalise tempting visitors to her Spanish hammock, the concierge beating on the ceiling below, the fancy-dress suppers and the chain-dances that went right down the street—it is a melancholy work. "We were young, always full of spirits, often rich . . . But there I strike a more sombre note. Our palace is razed to the ground. I picked over the debris in the street last autumn." Nerval says the Doyenné marked the first of the "seven châteaux" of a poet's life, each of which was to be destroyed in turn.

Gautier's memoirs of this time are typically flamboyant by comparison. Nerval, he says, led a mysterious and scholarly life; he would read through the night with a candlestick tied to his head, and sleep at the foot of an enormous Renaissance four-poster bed, carved with salamanders and other symbolic devices, until the goddess of his dreams should descend to take her place between the sheets. "This monumental bed later proved a great embarrassment to Gérard's nomadic life, and for a long time it remained in my apartment, since I was the only one who afterwards owned a room big enough to house it." Balzac used the story of this bed in one of his novels, and the whole period of the Doyenné became richly embroidered with literary legends—many of them exaggerated.

For Nerval the salient fact was that he had spent his inheritance. Most of it was lost when *Le Monde Dramatique* went bankrupt after a year of publication, in June 1836. He did, however, collaborate with Dumas on a comic-opera, *Piquillo*, which had its Paris première in October 1837, and in Brussels three years later. The lead-singer was a blonde cantatrice from Boulogne, Jenny Colon, with whom Nerval fell wildly and fashionably in love. Financially the piece was a success, and Nerval eventually earned some six thousand francs in royalties, which paid off some of his debts. But two other serious melodramas, *L'Alchimiste* and *Leo Burckhart*, both premièred in 1839, were comparative failures. The latter, a play set in Germany concerning a political intrigue, with Faustian overtones, was intended as Nerval's masterpiece, and its withdrawal from the Porte-Saint-Martin theatre after only twenty-six performances profoundly depressed him. He was now thirty-one, and had failed to establish himself professionally in the theatre, as he had hoped, being dependent on collaborative work, dramatic reviewing and other piecemeal newspaper work, much of it arranged for him by Gautier in *La Presse*. Dr Labrunie reproached him, and blamed his son's literary friends for leading him astray.

It was during these years that Nerval discovered his taste for travel, and, as Gautier said, began to lead the life of a nomad. His natural gifts as a poet and linguist, never really suited to the popular theatre, began to flower in a particular kind of romantic travel-writing. It was both learned and eccentric, starting by reports on foreign theatre, art galleries and folk festivals, as conventionally required by newspapers, but gradually evolving into a series of picaresque adventures in which his own personality—full of self-deprecating bohemian whimsy and melancholy humour

229

—came increasingly to occupy the forefront of the narrative. Such pieces of romantic self-dramatising became his unique art form, and it was as a traveller that I finally began to understand something of his true nature, and its mixture of helpless dreams and stubborn independence.

4

Nerval's journeyings began from the moment he inherited his grandfather's money. In the autumn of 1834 he left Paris, telling his father that he was going to visit relations in Aquitaine. In fact he travelled south-east to Avignon from where, carefully concealing his itinerary by messages sent to Gautier and other friends in Paris, he continued on into Italy, visiting Genoa and Florence before reaching Naples, where he stayed "living like a tramp" for ten days. He finally returned penniless and with split boots by ship to Marseille. The southern Mediterranean setting of Naples, and the ruins of Pompeii, were a revelation to him, and for the first time he felt the powerful, almost mystical attraction of Greece and Egypt and the Near East, which corresponded to some childlike hunger for faith in his make-up.

For the first time, too, in several of his long travel-letters, I could at last catch his real voice. It was full of enigmatic anecdotes and humorous self-descriptions, such as his return to Marseille with "five *sous*" in his pocket, and a little leather valise containing "two lemons, some apples and pears . . . and an old pair of yellow gloves". It was also at Naples that he seems to have had his first sexual experience, during a strange half-drunken night in the apartment of an Italian seamstress he met in a café after a visit to the theatre. This incident was later to take on immense psychological and symbolic significance for him, and he would write no less than five different versions of it between 1837 and 1853. In his letters of the time he gives only hints—a jealous husband who gets drunk on Lacrima Christi wine, a beautiful *Judith* by Caravaggio that took his heart at the Naples museum, and the "hot cinders of Vesuvius which contributed considerably to the demoralisation of my boots". But all these details, including the lemons, "sank into the bark" of his memory, to be later transformed in his stories and poems.

In July 1836, immediately after the collapse of *Le Monde Dramatique*, Nerval was again abroad, this time with Gautier on a wild trip into Belgium, which was intended to provide the materials for a rakish novel provisionally entitled *Confessions galantes de deux gentils-hommes périgourdins*. Nerval fell ill in Brussels and the novel was never written, but Gautier cleverly used the material in despatches to *La Presse*. The articles are enlivened by humorous accounts of Gautier's unidentified travelling companion, an eccentric young man called "Fritz" who has a passion for all things Gothic and Teutonic, and is continuously getting into scrapes. At one point Fritz is thrown out of a Brussels café for "priapism". Fritz has fallen in love with the well-endowed blonde woman of Rubens's paintings, and he seeks everywhere for her equivalent in real life: he is "in pursuit of the big blonde". Farcical overtones of *Faust* and Hoffmann's *Tales* are woven in; but it is clear that Gautier has already discovered what wonderful copy Nerval provides. "Fritz" does not seem to have minded, as yet.

In August 1838 Nerval was on the road once more, this time through Switzerland into Germany, alone. After a short stay in the elegant old spa-town of Baden, he followed the course of the Rhine northwards, through Strasbourg, Mannheim and Frankfurt. I was interested to find him retracing the steps of Dr Labrunie's retreat with the Napoleonic army in 1813–14. In Frankfurt he met Dumas, and they researched German material for the play *Leo Burckhart*. He also wrote one of the earliest extant letters to his father, justifying his journalistic travels—"It is unbelievable to find to what degree French men of letters are welcomed and honoured in Germany"—and holding out the hope of a future commission from the French Government, "part-literary and part-political".

After the failure of *Leo Burckhart* Nerval quickly returned to Germany in October 1839. Travelling through Geneva and Zurich, he now pushed much further to the east, via Munich into Austria, reaching Vienna in November, where he remained for four months. He began to write a Vienna newsletter for the columns of *La Presse*, at the same time compiling a Government report on the translation and reception of French books in Germany, and questions of international copyright. To his father, he wrote long letters of self-justification, emphasising his professional seriousness and denying the colourful rumours that were already beginning to circulate in Paris about his adventures. Some idea of what these rumours were, and the way his friends joyfully embellished them, may be gathered from an ecstatic letter of Gautier's written from Paris in January 1840. In it, one can catch that mixture of worship and mockery with which Gautier still regarded his former hero from the Lycée Charlemagne. Nerval still retained all the magic of adolescence;

indeed, I began to wonder if Gautier would ever allow his old friend the prosaic business of growing up:

> I am waiting with the utmost impatience the history of your love-affairs and conquests. In your first epistle [*ie newspaper article*] you pretend to know the ladies of Vienna only by sight; this is a most immaterial method, and by now you should have passed to other means . . . Tell me what you eat, and especially what you drink; where you perch; how much human flesh costs, and whether the gorgeous ladies of that happy city give you a tight fit or a loose one; if the gin is strong and if the Rhine wine is good. Tell me what pleases you and what bores you—if a gentleman who has the happiness of always being in the company of Mr Gérard *can* ever be bored. Finally, tell me if you have found the *big blonde*, the blonde we have drunk so many steins of beer in pursuing. What a wonderful thing if we could go to Turkey together! What fine turbans and beautiful haiks we would buy . . . we would soon be far more expert in Eastern Passion than Alphonse Royer and we would take a small harem in common—not being jealous of each other—and inundate the newspapers of Europe with an enormous flood of copy. It would be fantastic!

In less than three years this dream would be fulfilled in its own fashion. That is to say, Nerval would actually be in Constantinople making notes on the "Nights of Ramadan", while Gautier would be safely at home in Paris enjoying the success of his Turkish ballet, *La Péri*.

Some account of Nerval's four months in Vienna later appeared in his *Amours de Vienne* (1852); and one particular episode in a story he wrote, *Pandora*, halfway between a romantic assignation and a Hoffmannesque nightmare, in which he is seduced by a *demi-mondaine* beauty with a clinging décolletage "of silk and Levantine purple", who drives him to distraction with sexual desire and guilt. But in general the visit does not seem to have been either happy or productive, and Nerval returned in March 1840 penniless once again, having to walk the last stage of his journey to Strasbourg because he had insufficient money for the coach. He walked ten leagues a day for four days, "between the hotel du Soleil and the hotel du Corbeau". Nerval hid this situation from his father, though in several long and eloquent letters he once again tried to defend his career as a struggling writer. These letters seemed to me a classic statement of the writer's dilemma in the nineteenth century:

Literary men like Lamartine, Chateaubriand, de Vigny, Hugo, all have private incomes or family money, or assured livelihoods from some other source. It is such people who have the most success, and who even earn the most money, because they have it to start with. They have not been constrained to waste all their energies on sterile work like cheap novels and newspapers, which are always attractive because of the ease of execution.

If a young man took up "commerce or manufacturing business" he could expect "all possible financial sacrifice" from his family; and even if he did not succeed at first his family would "complain but go on helping him". A man who set out to be "a doctor or a lawyer" could expect to work for several years without sufficient clients or patients to support him, and his family would "take the bread out of their own mouths" to keep him going. "But no one considers that the man of letters, whatever he does, however high his ambition, however hard and patient his labours, has need of support just as much in his chosen vocation. Or that his career, which may be eventually as solid in material terms as the others, will probably have—in our times at least—an initial period which is quite as difficult."

No doubt Dr Labrunie read these appeals with growing irritation: had not his son just squandered a family inheritance of thirty thousand francs, and then gone gadding about through the cities of Europe? What about Nerval's tiresome friend Théophile Gautier? At least he had published a popular novel, *Mademoiselle de Maupin* (1835), however scandalous it might have been, and now wrote a regular theatrical column in *La Presse*. Gautier was a thoroughly *professional* author.

Yet Nerval's defence, however partial in his own case, carried a wider justification for his own generation. The fate of contemporaries like Henry Murger, who died in poverty and sickness, bore it out; and even successful major writers like Baudelaire and Balzac —the latter the most prolific of all professionals—suffered keenly from material want. Murger himself wrote in the touching Preface to his single masterpiece, *Scènes de la Vie de Bohème*:

Today, as in all previous times, any man who takes up the arts without other means of existence except the art itself will be forced to start off in the ways of Bohemia . . . and for the anxious reader or the timorous bourgeois we must repeat this truth in the form of an axiom: Bohemia is a necessary stage of the artistic life, it is the prologue to the Academy, to the State Hospital, or to the public morgue.

Nerval finally put the position, realistically and without sentiment, in terms that even Dr Labrunie might have understood, and that carry conviction even today:

> All literary work consists of two kinds. There is literary journalism, which brings a good living and gives a solid, recognised position to anyone who pursues it assiduously; unfortunately it doesn't lead on to anything higher or more lasting. Then there is the writing of books proper, plays, studies of poetry and so on, which is all slow and difficult work; it inevitably requires long preparatory labour and a certain period of research and study without any immediate fruits. Yet here alone lies one's literary future: a reputation and a happy and honourable old age.

With an obstinate determination that I found more and more characteristic, Nerval refused to take up a regular column open to him on the Paris newspapers like Gautier or Janin. "I tremble at the idea of having to take up again the yoke of a *feuilletoniste*." Instead, he persisted in maintaining his freedom as a travel-writer, and in 1842 planned a grand voyage to the Near East, as he had so often imagined it with Gautier in the golden days of the impasse du Doyenné. He departed from Marseille in December 1842, taking with him a mass of carefully prepared equipment, including camp-beds, cutlery, Arabic guides and dictionaries, a daguerreotype camera complete with glass slides and chemical kit, and even a pair of blue-tinted glasses for the desert.

"Orientalism", as the French called it (meaning the Near East and North Africa, rather than China and Japan), was much in vogue, and he had chosen an opportune moment. The fashion for the East had been started in France by Napoleon's Egyptian campaign, and the many marvellous accounts that his soldiers had brought home. Both Chateaubriand and Lamartine later made extensive tours there, travelling *en grand seigneur* with extensive retinues, like Byron in Greece. Delacroix exhibited his *Femmes d'Alger* at the Salon in 1834.

But Nerval's plan was to travel as simply as possible, with a single companion, Joseph Fonfrède, from Bordeaux, using a special pass on French ships, and living, eating and even dressing in the style of the local population. He would study local customs and religious festivals and make extensive notes on the literature and mythology of Egypt, Syria, the Lebanon, and Turkey. This long period of research, which lasted for almost a year, resulted in his second major work, a two-volume *Voyage en Orient*, which was successfully serialised in the prestigious *Revue des Deux Mondes* between 1846 and 1847, and in various other journals such as *L'Artiste* and *Le National*, finally appearing in a definitive edition published by Charpentier in 1851. Overall, the project and the book was to occupy him for a decade.

I now began to consider if I too should leave Paris and embark on an Eastern pilgrimage with Nerval. It would be the most ambitious of all my journeys, and I should finally be adopting the life of a nomad myself.

For some weeks I had plans to take the old Orient Express as far as Istanbul, then cross the Bosphorus into Turkey and Syria. I become increasingly restive in my attic room, and roamed Paris through the perfumed nights of June, smelling the indefinable Arabic scent of nougat, chestnuts, Moroccan wine and coffee that fills the backstreets between the place d'Anvers and the boulevard Montmartre. I woke up on park benches, haunted railway stations, befriended bargemen down by the pont d'Austerlitz and drank at little cafés that stay open between the all-night PTT and the old newspaper offices of *La Presse* near the place du Caire. Sometimes I posted articles to London to pay for my food and rent, but Françoise said I didn't eat properly, and my Irish friends took me pointedly to wedding feasts and funeral wakes. "Don't let the ghosts get you," they said. Yet always I finished up alone, back in my attic, turning my books and papers under the solitary lamp. An entry in my notebooks asked: "Why is it always 4 a.m.?"

But as I read Nerval's letters during the year previous to his departure I discovered something that put his whole journey in an entirely different perspective, and tied me more than ever to Paris and the little streets leading up to Montmartre.

Nerval's friends, like Gautier, had always implied that his madness came upon him slowly, and did not really begin to affect his career until the last years, when from 1851 onwards he more or less regularly sought treatment and shelter in a special asylum run by Dr Emile Blanche at Passy. Gautier specifically made the suggestion that it was the very experiences of his Eastern tour, and the dabbling in Egyptian mythology and Druse religion, which slowly unhinged his mind, like some latter-day Lady Hester Stanhope, unfitting him for the world of Western materialism.

But his letters revealed something quite different, and far more tragic. Nerval had first "gone mad" in 1841, before he ever set out for the East. He had undergone a violent breakdown during the festivities of *mardi gras* in Paris in February of that year, been arrested by the night-patrol and interned at a clinic in the rue

Picpus. The following month he had a relapse, and after further violent scenes was admitted as a voluntary patient for eight months at the private asylum of Dr Esprit Blanche (the father of Dr Emile) at the rue Norvins, just off the present site of the Sacré Coeur in Montmartre.

In other words, Nerval's great journey had begun before he left Paris: but it was essentially an inner journey, a *voyage à l'intérieur*, through the unsettled regions of his own mind and memory. It was this metaphysical pathway that I now determined to pursue: a track that went into the dark places, bordered by a hidden stream that came from a single consciousness. I also felt, obscurely, that this passage from outer to inner travelling marked some vital transformation or watershed in the history of Romanticism. The imagination of the Hero had finally doubled back on itself, and the rivers and mountains, the visions and revolutions had become in this last phase those of a purely internal landscape, or moonscape, the world of dreams. So for the second time I jumped over a low wall into the blackness below.

There was, too, a subtle shift and doubling back on itself of the biographical evidence. For in fact Gautier knew all about this early breakdown, since it was he who had come to collect Nerval from the military station at the place Cadet. I now realised that he had been carefully adjusting and editing the life story of his old friend, to give it a more conventional and acceptable pattern. The literary relationship between the two of them took on a new depth and complexity.

5

What exactly had gone wrong with Nerval? Later French critics and biographers, referring to the pattern of violent outbursts, visual and auditory hallucinations, together with a manic-depressive cycle that ended in suicide, were inclined to label him as a schizophrenic. But British and American psychologists in the 1960s had gone far to discredit the whole concept of schizophrenia as a diagnosis. Instead, writers like R. D. Laing and David Cooper had laid new emphasis on the human surroundings that produced an "unstable personality", especially through intolerable or contradictory pressures from other members of the family, or close working colleagues. They spoke of "disjunctive relationships". Laing described the experience of "schizophrenia" in terms of an inner journey, during which the old personality is more or less consciously broken up, in order to find a new identity freed from the contradictions of the former self. It seemed to me that something of this nature was happening to Nerval; and by the end he was himself describing it in such terms: "I compare this series of trials that I have gone through to that which the ancients understood by the idea of a descent into hell." But such a journey into the underworld did not, unhappily, guarantee either salvation or cure.

Eyewitness accounts say that Nerval's first breakdown took the form of a violent outburst late at night in the café Lepeletier, during which "chairs and a mirror" got broken. Nerval himself later said that he was overcome by the excitement of the *mardi gras* carnival, had delusions of "mystical systems" which he could control, and walked off down the boulevard following a star in the East, and throwing off all his clothes. It was at this point that he was first arrested.

The soldiers treated him kindly, put him in a camp-bed and hung up his clothes to dry, while someone was despatched to find Gautier in the rue de Navarin nearby. They may well have thought that Nerval had simply drunk too much during the festivities. However, further outbursts at the clinic, and obsessive talk of astrology, numerology, mythological identities—in one hospital note Nerval signed himself "Napoleon"—convinced Dr Blanche that his patient was deeply ill. Writing to Dumas's wife in November, at the end of his treatment, Nerval himself said that the doctors had defined his sickness as "Theomania or Demonomania". One of its most worrying aspects was that Nerval at first would not accept that he was ill at all. In March he wrote that his sickness was "nothing very extraordinary", and that he had "already experienced for a long time previously quite similar attacks of nerves". Certain odd episodes on his journeys in Belgium, Germany and Austria might indeed be explained by this. Yet Gautier always insisted that there was nothing in his published writing that suggested the least irrationality, and he always considered Gérard to be the ideal travelling companion.

Knowing as I did by now something of Nerval's purely literary fascination with mythology and "mystical systems", it seemed to me that the "theomania" that must have astounded his doctors, was purely symptomatic. His mind was naturally, and as it were professionally, stocked with such materials. The question was, what made it all bubble over in such violent and manic confusion?

One answer seemed to me, simply, the extreme difficulty of his professional situation—continually in debt or penniless; under constant pressures from editors; having repeatedly failed in the theatre; yet having to live out the image of the insouciant, romantic traveller dashing off brilliant copy in distant cities between amorous assignations—as Gautier and other friends wanted to think of him. Nerval was constitutionally a "loner": he loved travel and poetry and solitude, and found regular newspaper work a bore and an anxiety. But he had very little psychological or emotional support for the kind of life he was trying to lead: no doting parents like Gautier's, no faithful wife like Murger's, no exotic lover like Baudelaire's, no attached sister like Wordsworth's. He was a deeply isolated personality, and many writers have taken to alcohol, drugs or lunacy under similar pressures.

Added to all this were the contradictions of the French society in which he was living: a society which increasingly idealised the "pure" unworldly artistic personality, the bohemian in his garret or attic studio, and yet which set enormous store by material achievements, popular success, public honours, high incomes. It took a prolific genius like Victor Hugo to encompass such contradictions, by being the leader of the Romantic rebels and at the same time receiving a pension from the King in 1822 and being created a peer of France in 1845.

So much of Nerval's sense of isolation and guilt seemed to be expressed in his relations with his father. At one level Dr Labrunie—the doctor, the soldier, the old Napoleonic campaigner —represented the judgment of society itself on a wayward son; at another, he was Nerval's most intimate friend, his confessor, the person who represented all the warmth of hearth and home. The first letter that Nerval wrote from the rue Picpus—"my dear Papa, at last I am permitted to read and write"—was to Dr Labrunie. It is a moving document, full of love and reassurance, but at the same time deeply reproachful. "Among so many people who have shown kindness towards me," he writes, "you appear to be the only one (and I say this only to you) who has continued to blame me for my behaviour and to doubt my future." He begs him at least to disguise this disapproval from his friends, his doctors and the people who can help him in his literary career:

I cannot tell how far my dislike for the profession of a doctor may have lowered me in your esteem, but I believe that the evil (if it is one) is irreparable by now, and we have had words on the subject so often that surely the matter should be closed. I can imagine the disappointment you must have felt about it, a dozen years ago, but all such griefs wear themselves out in time, and I was surprised during my illness (for I was always perfectly conscious, even when I could not speak) to hear you telling people about them in such detail, when they had no real need to know these things.

It is a revealing picture: the silent, "crazy" son and the voluble, stern, complaining father. The missing figure is, of course, the gentle, mediating mother: *mamma mia, medicate* . . .

In many ways, Nerval's breakdown actually brought into the open those contradictory or "disjunctive" relations which were tearing him apart. This was nowhere more evident than in the newspaper world, where the temptation to turn him into colourful copy now became overwhelming. Previously Gautier had done this with tact and humour, and indeed with Nerval's tacit compliance; in a way it was part of their collaboration, of their friendship. But now Jules Janin, the theatre critic on the *Journal des Débats*, who had followed Nerval's career closely and with some encouragement, could no longer resist the opportunity to write a devastating—and brilliantly funny—editorial on the fate of the Jeunes-France generation. His general theme was that the poets and artists of that supposedly wild, post-war, Romantic new wave had, ten years after, all suffered the "singular destiny" of becoming "administrators, ambassadors, academicians, or even priests". But among the happiest "of this poetic tribe" were two who were now "permanently locked up in the madhouse of Dr Blanche"—the actor Anthony Deschamps, and Nerval. Janin then proceeded to write a long fulsome mock-obituary of the young poet and playwright who might have been the glory of French literature. In this sense Nerval became the tragi-comic apotheosis of his generation: the Romantic writer who had finally been recognised by society as a simple madman. Janin's was a cruel betrayal, and all the worse because it was done cleverly and amusingly, for a fascinated and not unsympathetic bourgeois readership.

Nerval did not discover the true content of this long article until four months after it was written. His friends kept it from him, merely saying that Janin had written a kindly piece, which made light of his illness. Nerval even sent thanks to Janin via friends, remarking that his friendship was unalterable: "It was he who put pen and bread into my hand; he is continuing his good works." When he did finally read the piece his bitterness and sense of betrayal were overwhelming. In August 1841 he wrote a long open letter to Janin at the *Débats* for publication. It is notable that this letter was approved by Dr Blanche, for it carries the "passed" stamp of the asylum. It seemed to me a key passage in Nerval's biography, for it shows his own identity being taken out of his hands, carefully packaged, and cleverly served up for the avid consumption of Parisian readers. At the same time, Nerval managed to state his case with admirable calm, and even a kind of smiling acceptance:

> You have greatly compromised us in the eyes of our friends in Paris and abroad. Anthony will very willingly forgive you, but what shall I say—I who owe you so much gratitude for your help? . . . Last February, following a journey in Northern Europe, I was struck down by a sudden illness and rumour said that I had died of an apoplectic fit. Several newspapers spread this story, thanks to the singular nature of the attack which took place in the street during the middle of the night. You then decided to publish a biographical article about me, twelve columns long, in which you placed me so high and held me up to the admiration of Europe, that I had either to hide myself away or die of shame because I was not really dead after all, and had been heaped with such unmerited renown . . . Nearly all my friends have followed your example, and everyone agreed to make me into a sort of prophet, or mad visionary, whose reason had been lost in Germany undergoing the initations of the secret societies, or in the study of Eastern symbols . . . Since that time, those of my friends who do not believe in my death (and there are those who obstinately insist on it, so they do not *recognise* me in the street) continue to bemoan my *lost reason*, and greet me with expressions of condolence: "What a tragedy!" they say around me, "a young writer of such style and promise! Such a fine intelligence wiped out without hope of recovery! And he has left us hardly anything . . . What a tragedy!" And it is in vain that I speak, I reason, I write even. "What a terrible pity!" they still repeat, "France has lost a genius who might have done her honour . . . only his friends really knew him!" With the result, my dear Janin, that I have become the living tomb of that Gérard de Nerval whom you loved, supported and encouraged for so long. May my complaint reach your heart!

I doubt if anywhere else in the history of biography can one find a subject who so bitterly and eloquently accuses his own biographer —from beyond the grave, as it were. To be consigned to death, or madness; to be made—in that haunting phrase—*le tombeau vivant* of your own identity, for the purposes of the literary stock-market:

here indeed was a novel fate, vividly expressive of the confused values of the time.

Here too, my own position as biographer began to be shaken with doubts, and I first glimpsed the labyrinth into which I was stepping. Who exactly was the man I was trying to write about? Was the real personality entirely hidden? Was he the tragi-comic creation of his own "friends"? (How repeatedly that word occurs now in Nerval's letters, taking on more and more doubtful meaning. How can your "friends" be those who do not *recognise* you?)

Moreover, the more I reflected on this public letter, the more subtle its implications became. Was it wrong, after all, to accept it at face value? Was it, itself, the product of an unbalanced mind, a paranoid expression of grief and guilt, an unfounded belief that the whole literary world ("Europe", even) was mocking and persecuting him? How does one square it with the fact that Janin decided not to publish the letter in the *Débats*, yet persuaded the Government to grant Nerval financial aid from the cultural funds for his great Eastern voyage? Or again, was the letter in fact a brilliant piece of self-publicity? Was Nerval somehow *himself* exploiting the exotic reputation he had earned as *une sorte de prophète, d'illuminé*, and deliberately trying to put it to literary use?

This last suggestion may seem far-fetched; but there was one particular consequence of his eight months in the asylum at Montmartre which gave me pause for thought. Hitherto, it may have been noticed that while I refer to "Nerval", all his friends including Gautier talk about "Gérard". It is almost as if we have been talking about two different people. There is a reason for this discrepancy. From the very beginning Nerval never used his family name—Labrunie—to sign published work. Instead he used a number of noms-de-plume, including Fritz, Aloysius, the initials G.G., and most usually his Christian name—Gérard—*tout court*. This is not so surprising as it sounds, for many of his contemporaries used the most exotic made-up names during their bohemian phase, often so as not to shock their families.

Whether Nerval had a particular reason for not wanting to use his father's name, besides simple propriety, is another question; the impulse to alter or suppress a family name can sometimes have deeper psychological meaning, similar to the conviction that one is an illegitimate child, fathered secretly by some great historical figure. The madhouses of Paris were full of Napoleon's unrecognised offspring.

Be that as it may, Nerval always consistently signed his private correspondence "Gérard" to friends, and "Gérard Labrunie" to his family, and there seems nothing odd about this. However, during the asylum year of 1841 this suddenly changes. He composes the symphonic and haunting name, *Gérard de Nerval*. He does, quite literally, find a new identity. In a letter to Edmond Leclerc of 8 March, Nerval signs himself with the wild humour typical of his manic phases, "a madman who believes himself wise and who would be if . . . Gérard". He then adds as a postscript: "Incidentally, here at Madame de Saint-Marcel's I am addressed as M. Gérard de Nerval, because it is my wish."

Later, in letters to magazine editors, and to the director of the Beaux-Arts, he experiments with "L. Gérard de Nerval", "G. Nap. della torre Brunya" (an early reference to the *"tour abolie"* of his sonnet) and "Gérard L. de Nerval". Only to his father does the signature always remain, *"ton fils bien affectionné*, G. Labrunie". Thus in his public letter to Jules Janin that striking phrase *"le tombeau vivant de Gérard de Nerval"* takes on a particular importance, as the intended introduction of a new literary persona to his readership, in the final form of his new name.

Its source is of course the Valois of his childhood. By adopting the name of his uncle's paddock at Mortefontaine, the clos de Nerval, and using the aristocratic *de* (just as Balzac invented "Honoré de Balzac"), Nerval granted himself a new patronym and a new genealogy, full of romantic overtones. It was moreover a genealogy connected with his mother's side of the family, for two of the Laurent grandparents had already been buried in the clos de Nerval in 1836. It is impossible not to detect in this some gesture of disinheritance—"El Desdichado"—towards his father, and the Labrunies of Aquitaine. Nerval was choosing to dig up and replant the very roots of his identity in the magic places of his earliest childhood. Eventually this was to influence the entire direction of his writing, and his final travels. In a certain sense, the asylum at Montmartre *had* seen a man called Labrunie die, and another man, called Nerval, born. But for me as a biographer this left a strange and unsettling question: which was the *real* one?

Jules Janin himself must have been deeply perplexed. For with the public letter from Gérard de Nerval came a private one from Gérard Labrunie, and its passionate tones are unmistakably sincere. "My dear Janin," it ran,

> excuse me for writing to you with some bitterness . . . but insert my letter [in the *Débats*] or at least quote and analyse it; for my complaint is just. I am as grateful to you as ever, but none the less deeply hurt at having to appear as a *sublime madman*, thanks

to you, to Théophile, to Lucas, etc. I shall never be able to present myself in any society, never be able to get married, never be able to obtain a serious hearing. Repair the evil by withdrawing your praises or frankly admitting your error! Print my letter, it must be done. I am counting on you.

But Janin, the "friend of his heart", never did so.

Nerval's crucial breakdown just before his voyage to the East had, therefore, at least three aspects: a medical or psychological one described as "Theomania"; a sociological one, in which he is the victim of the professional pressures of his uncertain career and the disapproval of his father; and a literary one, in which the breakdown of his old identity as G. Labrunie is really the prelude to his creation of a new author, Gérard de Nerval. All this was sufficiently complicated as it stood. But I gradually discovered there was a fourth interpretation, and this was Nerval's own. He said he had been driven mad by his unrequited love for Jenny Colon, the actress who had starred in *Piquillo*. Or, at least, for the woman that Jenny *represented*. This was something entirely new to me.

The part that Jenny, or her avatars, played in Nerval's insanity was not revealed until the autobiographic work *Aurélia*, written in the last months of his life. No letters from Jenny to Nerval are known, nor is there any mention of her in any of the letters Nerval wrote from the asylum in 1841. It might therefore be natural to suppose that *l'affaire Jenny* was an invention of Nerval's, dating from long after the event, or at least made into something imaginatively important only in retrospect. The biographical truth is hard to discern; and extraordinarily little is known of the woman herself.

Jenny sang the lead in the 1837 production of *Piquillo*, and again in the production of December 1840 in Brussels which Nerval visited just before his breakdown. In the interval she had married a flautist in the theatrical company, a M. Leplus, and Nerval later said this had been a severe blow to him. He had admired her, he said, ever since 1834; and *Le Monde Dramatique* had been founded largely to further her career. Gautier also tells this story, though the fact remains that there was only one important profile of Jenny in the magazine, and this was written by Gautier himself, not Nerval.

During 1837 Nerval sketched a series of love-letters which still exist in the form of sixteen rough manuscripts preserved in the library at Chantilly, which I was eventually to track down. Unfortunately none of these letters is addressed, and there is no evidence that Nerval ever actually delivered them. Gautier wrote: "The story of his love affair will always remain obscure. He launched the periodical and wrote articles in it to bring himself in contact with his idol. He wrote wonderful, passionate love-letters to her: but he can only have slipped them into the postbox of his own pocket . . . Did he ever declare his love to her openly? I do not know."

It is possible that, even at this stage, the whole thing was largely a literary game of Nerval's, conceived à la Rousseau as an exercise in style and emotion. It is difficult otherwise to account for the fact that Nerval polished and adapted six of these love-letters for publication before going on his Eastern voyage; they appeared in the Christmas 1842 issue of a fashion magazine, *La Sylphide*, under the title of *Un Roman à Faire*, or, "A novel in progress". Meanwhile the real Jenny Colon-Leplus had died in June 1842, "exhausted by child-bearing", and was buried in the cemetery at Montmartre. But the "novel in progress" was to bear fruit in a different way, ten years later, in the story *Octavie*.

Despite all this literary artifice, there is some evidence that Nerval's passion for Jenny was genuine and even notorious in theatrical circles. In one of the oddest sidelights of the whole affair, there is a note of February 1841 from a journalist in Brussels which tells Nerval that his constant praises for Jenny in the *Gazette des Théâtres* have made the rest of the *Piquillo* company furiously jealous: "They are talking of drawing lots between the actors to choose who should come and stab you to death, in the manner of the secret societies."

A joke, no doubt. But it would have reached Nerval in Paris about a week before his breakdown.

6

Nerval's *Voyage en Orient* was a voyage of inner self-exploration as much as one of recuperation and research. He said that he went east to forget his troubles and to renew himself, both physically and morally. He wrote to Dr Labrunie, who did not entirely approve of the expedition: "I had to leave all that behind me by some great enterprise which would efface the memory of it, and give me a new physiognomy in other people's eyes." But from Cairo he wrote ecstatically that "the sun is really brighter in these countries than our own. It is as if I had not seen a sun like this since my earliest childhood, when all our perceptions are more intense and fresh. Living here is almost like growing ten years younger."

Nerval remained in that city for three months, then took ship for

Beirut, arriving there in mid-May. A further two months were spent in Lebanon, some of it travelling by mule in the desert, visiting the Druses and Maronite Christians. At the beginning of July he sailed again from Beirut, stopping off at the islands of Rhodes, Cyprus and at Smyrna before reaching Constantinople on 25 July. Here he remained for a further three months, delaying his departure so that he could stay for Ramadan. His travelling companion, Joseph Fonfrède, left him to return early to France, supposedly because of legal matters connected with his family. Nerval and Fonfrède seem to have got on excellently throughout, the younger man (Fonfrède was twenty-five) providing them with many colourful adventures, notably with a slave-girl he hired in Cairo. Nerval said her breasts were tattooed with images of the sun, and Gautier—true to form—later claimed that Nerval had promised to bring her back for him as a present. As "Zetnayb", she became a central figure in the published *Voyage en Orient*. It is one of the great gaps in Nerval's biography, however, that Fonfrède's journal or letters were not preserved: few people could have got to know Nerval so well. Indeed, apart from some fragmentary "Notes de Voyage" Nerval's own record of this entire year consist of some twenty letters written either to his father or to Gautier. This absence of documentation is itself vaguely disquieting, and no letters at all belong to the months spent in Lebanon.

In the *Voyage en Orient* this period is largely covered by the strange "Legend of Calif Hakim", an account of hashish-taking, madness and double identities which seems to have strong autobiographical overtones. The travel notes are full of revealing passages, though never more than fragmentary. In one place I found: "I feel the need to assimilate all Nature into myself (*foreign* women). Memory of having lived here before. Night of Vienna. To pursue the same features in many different women. Lover of an eternal type. Destiny . . . The actress who *cheated* him in all her roles. To the ends of the earth."

In another place, also unidentified, there was a passage which would be closely linked with the eventual accounts of his madness in *Aurélia*: "Dreams and madness. The red star. The desire for the East. Europe rises. The dream is realised. Seas. Confused memories . . . It is *men* who have made me suffer. A climate where my head may rest. Loves abandoned in a tomb. Her. I fled from her, I lost her, I made her great. Italy. Germany. Flanders. The boat to the East."

Here I felt I could again overhear Nerval's inner voice, talking to himself, grief-struck and obsessive, muttering on and on in that eternal dialogue with the self that exists in all of us, but which must be constantly restrained if it is not to unhinge us from reality.

Yet Nerval the travel-journalist remained as resourceful as ever. The posts between Paris and the East were slow and extremely unreliable, so he found a novel way to communicate with Gautier and maintain his new literary persona as Gérard de Nerval. On reaching Constantinople he had found in one of the French libraries a back-number of *La Presse* in which Gautier reviewed his own work, the ballet *La Péri*, in the form of an open letter, "To my friend Gérard de Nerval in Cairo". Nerval immediately answered it by gaining access to the columns of a local paper, *Le Journal de Constantinople*, and writing a return article, "To my friend Théophile Gautier in Paris", knowing that copies of this paper —"the best circulating news-sheet in the Bosphorus"—would travel far more quickly and safely than private correspondence. In fact Gautier read this piece in Paris within three weeks, and it is one of Nerval's finest and most evocative travel-letters, even though he modestly describes himself as "rusty". Having whimsically filled in the local colour—British tourists wearing rubber mackintoshes, hashish-eaters swathed in striped Bedouin blankets and sinuous *alma* dancers who turn out to be male—Nerval delivers up a marvellous and ironic farewell to the Romantic illusions of Orientalists and the would-be pursuers of Eastern exotica:

O my dear friend, how well we have acted out the fable of the two men: one who runs to the ends of the earth in pursuit of his fortune, and the other who tranquilly awaits it in his own bed at home! It's not my fortune that I pursue, but the ideal—colour, poetry, love perhaps; yet all that comes to you, who have stayed behind, and escapes me, who has run without ceasing. Only once, being imprudent, you spoilt your ideal of Spain by going to see it ... But I have already lost, kingdom by kingdom, province by province, the most beautiful half of the universe, and soon I shall not know any more where to seek a refuge for my dreams. But it is Egypt that I most regret having hunted from my imagination, to let it find sad lodgings in my memory! You still believe in the magic ibis, the purpled lotus, and the yellow Nile ... Alas, the ibis is nothing but a desert bird, the lotus a vulgar onion plant, and the Nile a murky red river with slate-grey reflections.

Nerval goes on to praise the Egypt that Gautier has created at the Paris Opera for his ballet—"the veritable Cairo, the immaculate

Egypt, the East that has escaped me"—finally reversing the worlds of reality and of theatrical illusion in a paradoxical and nostalgic grande finale:

> The works of the Pharaoh, the califs and the sultans have dis-appeared almost entirely beneath the dust of the khamsin [south wind] and the hammers of a prosaic civilisation. But beneath your enchanted gaze, O magician, their reanimated ghost rises up once more with its gardens, its palaces, and its ideal—well, almost—*péris*! It is *this* Egypt that I believe in, and not the other one. The six months that I spent in the other Egypt have slipped silently away: already lost in a non-existent world [*le néant*]. I have seen so many countries fall away into the darkness behind me, like so many wooden theatrical sets. What will be left to me?—nothing but an image as confused as something one has dreamed.

Gautier would have liked all that, the romantic dreams and the fashionable world-weariness, and the continuing mythology of their collaboration—the Gemini, the "two men in the fable", acting out the story of their lives. It was also flattering—"O magician!"—using exactly the same form of compliment that Baudelaire would use a decade later in dedicating the *Fleurs du Mal* to Gautier, "*au parfait magicien ès lettres françaises*". And of course there was the blazoned signature with the dateline, Constantinople: Gérard de Nerval.

Yet Nerval did not take all "*trop au sérieux*", as he explained in a letter of October to his father. It was, he said, "one paradox in answer to another", and the sort of thing that was expected by the newspaper public in these kinds of "*jeux d'esprit*". He did not really feel like that about Egypt and Lebanon. His attitude was much more practical and down to earth: what really counted was Gautier's kindness in dedicating his ballet to him publicly, so to speak, through *La Presse*, and giving publicity to his voyage: "I feel this all the more since my illness was only too well known, and it is vital that my return to health should be publicly noticed. Nothing can prove it better than this difficult journey through the hot countries of the East."

So the split personality—Gérard and Nerval—remains in evidence.

Nerval left Constantinople at the end of October 1843, returning via Malta and Naples, where he stayed for a fortnight renewing his memories of 1834. The significance of this last stop-over was lost on me at first. He passed Christmas at Nîmes in the family of his old friend from the Doyenné days, Camille Rogier, finally returning to Paris in the first week of the New Year 1844, where there was a moving but uneasy reunion with his father. Now there lay ahead the long task of working up his notes and impressions, reading up on every aspect of Eastern customs and religion and slowly drafting the three long studies of Cairo, Beirut and Constantinople which would be serially published, and then eventually become the definitive version of his book, *Scènes de la Vie Orientale*, provocatively entitled, "Les Femmes de Caire", "Les Femmes de Liban" and "Les Nuits du Ramazan".

The whole process took six long and increasingly difficult years. Far from establishing his return to health and "normality", it gave him an increasingly eccentric reputation as the Last of the Romantic Travellers, the dreamer and "initiate", the man who had "gone East" and never quite come back. Once again it was Gautier who summed up, and brilliantly exploited, this new persona:

> From the mists of Germany Gérard de Nerval passed into the blazing sunshine of Egypt . . . Coptic marriages, Arabian wedding feasts, evenings among the Opium Eaters, the customs of the Egyptian fellaheen: all the details of the Mohammedan world are caught with the same sensitivity and acuteness of observation . . . His chapters entitled "The Legend of Calif Hakim" and "The Story of Balkis and Solomon" show the extraordinary degree to which he had succeeded in penetrating the profoundly mysterious spirit of these strange tales, in which each object contains a *symbol*. One could even say that he took from them certain occult meanings intended only for the *neophyte*, certain cabalistic formulae and overtones of the *Illuminati*, which made one believe, at times, that he was writing directly of his own personal initiation. I would not be altogether surprised if, like Jacques Cazotte, the author of the *Diable Amoureux*, he had received a visit from some stranger making Masonic signs, who was quite confounded not to find in him a true member of the Secret Brotherhood.

Cazotte, incidentally, was arrested and guillotined during the Revolution.

Gautier is the first to make the link between Nerval's physical travels and his metaphysical ones: the implication is that he has journeyed through mysticism into madness, through the Orient into insanity, though typically the conclusion is turned away as a joke. Nerval was not *really* a member of the Brotherhood, just a bright fellow-journalist. But was he?

During these middle years of Nerval's life the solid ground began to slip away beneath my feet as a biographer. The "Eastern star" that is calling Nerval seemed to get a progressively deeper hold on his psyche—the symbol of his travels, or the symbol of his lost love, or the symbol of his dreams and madness. The 17th card of the Tarot pack shows a naked woman pouring water into a sacred river, beneath a night sky of huge hypnotic stars.

So I too began star-gazing. From my attic room, I found I could climb out on to the little ironwork balcony six floors above the street, and by standing on the top rail reach up to the guttering and pull myself on to the steeply sloping slate roof. Here I would establish myself on a flat stone platform between the chimney-pots. From this vantage point I gazed eastwards up the rue d'Hauteville, as the long summer evenings yielded their stars. The darkness thickened over the distant roofs and tufted TV aerials while the top section of the architrave of the gare de l'Est shone on the horizon, its Second Empire frieze of allegorical gods and goddesses— L'Industrie, Le Commerce, L'Agriculture—lit from below by hidden lamps, so they hung strangely yellow and illuminated against the deepening black of the sky. I read again and again Nerval's accounts of his first breakdown in 1841 (from the various drafts of *Aurélia*) describing how he had left the café Lepeletier after talking excitedly of "music, painting, the generation of colours and numbers", and rushed into the rue d'Hauteville telling his friends he was going "to the East":

> And I began to search in the sky for a Star that I thought I knew, as if she had a particular power over my destiny. Having found her, I continued my walk following the streets in the direction in which she was visible, hanging there, and moving so to speak ahead of my fate, and wishing to have my eye on her at the very moment that death struck me down . . . Here began for me what I shall call the overflowing of dreams into real life.

Here at last began for me too the overflowing of the irrational into the normal forms of biography. All the logical and traditional structures that I had learned so painstakingly—the chronology, the development of character, the structure of friendships, the sense of trust and the subject's inner identity—began to twist and dissolve. It was becoming more and more difficult to tell, or to account for, Nerval's life in the ordinary narrative, linear way. Sometimes it seemed that those haunting Tarot cards—La Lune, L'Etoile, La Tour—expressed much more about him than any critical commentary.

There was a ludicrous incident on the roof that I afterwards connected with this growing realisation. Studying my eastward stars one night, I stepped backwards to bring a constellation clear of a distant tower—I think it was the church tower of Saint Vincent-de-Paul, in the place Liszt. Suddenly I became aware that I was standing on nothing but a bright square of transparent light. It was as if the dark roof had flicked aside like a camera-shutter, and my feet were resting on a lens of sunlight shining up from beneath. I hung there like the man in the cartoon who steps over a cliff without realising it. Then there was a sharp crack, the skylight folded in on itself, and I dropped like a condemned man from the scaffold. I landed in a roar of plastic curtain on the springy floor of the shower-cabinet below, perfectly unhurt and shaking like a leaf. The skylight glass was not broken, but the frame had collapsed inward on its hinges. My imperturbable friend and landlord sorted me out from the wreckage. All I remember him saying was, *"Tiens, tu descends assez vite de tes contemplations."* We drank stiff whiskies and worked out the repair bill. But I was shaken more than I could say; it was not only a skylight that had given way.

Nerval's *Voyage en Orient*, definitively published in 1851 when he was forty-three, was intended as the proof of his sanity, his claim to the literary recognition of his peers. Yet already his troubles had started again, and his whole attitude towards the nature of his travels was deeply ambiguous. Even on the boat sailing homeward from Malta to Naples, at the very time he was assuring his father of the practical solidity of his achievement, he had emphasised the inward, mystic quality of his experience in a letter to Jules Janin.

"In sum," he wrote, "the East bears no comparison with that waking dream I had two years ago; or rather, the East of that dream is further away and higher. I have had enough of running after poetry; now I believe that it is to be found on your own doorstep, and perhaps in your own bed. I am still the man who runs over the earth, but I am going to try to stop myself, and to wait . . ."

Nerval had worked immensely hard during these intervening years. He had written a series of six long biographical essays, on the eccentric and occult figures of the seventeenth and eighteenth century, including Jacques Cazotte, Cagliostro, and the expert of the Paris night, Restif de la Bretonne. These were collected in 1852 under the title of *Les Illuminés*, which has for its general theme the decline of religious and magical beliefs in France, a subject dear to his heart. He had also written a pioneering study of French ballads and folklore, "Chansons et Légendes du Valois", which shows a profound understanding of the old musical and magical roots of poetic inspiration. Here he applied his gift for travel-writing on a place close to home, so that the Valois itself becomes a mysterious land, shrouded in mists and legends, though it was now a mere half an hour away on the newly constructed chemin de fer du Nord that Nerval so detested.

More painfully, Nerval had also turned back to the theatre, with delusive hopes of popular success. In 1847 he had worked on an opera, *Les Monténégrins*, which had a short and unsuccessful run at the Opéra-Comique in April 1849. He fell ill immediately afterwards, perhaps with memories of *Piquillo*, and spent a few ill-omened weeks in the care of another physician, Dr Aussandon. However, he recovered bravely, and was able to take over Gautier's post as dramatic critic on *La Presse* during the summer weeks while his friend was pursuing a romantic liaison in London. The following May, 1850, a further theatrical collaboration with Joseph Méry, *Le Chariot d'Enfant*, also failed, and again Nerval spent some time in the care of Dr Aussandon. It seems strange that none of his friends, and particularly Gautier, took him aside at this time and persuaded him to leave the theatre well alone.

After a short trip in Germany, as far as Leipzig, Nerval returned with the idea for a third drama, *L'Imagier de Harlem*, a modern retelling of the Faust story, which he intended for the Porte-Saint-Martin theatre in the autumn of 1851. Overwhelmed with work — besides *L'Imagier* he was also trying to complete the last of the essays for *Les Illuminés*, which had overrun its deadline for the *Revue des Deux-Mondes* — Nerval suffered a bad fall down one of the street-steps in Montmartre, wounding his chest against an iron banister, almost certainly during one of his manic phases. It was at sunset, within sight of Montmartre cemetery, and he says he was thinking of Jenny Colon. It was from this fall, on 24 September 1851, that Nerval himself dates the return of his madness in Section Nine of *Aurélia*.

Now, for the first time for ten years, Nerval returned to the clinic of Dr Blanche. The institution had moved from Montmartre to the other side of Paris at Passy, to occupy the one-time Hôtel de la Princesse de Lamballe set in a large garden at No 2 rue de Seine. Direction of the clinic had been handed over by Dr Esprit Blanche to his son Emile, a man some years younger than Nerval himself, who would prove the most gifted psychotherapist of his generation. Among Dr Emile Blanche's most distinguished artistic patients besides Nerval would be the composer Gounod and Guy de Maupassant. For the next four years Nerval was a regular patient at the clinic, and the relationship he formed with the younger Blanche became one of the most important in his life. Blanche helped Nerval fulfil himself as a writer more than any other person except Gautier; he provided a stable friendship that was part parental and part brotherly; and he gave Nerval the nearest thing to a home that he had had since the Doyenné days.

Certainly the world outside had become cruel. *L'Imagier de Harlem* was a failure, despite an impassioned plea which Nerval sent to Jules Janin for his critical support on the eve of the production. Janin's review was hostile and other critics were starting to write his obituary again. Jules Champfleury, the future champion of Realism, had already composed an article in May 1849 which professed to foresee Nerval's literary fate:

> Gérard's name is marked in red in the dossiers of the undertaker critics who do so well at funeral speeches and the suicides of their colleagues. When he is dead, Gérard will be a Great Writer. They will lay the blame on society, or the Government. "Poor Gérard! What a beautiful spirit!" etc. But while Gérard is still living he passes unnoticed. The critics who will in future pour crocodile tears over the *Scènes de la Vie Orientales* have not a word to say at present. They await the obituaries.

It was meant satirically, but the blade was double-edged, and must have wounded Nerval deeply.

His collaborator Joseph Méry recalled how, one day soon after the failure of the *Imagier*, Nerval came to visit him and broke out into bitter, almost hysterical laughter: "'There is only one play that ever succeeds in Paris. It's been seen for thirty years, and the public wants to go on seeing it. You take a mother and her son — Act I, the son is lost; Act V the son is found again. The mother cries — my son! The son cries — mother! The audience bursts into tears, and the dramatist receives a cloudburst of money.'"

Did Méry see the full psychological significance of this cry of fury and disappointment, or understand the reference to the son and the mother? He only notes that Nerval ran out of the apartment and down the stairs, saying he never wanted to see Méry again.

"Gérard, why ever not?"

"Because you tried to console me," came the reply.

It was the end of his theatrical ambitions and all hope of popular success.

7

But at the very moment that Nerval saw his public career founder, he entered into the final and most brilliantly original phase of his autobiographical writing. Freed from newspaper criticism and dramatic scripts, he reverted to his first and most natural form —what I came to think of as his *promenades*. Rousseau invented this term to describe the occasional or confessional essays he produced in his last years. Nerval's *promenades* are all essentially short pieces of travel-writing, none of them more than fifty pages, but each developed in a completely individual way—as short stories, critical essays, personal memoirs, studies of myth or customs or frankly confessional pieces. In fact often he mixes these forms, combining romance with autobiography or sliding a personal reminiscence into a scholarly or descriptive passage. What remains constant is the voice of the narrator, the voice of Gérard de Nerval, the traveller telling his tale and recounting his most private thoughts and reflections.

The finest of these *promenades* is the love-story of his childhood and adolescence, *Sylvie*, subtitled *Souvenirs du Valois*. It recounts a series of return journeys to Mortefontaine, layering one memory on top of another in a complex time-scheme greatly admired by Proust. It forms a pastoral romance, evoking the country manners of the Valois villages, in a way that attaches it to the classic prose of the French eighteenth century, like Bernardin de Saint-Pierre's *Paul et Virginie*. Yet its psychology, and its symbolic structure, are so subtle and modern as to appear almost contemporary, reminding one of nothing so much as a film such as Ingmar Bergman's *Wild Strawberries*.

Sylvie was not the first of this masterly series of *promenades*, nor the last. It was not, in other words, an exceptional production—as Gautier was inclined to suggest—struck off in the failing light of Nerval's sanity. On the contrary, it formed part of a regular cycle of creative periods which alternated with the worst months of manic hallucinations and prostrating illness. To begin with, not all these took Nerval to the asylum at Passy. Sometimes his friends were still able to cope. At the beginning of 1852 he spent some weeks with Gautier at the rue de Navarin; and at the end of the year there are notes between Nadar and another friend, Eugène de Stadler, showing that they took turns to sit up all night with Nerval. An unpublished notebook entry of Nadar's, in the Bibliothèque Nationale, describes Nerval being cared for by Stadler: "I can still recall that small, high bedroom in a fourth-storey flat in the place Pigalle, the full summer sun flowing in with asphyxiating heat, and Stadler's only bed; I shall always see before me the good Samaritan rubbing [Nerval] all over with a greyish ointment, his body like a living corpse, in a bath of sweat . . ."

Between these attacks of 1852 Nerval managed to write *Les Nuits d'Octobre*, describing three nights of walking round the backstreets of Paris, including Montmartre, Les Halles and Pantin; and a train journey out to Meaux. The style here is humorous and sometimes surreal, as with the fair at Meaux, where "a very fine woman with merino sheep fleece for hair" is on display at a side-show. There is a hallucinatory section, entitled "Capharnaum":

> Corridors—corridors without end! And staircases—staircases which go up, or go down, or go up again, and which always end sunk in deep black water, whipped up by wheels, beneath the immense arches of a bridge . . . seen through a mass of inextricable wooden scaffolding! I climb them, I descend them, I run through the corridors—all this for several eternities. Is it the punishment to which I have been condemned for my faults? I would rather live!!! But instead—my head is being hit with great hammer blows. What does it all mean?

Perhaps these are only distorted glimpses of the Seine at night, with its bridges and barges, its steps and alleys; but I found something terrible in them, like the engravings of Piranesi's imaginary prisons or the worst opium visions of de Quincey. They were travel-writings of a new kind: interior journeys, journeys through dreams and nightmares, and they seemed to portend Nerval's final night in the backstreets round the dismal rue de la Vieille Lanterne. Yet *Les Nuits* is in many ways a light-hearted, diverting work, and in its opening section describes the path that Nerval had mapped out for his future *promenades*:

> As time goes by, the passion for long and distant journeys fades, provided that one has not been travelling for so long that one

becomes a foreigner in one's own land. The circle of travel shrinks steadily, getting nearer and nearer to one's home ground . . . I have grown fond of those little villages a dozen or so leagues outside the radiating centre of Paris, like modest planets. Ten leagues is far enough to ensure that you aren't tempted to come back the same evening . . .

This shrinking of the circle was now to be Nerval's pattern until the end. It was an inner shrinking too, for as his imagination withdrew from distant adventures he fastened on his own memories, and consumed himself until he feared nothing would be left. He wrote to George Bell, another of the friends who tried to support him in his extremity: "What I write at the moment turns too much in a tightened circle. I am feeding off my own substance, and do not renew myself."

Les Nuits was published serially in *L'Illustration* during the winter of 1852, following which he was hospitalised for nearly two months in the Maison Dubois, a municipal hospital in the rue du faubourg Saint-Denis. The official diagnosis was "erysipelas", a fever and general inflammation of the skin, sometimes known as St Anthony's fire, and often associated with acute nervous disorders.

The alternating pattern of illness and creation became steadily more pronounced. In the early summer of 1853 Nerval travelled in the Valois and worked on *Sylvie*, which was published in the *Revue des Deux-Mondes* on 15 August. Exactly ten days later he was taken on as a long-term patient by Dr Emile Blanche at Passy, where he remained, with occasional remissions, until the spring of 1854. During one of the brief periods of lucidity he delivered several poems he had written to Alexandre Dumas who was now editing a magazine, *Le Mousquetaire*. Dumas published one of them in December.

It was the sonnet "El Desdichado", the story of his life told in fourteen poised and noble lines, each phase of Nerval's private sufferings transfigured into symbolic language, as if it were some great folk-myth of Romanticism. In the first section comes the disinheritance of the Hero, the loss of his visionary estates, the death of his beloved; in the second, the consoling memories of his great journeys, and the healing powers of nature; in the third, the questions of his identity and purpose, the fatal kiss of the Muse, and the perilous immersion in the seductive grotto of his dreams; and in the fourth and last, the epic attempts to swim the river of madness and death and the unceasing efforts to find eternal harmony in a universe divided by desire and renunciation, through the magic lute of Orpheus—the poet's lyre of words, his only hope of salvation:

> *Je suis le Ténébreux,—le Veuf,—l'Inconsolé,*
> *Le Prince d'Aquitaine à la Tour abolie:*
> *Ma seule Étoile est morte,—et mon luth constellé*
> *Porte le Soleil noir de la Mélancolie.*
>
> *Dans la nuit du Tombeau, Toi qui m'as consolé*
> *Rends-moi le Pausilippe et la mer d'Italie,*
> *La fleur qui plaisait tant à mon coeur désolé,*
> *Et la treille où le Pampre à la Rose s'allie.*
>
> *Suis-je Amour ou Phébus? . . . Lusignan ou Biron?*
> *Mon front est rouge encore du baiser de la Reine;*
> *J'ai rêvé dans la Grotte où nage la Sirène . . .*
>
> *Et j'ai deux fois vainqueur traversé l'Achéron:*
> *Modulant tour à tour sur la lyre d'Orphée*
> *Les soupirs de la Sainte et les cris de la Fée.*

Dumas accompanied this sonnet with a long editorial article, in which he mockingly described Nerval as feeding on dreams and visions like an opium-eater of Cairo.

> Sometimes he believes he is Solomon, the King of the Orient, who awaits the Queen of Sheba; sometimes he believes he is the Sultan of Crimea, the Count of Abyssinia, or the Baron of Smyrna; and sometimes he simply believes he is a madman, and explains how he became so, but with such joy and enthusiasm that everyone else wants to become mad too and follow their fascinating guide through the Land of Chimeras, with its green oases far cooler and more shadowy and inviting than those on the dusty road from Alexandria to Ammon.

It was, in effect, the third mocking obituary that Nerval had received in his lifetime.

But Dumas also encouraged Nerval to think in terms of collecting together his scattered pieces of prose and poetry. This resulted in his two major volumes of 1854. The first was *Les Filles du Feu*, a linked anthology of eight prose pieces, including *Sylvie*, the essays "Chansons et Légendes du Valois" and "Isis" (concerning Egyptian mythology). There were also *Octavie* and *Pandora*, the two love-stories set in Naples and Vienna. The book was dedicated to Dumas in a long Preface, in which for the first time Nerval openly discusses his madness. The second volume was *Les Chimères*, a collection of seven mystic sonnets, including "El Desdichado"; and a sequence of five religious sonnets, *Le Christ aux Oliviers*, probably written in the Lebanon in 1843. These two books became Nerval's most famous titles, and had they been properly recognised at the time would have assured his reputation and given him the peace of mind that alone might have saved him.

In fact Nerval was more restless and unstable than ever. He was working at another autobiographical work, the *Promenades et Souvenirs*, which describes the memories of childhood evoked by a series of short, probably therapeutic trips to other places round Paris—St Germain-en-Laye, Pontoise, Chantilly and Senlis. But the need to attempt a further "*grand voyage*" overcame him, and, despite the misgivings of Dr Blanche, in May 1854 he set out for Germany. This was to be his last major journey, taking him as far as Nuremberg and Leipzig, and possibly to Glogau where his mother was buried. It produced a sequence of some forty letters, mostly written to Dr Blanche and to Dr Labrunie, which are among the most revealing and tragic that he wrote. Here the tension between being "Gérard", the wayward son, and "Gérard de Nerval", the romantic travel-writer, becomes almost unbearable.

To his father he is reassuring, explanatory, serious and frequently sad; to Dr Blanche he is mercurial—cheerful or gloomy, teasing or apologetic, calm or exalted. To Dr Labrunie he writes: "My situation is good, though dependent on the future . . . My works are a capital which I shall increase, if it please God, and which after my death will be enough to acquit me towards mankind . . . Napoleon said that everything has to be paid for. It was Balzac who taught me this saying. And Balzac paid for everything in the end; he died *honoré*, as was his first name."

To Dr Blanche he sends greetings and asks to be remembered to the lady patients at the asylum:

Explain to them that the pensive person they used to see drifting, morose and uneasy, through the day-room and the garden, or at your hospitable dining-table was assuredly not me. From the far side of the Rhine, I reject that double-dealer [*sycophante*] who stole my name and perhaps my face. When the ladies see me again, I hope I shall be worthier, wittier, more attentive and more seductive—more affectionate, I should say.

He admits to Dr Labrunie that his illness, "that is to say, my exalted states", sometimes returns. "I am taken for a prophet (a false prophet), with my occasionally mysterious talk and my frequent air of distraction." He has become well-known and much spoken of, "though thanks, it is true, to my *misfortunes*". But he is better, and the proof is that he can write to his father "so easily and so logically". His trip is doing him good, above all because it has allowed him much solitary reflection "about other people and about myself", and the time to make "good resolutions". Yet though he can write logically to his father it is only to Blanche that he writes emotionally. His letters to Blanche often make him cry as he writes: "My heart aches in thinking of you, and of my father. Write back to me what I must do, because I suffer deeply, and from the bottom of my heart. If there is always a last moment to repent, well then, I repent! But I am still walking in the darkness, and it is your answer and counsel that I am waiting for."

He tries to put things—his whole life—right with his father, but he can only do so stiffly, and formally: "I want you to be perfectly at ease concerning me, but I reproach myself bitterly for all the anxiety that I have so often given you. At last I see clearly that one must give up the ideas of one's youth, and try to make oneself a position appropriate to one's age and abilities."

What does this mean—changing, or giving up? His whole writing career, perhaps? Nerval does not say; Gérard does not say. But to Blanche he is more heart-felt, and more desperate. He admits that he has written to his father, "affecting a calm that I don't really have". His visions have begun again, and he doubts if he will ever be able to attain "the peace and the future that you speak to me of". His writing projects were serious ones, "and still are serious". But he will come home, because "now I count on being better at Paris".

Contrary to what I expected, there is virtually nothing in these letters about his mother. "My principal torment in my moments of solitude," he writes to Blanche, "has always been the thought of my father. Don't imagine that I tell you this to soften you in my favour. But the evils that I have made him suffer continually weigh upon my heart. If I should be destined to act out the most painful expiation that could be imagined I would willingly submit to it, for this reason alone."

Dr Blanche must have seen this as a veiled threat of suicide, but he could do little except urge his patient to return to Paris. Nerval's sense of guilt towards his father had become one more element in the growing mythology of his own life. Blanche knew equally that

Nerval still *blamed* his father for not supporting his literary career. These contradictions formed part of the complex pattern—soon to be developed in *Aurélia*—which expressed Nerval's fundamental sense of abandonment, going right back to his mother's tomb in "cold Silesia". Blanche's kindly letters of reply could not reassure him.

No letters from Dr Labrunie are known, and I also looked in vain for a letter to or from Gautier. There was something of a further mystery here, for in these last months references to Nerval's oldest friend become surprisingly scarce. Those there are have an unexpected tone of bitterness. Writing to George Bell from Strasbourg Nerval mentions that he has offended his "best friend" by describing him somewhat hyperbolically in memoirs of the Doyenné, *Les Petits Châteaux de Bohème*. "I thought I had made an *Adonis* of him," protests Nerval. In fact he had compared Gautier to an Indian Bacchus, and described him as putting on weight (both of which descriptions were just). In another letter from Leipzig he asks the publisher Sartorius simply to pass on his news to Gautier: "I have a travel-letter for him but it will be published, dated from Karlsruhe, and I don't want to waste more copy in writing private letters."

That their friendship had been reduced, apparently, to this cold professionalism suggested that something had gone very wrong. The newspaper letter from Karlsruhe was never written, and the last known note from Nerval to Gautier is a formal introduction of a newspaper colleague sometime in autumn 1854. It is signed "Gérard de Nerval", a signature which Nerval had never used to his friend before, and is virtually a gesture of hostility.

I puzzled over this for many weeks until I finally found the sad solution in the archives of the Bibliothèque Nationale, in Nadar's notebooks. That Nerval felt exploited by Gautier was clear to me: it is a central thread in his story, though Nerval surely had greater cause to blame his "undertaker critics", Janin, Champfleury and Dumas. But perhaps he forgave them more readily as they were, after all, primarily professional friends, and the damage they had done was inextricably involved in the creation of his public persona as Nerval.

But Gautier was a friend—*the* friend—of his youth, *un ami de coeur*; almost his brother. Gautier, it must have seemed, was guilty of a family betrayal; a failure to love him and support him comparable to the failure of his father. How far Nerval was justified in thinking like this was difficult to establish objectively. But the consequence was one of those tragic actions of Nerval's madness which gave me the sense of having lost his true identity in the labyrinth of his delusions. The incident probably occurred in 1853, and it is told in a single-sentence aside by Nadar. The fact that Nadar never referred to it again, in any of his published writings, paradoxically convinced me of its authenticity. He wrote: "The door of my dear friend Théophile Gautier was closed forever to [Gérard], by the memory of a knife-blade drawn against him in one of those outbursts of demented fury."

I read this with a cold shock, that nothing else in Nerval's life had produced. He had actually tried to kill his old friend. It is one of those actions that challenges one's whole notion of a person's character. More and more I felt I was following Nerval into the dark, and had lost him on that inner journey.

By 1854, Nerval was already the subject of a published biography by the hack Eugène de Mirecourt, a copy of which he discovered in a library at Strasbourg before coming back to Paris. It was accompanied by an engraved portrait, possibly based on an unknown daguerreotype, on which Nerval drew a pentangle against enchantment, and wrote "*Je suis l'autre*", a formula which antedates Rimbaud's "*Je est un autre*" by thirty years. His growing sense of being two people, already clear in his correspondence with Dr Blanche, comes out with apparent naturalness in his description of the biography to his father:

> I am presented like the hero of a novel, and the whole pamphlet is full of exaggerations, no doubt well-meaning, and incorrect facts, though these are of very little importance, since the whole thing describes a conventional "personality" . . . One can't stop people talking, and this is how history gets written. All of which goes to prove that I have done well to keep my imaginative life [*vie poétique*] and my real life apart.

Nerval eventually returned to Paris in July 1854, full of good intentions. "How often I have planned to reform my life," he told his father, "but never more seriously than now." To Dr Blanche he wrote from Bar-le-Duc, "I still hope to show myself worthy of your care." He had a little less than seven months to live.

In the mass of unreliable and picturesque anecdotage that surrounds these last months, three dates are of outstanding importance. On 19 October 1854 Nerval voluntarily released himself from Dr Blanche's care at Passy, claiming that he would stay with a relative at Saint-Germain. On 1 January 1855 the first part of *Aurélia* was published in the *Revue de Paris*, finally making his madness public property in the literary world. And at dawn on 26 January, Nerval's body was found hanging by a piece of kitchen cord from the bars of a grilled ventilation window, halfway down the steps of the alley leading to the Seine known as the rue de la Vieille Lanterne.

According to Gautier, the partially corrected proofs of part two of *Aurélia* were in Nerval's jacket pocket. The mortuary records, which have been found, do not confirm this story, though they show that Nerval had no topcoat on despite the fact that it was a snowy night with a temperature of minus eighteen degrees. There was no suicide note, though everyone who knew Nerval well—including Gautier, Nadar, Stadler, and Dr Blanche himself—agreed that he died by his own hand. The second part of *Aurélia* was duly published in the *Revue de Paris* in February, creating a sensation; and Gautier carefully edited a version for book publication—adding the "Letters to Jenny Colon" of 1837—which appeared later that summer under the title *Le Rêve et la Vie*. Gérard Labrunie had finally passed into the *"vie poétique"* and legend of Gérard de Nerval.

Writing officially to the Archbishop of Paris—there were clerical complications whether a suicide could be buried in the consecrated ground of Père Lachaise—Dr Emile Blanche gave the following summary of the case:

M. Labrunie (Gérard de Nerval), aged forty-five, a man of letters born in Paris, had been seized on repeated occasions during these last years with an attack of mental alienation for which both my father and I gave him treatment . . . On 19 October 1854, at his own insistence, I released him into the care of his aunt, Madame Labrunie. She was forewarned by me that M. Gérard was still in need of a degree of surveillance, and on this basis she agreed to take him in and look after him. In truth, M. Gérard de Nerval was not so ill that he could be held, against his will, in a lunatic asylum. Yet as far as I was concerned he had not been sane for a long time. Believing that he retained the same energy of imagination and the same capacity for work, he thought he could live on the earnings of his literary output, as before. He worked harder than ever, but perhaps he was disappointed in his hopes? His independent nature and his self-respect prevented him from accepting financial aid, even from his most tried and trusted friends. Under the influence of these moral pressures [*causes morales*] his reason was steadily undermined. But it was above all because he saw his madness face to face. I do not hesitate therefore to inform you, My Lord, that it was certainly in an extreme attack of madness that M. Gérard de Nerval put an end to his days.

As I read this calm, carefully worded medical statement, which succeeded in blaming no one for the tragedy, one ironic detail struck me. Blanche uses three different names to describe his patient. Even Nerval's own doctor did not know what to call Gérard at the end. What chance had his biographer?

8

This is not a rhetorical question. Nerval's story, as I have recounted it, makes a superficial sense, and the outlines of a personality emerge to some degree. He was a brilliantly gifted writer, a modest and charming man, but so deeply wounded in his private life that he was never able to settle down and establish himself—either domestically or professionally. The rootlessness of his condition in many ways represents the larger transformation that was painfully coming over the whole of Europe since the Revolution and the Napoleonic Wars. France was changing from a traditional to a modern, industrialised society, with its popular press, its railways and steamships, its banking and commerce and its increasingly materialistic values. The spirit of Romanticism was being overcome by Realism, like a candle being carried into a room fitted with electric light. One is tempted to say that, had Nerval been born earlier, he would have been saved by religion; had he been born later, he would have been saved by psychoanalysis.

His agonised sense of being lost, of being in purgatory, surrounded by a world of symbols that he could never quite organise or interpret, is memorably expressed both in writing about the mystical madness of his adulthood in Paris and the magic geography of his childhood in the Valois. Wherever he travelled, he saw images of his own "disinherited" spiritual state. Whether it was in the romantic mythology of Germany with its Lorelei and mother-goddesses; or in the fertility cults of Egypt celebrating Isis and Osiris; or the Gnostic revelations of the Druses of Lebanon; or the memories of a classical golden age in Greece and southern Italy; or in the beautiful poetic superstitions and legends of the Valois—"where the heart of France has beat for a thousand years"—Nerval found evidence of a lost paradise no longer available to modern man.

He could see this in the smallest, most familiar things, like the little villages of the Ile de France isolated by the chemin de fer du Nord:

> those poor abandoned villages which the railways have cut off from the circulation of daily life. They draw back into themselves, casting a disillusioned glance on the marvels of a new civilisation that condemns them or forgets them . . . they are like those circles in Dante's *Purgatorio*, frozen in a single act of remembrance, where the actions of a past life are repeated and repeated in an ever-shrinking centre of consciousness.

Or he could describe this loss in the largest, most philosophic, reflections on the ruined temples and shrines all over the globe:

> If there is, to be sure, something more terrifying than the history of the fall of great empires, it is the history of the death of religions. Volney himself was overcome by this feeling as he visited the innumerable ruins of once-sacred buildings. The true believer may still escape from this impression, but with the inherent scepticism of our age all of us must sometime tremble to find so many dark gates opening out on to nothingness.

But the coherence of Nerval as a historical figure, speaking so eloquently but quietly for the failing vision of Romanticism in France—this coherence begins to quiver and dissolve the moment one tries to approach him more closely and intimately. His two names, which might seem no more than a literary device, do genuinely represent a profound ambiguity in his "real" identity. Was he one of the last of the Romantic heroes; or a poor, suffering, psychotic misfit? Was he the picturesque personality—"*le doux rêveur*"—described in the newspaper columns of his friends; or the anxious, guilt-laden, motherless son revealed in the long letters to his father and his physician?

This duality takes on a further, terrible twist in his last completed work, *Aurélia*—what Gautier called "the memoirs of Insanity dictated to Reason"—where the idea that he was a double personality, one condemned and one saved, becomes a central and inescapable obsession:

> . . . What was this spirit that was both within me and outside me? Was it that Double of the legends, or that mysterious brother which the Orientals call the *ferouer*? Had I not been curiously

struck by the Teutonic story of the knight who did battle all night in a dark forest with an unknown assailant—that turned out to be himself? A terrible idea seized me: mankind is cursed with a double nature, I told myself. One of the Fathers of the Church has written: "I feel two men within me" . . . In every man there is a spectator and an actor, the one who speaks and the one who answers. The Eastern mystics have seen in this idea two implacable enemies: the good and the evil genius. But am I the good one, or the evil one? I ask myself. In any case, *the other* is hostile to me. Who knows if there are not certain circumstances, or certain times in life, when these two spirits inevitably separate?

Here is Nerval in the full grip of his insanity, rushing headlong from German legends and Oriental mysticism to the *Confessions* of St Augustine and the dualistic philosophy of Romantic drama. His very madness lies in the conventionality of the *doppelgänger* idea, which seizes him like a wholly new and terrible revelation. This is the mythomania spoken of by his doctors; but it is also at the centre of his self-understanding. How could a biographer present this? Should one write the lives of two separate people, as Nerval himself sometimes experienced them?

The immediate answer was, of course not. The biographer must integrate the facets of his subject until he becomes the self-same man that others knew and loved and remembered. Yet it was clear to me that any biography of Nerval must account fully for his madness and suicide, both from without and within. To do this all paths led directly back into his childhood and adolescence. Even if one accepts the story of his love affair with Jenny Colon at face value, and in the way he presents it in *Aurélia* (and in the way Gautier embroiders it), it is evident that such an experience of unrequited love could never have affected Nerval so profoundly and disruptively, if it did not correspond to—or nourish itself on—damaging and wounding experiences of love lost or rejected from his earliest moments. I was thus, in a way, committed to psychoanalysing Nerval for myself; to achieving what even Dr Blanche had been unable to do. And as my months went by in Paris, I became more and more convinced that was exactly what could *not* be done, and that I had reached the limits of the biographical form, as a method of investigation. Instead, I found myself slipping further and further into a peculiar and perilous identification with my lunatic subject, as if somehow I could diagnose Nerval by becoming him. As if self-identification—the first crime in biography—had become my last and only resort.

If this sounds melodramatic, the problem can be shown simply in terms of sources. I have already explained how nearly everything we know about Jenny Colon depends upon Nerval's retrospective view of himself, written in the last four years of his life, which is to say during his madness. So there are very few first-hand sources for what Nerval claimed was the most important emotional relationship in his life. The position is even more difficult for his childhood and teens. Virtually everything we know has to be extrapolated from *Sylvie* (1853), *Promenades et Souvenirs* (1854) and *Aurélia* (1855), where autobiography, romance and hallucination are inextricably mixed. For example, the travel-letters written from Germany between 1810 and 1812 by his mother, which letters Nerval says had such a shaping influence on him, have never been discovered. Did they ever exist? There are no letters or journals from Dr Labrunie or the Boucher-Laurent circle of relations. No one recorded any reminiscences of Nerval's childhood at Mortefontaine, not even that faithful collector of antiquities, Uncle Antoine Boucher. Apart from a single five-line note (referring to the publication of *Faust*) there are not even any letters from Nerval himself before 1830, when he was twenty-two. (For comparison, there are over two hundred known letters from Shelley before his twenty-first birthday.) In fact Nerval did not begin to write regularly until he began to travel, and a continuous correspondence really only exists from the time of his first journey to Naples in 1834. This was one more reason why that early Italian visit began to seem so important to me, and the story *Octavie* promised me a final clue.

The consequence of this is that the biography of Nerval's youth, even in the apparently circumstantial way that I have given it here (and omitting many key incidents, such as the dance with "Adrienne" in the grounds of the château of Morte-fontaine, much beloved by Nerval's French biographers), is almost entirely an artificial construct. That is to say, it uses unverifiable materials from the end of Nerval's life to invent or imagine his beginnings. So I found myself effectively trapped within Nerval's own mind and memory. To write a novel based on Nerval's life from these materials would be perfectly satisfactory: it would have imaginative truth. But for me to write his biography meant entering into a solipsistic world, where the traditional structure of objective documentation, third-party evidence, and chronology dissolved.

So it was that I slipped into the literary labyrinth, and was slowly disorientated, and finally lost, until even my own Paris came to seem a kind of nightmare.

It is not a place to which I ever wish to return; but I can give briefly some idea of the forms in which I lost myself, and the "staircases and corridors" up and down which I ran. For a short time, influenced by the work of Michel Foucault on the history of prisons and madhouses, I thought I could present Nerval as a victim of his doctors: Dr Labrunie, Dr Aussandon, Dr Esprit Blanche at Montmartre and Dr Emile Blanche at Passy. The fact that Nerval himself was always torn between the two careers of medicine and writing gave this some authenticity; and it expressed that fundamental opposition between the spiritual and material values of the age—the poet versus the scientist—which I always saw as the background to his story.

The writing of *Aurélia* itself can be understood as Nerval's deliberate attempt to reconcile these two disciplines, the one imaginative and the other diagnostic. As he wrote: "If I did not think that the mission of a writer is to analyse honestly what he experiences in the grave crises of life, and if I did not see this as a useful purpose, I would stop here, and would not try to describe what I experienced from this time on, in a series of visions that were perhaps totally irrational, or simply insane . . ."

Nerval also partially attributed his cure to the help he gave in Passy to another patient called Saturnin, who was in a cataleptic trance and being force-fed. By himself acting as a doctor towards Saturnin he exorcised his own fear of the Avenging Double and achieved visions of his own salvation. It was Saturnin, "the poor sick youth, but with a face transfigured and intelligent", who brought him the final dream of his healing goddess. His star grows in the night sky, takes the form of Aurèlie, and walks between the two of them in a paradisal garden, where flowers sprout beneath her feet. She tells him: "The trial which you had to undergo has come to its term. Those numberless stairs where you exhausted yourself, clambering up and down, were the phases of your old illusions which confused your thought . . . It was necessary that your prayer should be brought to [the Holy Virgin] by a simple heart who was freed from all links with earthly things."

Yet this view of Nerval, as primarily a medical case seeking his own cure, soon lost itself in the incapacity of medical science to do more than attach labels to his sufferings. It left the world of his imagination untouched, and this is what Nerval himself had said: "There are doctors and bureaucrats here who try to prevent one from extending the field of poetry into the public highway. They only let me out and allowed me to move freely among reasonable people when I had formally agreed with them that I had been *sick*.

It was an admission that cost me a lot in terms of self-respect and even my sense of truth."

I next moved to the opposite extreme, and began to interpret Nerval's life almost entirely in terms of the magic world by which he himself was so fascinated. Much of this was influenced by the great Nervalian critic, Jean Richer, and his study *Gérard de Nerval et les doctrines ésotériques* (1949). But I went much further. Everything in Nerval's life came to have symbolic meaning, full of archetypes, alchemical processes, astrological signs, mystic correspondences and invisible harmonies. I interpreted the seven sonnets of the *Chimères* as the seven alchemical processes—"El Desdichado" was Calcination, "Horus" was Putrefaction, "Myrtho" was Solution, "Delfica" was Distillation, "Antéros" was Conjunction, "Artémis" was Sublimation and "Vers Dorés" was Congelation; and these seven mystic processes became the seven phases of Nerval's life, which corresponded to the "Seven Châteaux" through which he said every poet had to pass. The seventh château—"of brick and stone, dreamed of in our youth"—became the madhouse at Passy, which had once belonged to a Princess; and this corresponded with the châteaux at Mortefontaine or at Chantilly which had presided over Nerval's childhood, where Sylvie his first love had danced, and where "Adrienne" (Sophie Dawes) had ridden in her costume of Amazon or Isis.

Every woman and goddess in Nerval's story became a personification of his lost mother; every animal—the lobster in Paris, the parrot in the Valois, the scarab in Egypt—became messengers from the supernatural world. I even somehow incorporated the four voluptuous statues, representing the four rivers of France, which stand in the little garden outside the Bibliothèque Nationale, as the four stages of Nerval's travels—to Germany, to Italy, to the East, and to the land of Dreams and Madness. I saw his whole life as a pilgrimage, or journey of initiation, intended to reunite the spiritual and material values of his generation. As he himself wrote: "My role seemed to be to re-establish the universal harmony by cabalistic art and to seek a solution by evoking the occult forces of diverse religions."

Indeed, the further I went into this labyrinth of signs and rituals the more I came to believe that *Aurélia* was the complete and literal statement of his life. The key passage seemed the following:

> From that moment, when I felt sure that I was being subjected to the trials of a Sacred Initiation, an invincible strength entered my soul. I imagined myself a Hero, living under the direct gaze

of the gods. Everything in Nature took on a new aspect, and secret voices, warning and exhorting me, came from plants, trees, animals and the humblest insects. The talk of my companions took on mysterious turns of meaning which I alone could understand, and formless, inanimate objects lent themselves to the calculations of my mind. From combinations of pebbles, from shapes in corners, from chinks or openings, from the outlines of leaves, from colours, scents and sounds, I could see hitherto unknown harmonies springing forth. "How have I been able to live so long," I asked myself, "outside Nature, and without identifying with her? Everything lives, moves, everything corresponds . . . Though I am captive now, here on earth, I commune with the chorus of the stars, and they take part in my joys and sorrows!"

This wonderful but demented vision, a sort of deranged apotheosis of Romanticism, which Nerval experienced in the locked gardens of Passy, sometimes seemed to describe my own researches. I came to believe that my own biography would have magic properties, and I started to organise it in the form of a commentary on seven Tarot cards, each one covering a phase in Nerval's life, presented not chronologically but in a series of cycles. It started with La Lune, Les Amoureux and L'Etoile . . . and ended with La Tour and, of course, Le Pendu—the Hanged Man card that appears also in Eliot's *The Waste Land*. One late summer evening, at a café in the place Royal where we had our rendezvous, I showed my notebooks—seven notebooks in seven different colours—to my friend Françoise. Her face took on a curious expression. "*Ce n'est pas la peine de te rendre fou, chéri,*" she remarked quietly. "*Ce n'est-pas ta vie à toi, après tout!*" She swept me off to a late-night showing of *Les Enfants du Paradis* at La Pagode. And slowly I began to realise what was happening.

9

After many more weeks, full of strange occurrences which I prefer to forget, I abandoned my "magic" notebooks and returned to my point of departure: Nadar's photograph of Nerval, taken just before his suicide. I felt I had got no nearer to him, and was in despair. There he still sat in the upholstered chair, with his deep eyes and the crooked, ironic smile beneath his moustache. ("*J'embrasse ton vieux moustache,*" Gautier had once written to him in Vienna.) His lined face and thin balding hair seemed to show his sufferings, yet there was something kindly, almost boyish still in his features. His jacket was scruffy, his cravat badly tied, his shirt partly pulled out from the top of his trousers, like a schoolboy caught stealing apples. I noticed for the first time that he was holding the stub of a little cigar or papier-maïs, and that his index finger was dark with nicotine. It was funny: in all those dozens of memoirs and articles I had read by his friends nobody had remarked on the fact that Gérard smoked heavily.

Time was running out for me; for both of us. I had wandered the streets of Pontoise, Saint-Denis, Dammartin and Senlis. No longer lost villages, but flourishing townships linked into the gridworks of *route nationale*, their fate had been reversed: reintegrated into civilisation they had suffered a transformation never envisaged by Dante. They had become suburbs of paradise like everywhere else, shopping centres and arcades where Nerval's footsteps were long lost. A few empty shrines alone remained—the sepulchre of St Denis, the gateway of Senlis Cathedral, the tomb of Rousseau at Ermenonville, "opening on to nothingness". But always I seemed to return to the gardens of the Palais-Royal, the raked walks, the iron benches, the diagonal shadows of the long galleries, *la fontaine qui coulait* and the little oxide-green statue of the naked goddess stung by a serpent, which stands in the middle of the tended municipal roses. "I continued on my way," wrote Nerval, "and arrived at the galleries of the Palais-Royal. There everyone seemed to be staring at me. A persistent idea had lodged itself in my mind: that there were no more dead. I hurried through the galerie de Foy saying: 'I have committed some fault,' but I could not discover what it was . . ."

My mind turned back to Nerval's suicide. Why had he finally done it? Why was there no suicide note? Suicides usually leave notes; but perhaps his whole work was a form of suicide note. Maybe this was the last link that I should try to trace back, the last footstep. The rue de la Vieille Lanterne was long gone—its place is now occupied by what is the orchestra pit of the Théâtre du Châtelet: for me another symbolic position. But suicide is frequently mentioned in Nerval's work. Perhaps if I could find the original place in which it occurred, all would be solved. This would be my last journey, I thought; the last mystery I could hope to solve.

Aurélia is full of thoughts of death, but most of these belong to the hallucinations of the 1850s: "When I reached the place de la Concorde, my idea was to kill myself. Several times I went down towards the Seine, but something stopped me from carrying out my plan. The stars shone in the firmament."

I did eventually find the strangest premonition of his hanging, dating from the first breakdown of 1841. It occurred, of all places, in Gautier's drawing-room in the rue de Navarin. Nerval had dined tranquilly with Gautier and the editor Alphonse Karr, but he could feel the evil moment coming, and he tried to ward it off with one of his occult talismen:

> I asked one of my friends for an oriental ring that he had on his finger, which I regarded as an ancient charm, and taking a silk scarf *I knotted it round my neck*, taking care to turn the stone of the ring, which was made of turquoise, on the exact point of my neck at which I could feel the pain. This point, as I thought, was the place from where my soul was in danger of leaving my body, at the instant that a particular ray of light from the *star* I had seen the evening before formed an astrological conjunction with the zenith.

In a sense, this is exactly what happened fourteen years later.

But I could go further back than 1841. I found in the story *Octavie* that Nerval claimed to have made a suicide attempt in Italy, during his very first journey of 1834. It had occurred on the Posilippo, that high cliff above the sea outside Naples which is associated with the prophetic cave of the Sibyl and also the tomb of Virgil, the first great classical poet who journeyed to the Underworld. These references fill the poems of the *Chimères* at the end of Nerval's life:

> *Dans la nuit du Tombeau, Toi qui m'as consolé,*
> *Rends-moi le Pausilippe et la mer d'Italie . . .*

So it was obvious that these formed a symbolic and biographical conjunction of critical importance in his life. Moreover, it was *Octavie* that had the most continuous history of manuscript revisions in all Nerval's work. Tracing the text backward (for now all my thinking about Nerval was concentrated on reverse time, *le temps perdu*) the incident appeared in the following sequence: lastly, in the *Filles du Feu* of 1854; previously in Dumas's magazine *Le Mousquetaire* of 1853; then in Gautier's magazine *L'Artiste* in 1845, under the title "L'Illusion"; then as Letter Three in the *Roman à Faire* published in *La Sylphide* in 1842; and earliest of all in a rough manuscript sketch of 1837, which was held in the great Lovenjoul Library at Chantilly. Each version saw various changes and expansions of the original incident, and I thought that if I could track down the very first version I might be in possession of the key to Nerval's suicide, and thus to his whole tragedy.

I took a train to Chantilly one burning hot morning at the end of August, my final *promenade*.

Chantilly, with its polished racecourse between two elegant straight streets, like an emerald in an L-shaped golden mount, has suffered perhaps the least of all the country towns of the Valois. Tradition and modernity have come to a compromise, with the Duc du Condé's great château in its lake full of lazing carp at one end of town, the railway station at the other. The tree-lined boulevards are very quiet except on racing days, though ancient gentlemen in mohair suits and gold-topped canes still help beautiful young ladies in Liberty-print dresses out of Paris-registered Mercedes and Rolls-Royces. "*Voilà, Angélique . . . nous-voici Hélène,*" they sigh, with tight moneyed smiles.

The Duc's stables, themselves as big as a castle, stand by the northern gate on the edge of the racecourse; and Spoelberch de Lovenjoul's library—a seventeenth-century country house with a little gravelled courtyard that Nerval would have loved—draws back into the cool shadows, almost anonymous, a few hundred metres into the town. The hotels and restaurants are many and expensive, so I wandered about as in the old days, waiting for fate to direct me.

Nerval beautifully evokes the place, comparing it to one of "those old aristocratic gentlemen with impeccable white shirt and faultless manners, whose proud demeanour covers a worn hat or well-darned clothes . . . Everything is proper, well-ordered, circumspect; and voices fill the high, sonorous rooms with harmonious echoes." An old concierge, sleeping in the sun with her dog near the château gates, told me of a place called Les Fontaines, beyond the southern limits of the town in a small wood, where I might find a bed for the night. It turned out to be a Jesuit retreat-house, set on the edge of a small lake, with conference rooms, kitchens, library and a long corridor of guest bedrooms, each with an iron bedstead, a writing-table and a wooden crucifix. I knew they would take me the moment I walked up the drive and saw the brothers hauling logs out of the woods. In ten years I had simply come full circle, and was walking back to La Trappe in another incarnation.

"We are giving a retreat for missionary nuns, and a conference on 'Les Routards'," the Guestmaster told me when I had explained what I was doing. He was a thin, intense man, dressed in the battered black suit of the Jesuit priest, with a yellowish complexion that suggested many years spent in the tropics. He chain-smoked with a hand that tremored slightly. "But we have a cancellation, and you can have a bed for a week if you want it." Behind him on the wall of his office was a world map, showing the concentrations of poverty and malnutrition. "You look tired after your researches. This may be a place for you to rest and reflect. Religious denominations do not interest us. Every traveller has his needs."

He took me to my cell, down the long corridor of pungent coconut matting, and told me the meal times. Going out of the door he stopped, and a gentle smile broke over his worn face. "Your Gérard de Nerval travelled a lot in Germany, I believe." He hesitated for a moment. "You are a historian, and you will appreciate the ironies of history. The Jesuit order purchased Les Fontaines very cheaply, in 1946. It used to belong to the Rothschilds. But during the war it was occupied by the German army, and it became the local headquarters of the police. That is to say, of the Gestapo. So after the war nobody wanted it. That was why the Jesuits bought it very cheaply, in the material sense." He hesitated again. "But in the spiritual sense . . ." The Guestmaster shook his head. "Now our guests come from all over Europe, and we try to help them, whoever they are. So you are very welcome. Our fountain flows. I hope you find what you are looking for."

Every morning for a week I walked to the Lovenjoul Library from the woods of Les Fontaines. The heat shimmered above the trees, and along the racecourse huge lawn-sprinklers played, their fans of water throwing up languorous rainbows of sparkling light. I found two manuscripts that concluded my researches. The first was a long travel-letter from Gautier, which described a trip he made to Italy in the summer of 1851, when Nerval's madness was beginning again. It was entitled "La Lettre à la Présidente"—La Présidente being Madame Sabatier, the famous courtesan who had been on various occasions the mistress of Baudelaire, Flaubert and Gautier, among others. The letter was a gross parody of all Nerval's delicate, amorous travel-writing; it was jocular and entirely obscene:

> The other evening Louis and I were visited by a young Venetian beauty, who having completed a number of preliminaries to satisfy herself that we were not police informers lifted up her dress and unhooped her stays, to allow us to run our eyes over her naked charms. Her breasts proceeded to explode into the room, crash straight through the floor, burst out into the via Condotti down the Corso as far as the piazza Venezia, leaving us

smothered in an avalanche of "lilies and roses" in the style of Dupaty . . .

The second was Nerval's letter of 1837, describing the night he first made love to a woman. The love-making goes without a word, and the story really begins the following dawn in Naples: "I tore myself away from this phantom who seduced and terrified me at the same time. I wandered through the deserted town, with the sound of the first church bells. Then, feeling the coming dawn, I took to the little streets behind Chiaia, and I began to climb the Posilippo above the grotto."

I worked slowly on this manuscript, comparing all six versions. Each evening I walked back along the racecourse, and dined at Les Fontaines with the missionary nuns, in a room full of small, polished wooden tables. The scrubbed faces of the nuns, framed in their starched wimples, glowed above the jugs of water filled with roses, as they told me of their homes—mostly in the Auvergne and the south and Aquitaine—and their missionary stations in the deserted regions of Chad and the Sudan. They had been away for seven years, and after this one summer at home they were going back again for another seven. Their devotion was simple and brisk; and heart-breaking.

In the later versions of his manuscript Nerval slowly turns the figure of his Neapolitan woman into a gypsy fortune-teller or sorceress. Her room becomes filled with mystical objects—the statue of a black madonna, ancient pictures showing the Four Elements "represented by mythological divinities", Etruscan vases and artificial flowers, old books on divination, dreams and the Tarot. But in the original version she is simply a woman who earns her living by embroidering vestments for the church.

It became clear to me that this beautiful, anonymous woman of the South had gradually been transformed in Nerval's mind —during the twenty years of his wandering, dreaming, searching life after 1834—into the embodiment of everything he had hoped love would give back to him, in return for what he had originally lost as a child. She was his mother, she was Jenny Colon the actress, she was the "big blonde" of his trips with Gautier, she was the slave-girl Zetnyab, she was the Goddess Isis, she was the Virgin Mary of his last consoling visions in the madhouse. Yet what she had finally brought him was—nothing, *le néant*, metaphysical emptiness, the sense of his own hopelessly divided and outcast self: the shadow man, the widowed man, the unconsoled child and lover.

His story in the 1837 manuscript unfolds indeed with almost childlike simplicity:

When I had reached the top [of Posilippo] I walked along looking down at the deep blue sea, the town with its early-morning noises still within earshot, and the two islands of Ischia and Nisita out in the bay where the sun was just beginning to touch the tops of the villas with gold. Tiredness was the last thing in the world that I felt . . . I paced along with big strides, I began to run, I rushed down the slopes, I rolled over and over in the damp grass. But in my heart I had the thought of death.

This sudden revelation is shocking, not because it is unexpected but because it seems like a second voice, the voice of *the other*, bursting out in Nerval's heart, never to be silenced again. The manuscript continues:

O God, I do not know what deep sadness was living in my soul, but it was nothing less than the cruel conviction that I was not loved. I had glimpsed the ghost of happiness, I had used up all the gifts of God, I was beneath the most beautiful sky in the world, in the presence of the most perfect Nature, and in sight of the greatest panorama that a man might live to see. Yet I was four hundred leagues from the only woman who had ever existed for me, and who still did not even know my name. Not to be loved, and never to have the hope of being loved! The unknown woman who had presented your image to me in vain, and who had served me for the chance encounter of an evening, she had loves of her own, her own interests, her own life; so she had given me all the pleasures that can exist—except for feeling and for love. And if love was missing, it all meant nothing.

If love was missing, it all meant nothing. This was the central revelation of his Naples experience, and it must have remained as the wound in his heart, the fracture in his brain, the unbearable confusion in his imagination, which he had spent half a lifetime trying to heal, to mend, to harmonise. This was why his Star was dead, his Tower fallen. Now I saw him, sharp as a figure on a bright and empty horizon, the Romantic Hero lost beneath the freezing Moon of his own entranced imagination. No parent, no friend, no lover could save him. And no biographer could come to his aid, could finally reach him through the bright cruel space of time.

The manuscript ends with his first act of suicide, an act that was not completed for another twenty years; so that his whole life could be seen as one long suspended act of falling:

> It was then that I was tempted to go to God, that I might demand the account on my incomplete existence. There was only a single step to take. At the place where I stood, the hillside was cut away like a cliff, with the sea groaning at its foot, blue and pure. There was no more than a moment to suffer. Oh how terrible was the dizziness of that thought! Two times I threw myself forward, and I do not know what power flung me back, still alive, onto the grass which I kissed. No, my God, you have not created me for eternal suffering. I do not wish to outrage you with my own death. But give me the strength, give me the energy, give me above all the resolution, which helps some to power, some to fame, and some—to love.

I left Paris later that autumn, as the last leaves were being swept along the quai. My kindly landlord had married, and my attic room had to be repapered for the expected baby. I wrote my life of Gérard de Nerval, four hundred pages of it, entitled *A Dream Biography*. But it was a confused production, beginning with Nerval's death and ending with Gérard's birth, and wisely no publisher ever touched it. I still have my seven coloured notebooks, covered with their Tarot signs. My taste for travel and my ear for footsteps had diminished, it seemed. I was thirty, and it was time to consider the way I should go myself.

I was sitting late one afternoon, after the Bibliothèque had closed, on a bench in the Palais-Royal watching the workmen clear out the plane-tree leaves from the stone bowl of the fountain. The water had been switched off. Couples strolled arm in arm in the galleries, stopping to look in the lit windows of the shops selling antiques and pipes and medallions. A stray dog, searching anxiously for its master, pattered lightly over the gravel and disappeared into the shadowed archway leading to the rue de Valois. Footsteps approached and a hand touched me on the shoulder. It was Françoise, come to meet me after work. We kissed lightly, as one does in France. "*Tu devais rentrer chez-toi,*" she said.

Author's Note

That dog pattering into the rue de Valois was of course the spirit of this mongrel book departing on a new adventure. It is difficult to give its genealogy, being part pure-bred biography, part travel, part autobiography, together with a bad dash of Baskerville Hound. It will be evident that people and places, and my own diaries and reflections, have shaped the creature as much as any literary texts. But the most important printed sources for the lives of my four protagonists can be found in the following works, which provide at least an elementary bibliography—and I hope an encouragement to further reading:

ONE. Robert Louis Stevenson, *Journal de route en Cévennes*, avec Notes de Jacques Poujol (Editions Privat Club Cévenol, Toulouse, 1978); *The Cévennes Journal*, edited by Gordon Golding (Mainstream, Edinburgh, 1978); *Travels with a Donkey in the Cévennes* (1879); *The Letters of Robert Louis Stevenson*, edited by Sidney Colvin (2 vols., Methuen, 1901); Margaret Mackay, *The Violent Friend* (Dent, 1968).

TWO. Mary Wollstonecraft: *Posthumous Works*, edited by William Godwin (4 vols., Johnson, 1798); *Collected Letters*, edited by Ralph M. Wardle (Cornell University Press, 1979); William Godwin, *Memoir of the Author of A Vindication of the Rights of Woman* (Johnson, 1798); Claire Tomalin, *The Life and Death of Mary Wollstonecraft* (Weidenfeld, 1974); John Alger, *A History of the English in the French Revolution* (London, 1912); *State Trials* (London, 1794).

THREE. Percy Bysshe Shelley: *Poetical Works*, edited by Thomas Hutchinson (Oxford University Press, 1968); *The Letters of Percy Bysshe Shelley*, edited by F. L. Jones (2 vols, Oxford University Press, 1964); *Mary Shelley's Journal*, edited by F. L. Jones (University of Oklahoma Press, 1947); *The Letters of Mary Wollstonecraft Shelley*, edited by Betty T. Bennett (vol I, Johns Hopkins University Press, 1980); *Shelley and His Circle, 1773–1822*, edited by Donald H.

Reiman (vols 5—6, Carl H. Pforzheimer Library, New York, 1973); *The Journals of Claire Clairmont*, edited by M. K. Stocking (Harvard University Press, 1968).

FOUR. *Nadar* par Jean Prinet et Antoinette Dilasser (Armand Colin, Paris, 1966); *Testi di Nadar* con Lamberto Vitali e Jean Prinet (Giulio Einaudi editore, Torino, 1973); Gérard de Nerval, *Oeuvres*, presenté par Albert Beguin et Jean Richer (2 vols, Bibliothèque de la Pléiade, Paris, 1960—vol I contains the poetry and correspondence, vol II most of the travel-writing); Théophile Gautier, *Portraits et Souvenirs Littéraires* (1875) and *Histoire du Romanticisme* (1874). Alfred Douglas, *The Tarot* (Gollancz, 1973) supplied much of my cartomancy.

For the use of copyright materials, and kind permission to consult and refer to manuscripts and archives my most grateful acknowledgments are due to the Bodleian Library, Oxford; the British Museum, London; the Bibliothèque Nationale, Paris; the Keats-Shelley Museum, Rome; The Carl and Lily Pforzheimer Foundation Inc., New York; the Bibliothèque Spoelberch de Lovenjoul, Chantilly; Mainstream Publishing, Edinburgh; Dent, London; Oxford University Press; Gollancz, London; Cornell University Press; University of Oklahoma Press; Johns Hopkins University Press; Harvard University Press; and the Bibliothèque de la Pléiade, Paris.

Other sources which have proved invaluable during my travels, or subsequently helped me clarify my conception of the book, include the fine maps and guides of Michelin; the incomparable *Dictionnaire Historique des Rues de Paris* by Jacques Hillairet (Editions de Minuit, Paris, 1973); the newspaper files of *Le Monde* and *The Times; The Quest for Corvo, An Experiment in Biography* by A. J. A. Symons (1934); *The Unquiet Grave* by Cyril Connolly (1944); *After Babel* by George Steiner (Oxford, 1975); *A Second Identity* by Richard Cobb (Oxford, 1969); and the *Symphonie Fantastique*, with its thematic Programme Note, by Hector Berlioz. The illustrative maps were drawn by Martin Lubikowski of MJL Cartographics. All translations from the French are mine.

For endless encouragement, expert help and inexplicable good humour my warmest thanks are due to Richard Cohen, a prince among editors; to Catherine Carver, for her sensitive reading and advice; to Elisabeth Sifton, for her patience and enthusiasm; and as ever to my old friend and advisor Peter Janson-Smith.

I have been greatly helped through the generosity of the Society of Authors; Ismena Holland; and Philip Howard of *The Times*, whose memo, "Dear Richard, where are you?" still travels with me. The Bridge House Factor has never failed.

Finally I should like to greet those friends whose kindness kept me together, in good weather and bad, at home and abroad. Some of them appear lightly disguised in this book, though none under their own names: Peter Jay of the Anvil Press; Sophie Vial of *Marie-France*; Pierre Voisin of the Librarie Sorbonne; Robert and Laurence de Bosmelet; Damon and Marie-Solange Pollard-Dubois; Françoise Dasques of IBM; and Alan Judd of Rovers International. To them all, the seventh card, the Chariot.

Richard Holmes
London, 26 January 1985

Index

Note: PBS refers to Percy Bysshe Shelley; RLS refers to Robert Louis Stevenson; MW refers to Mary Wollstonecraft.

Index